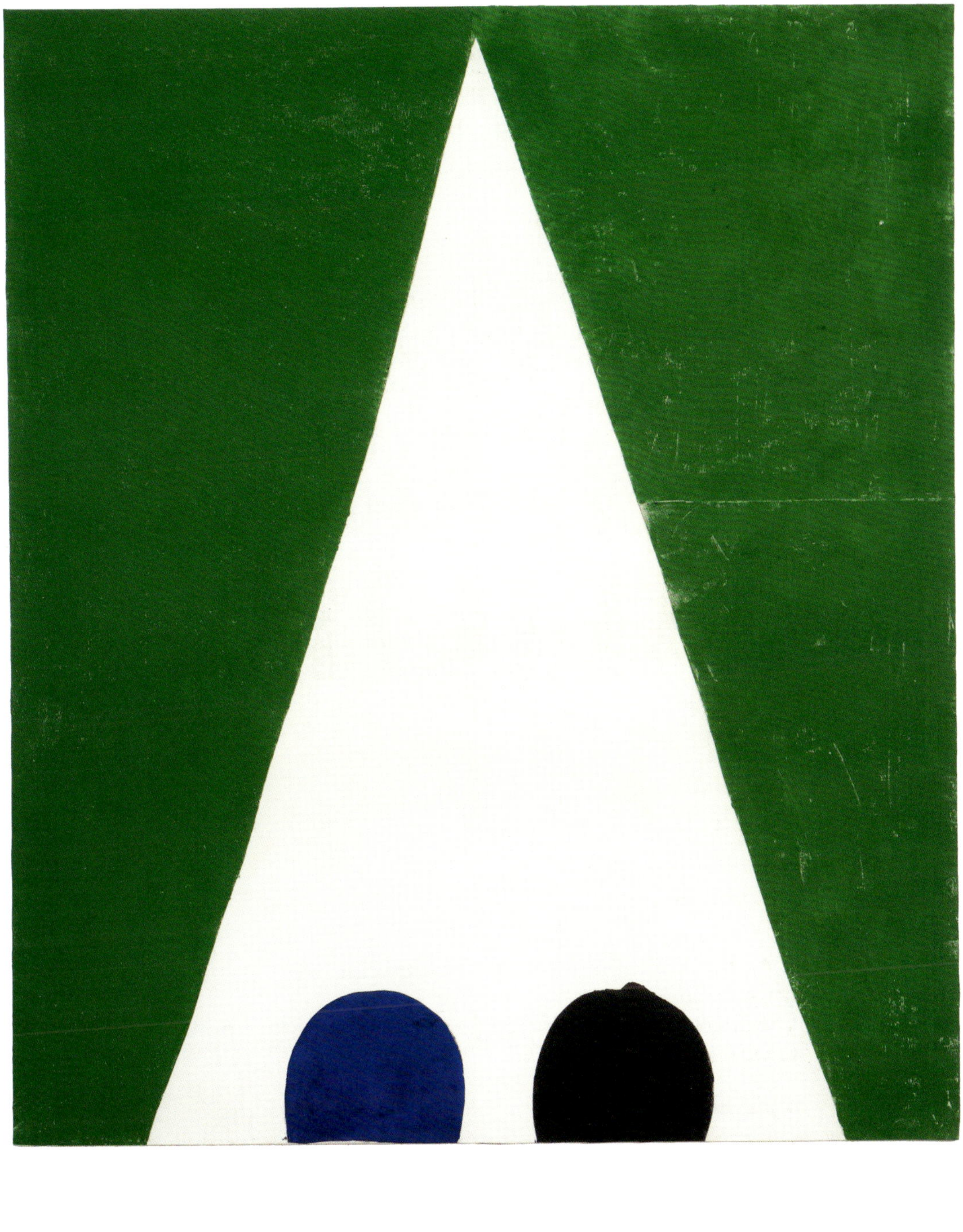

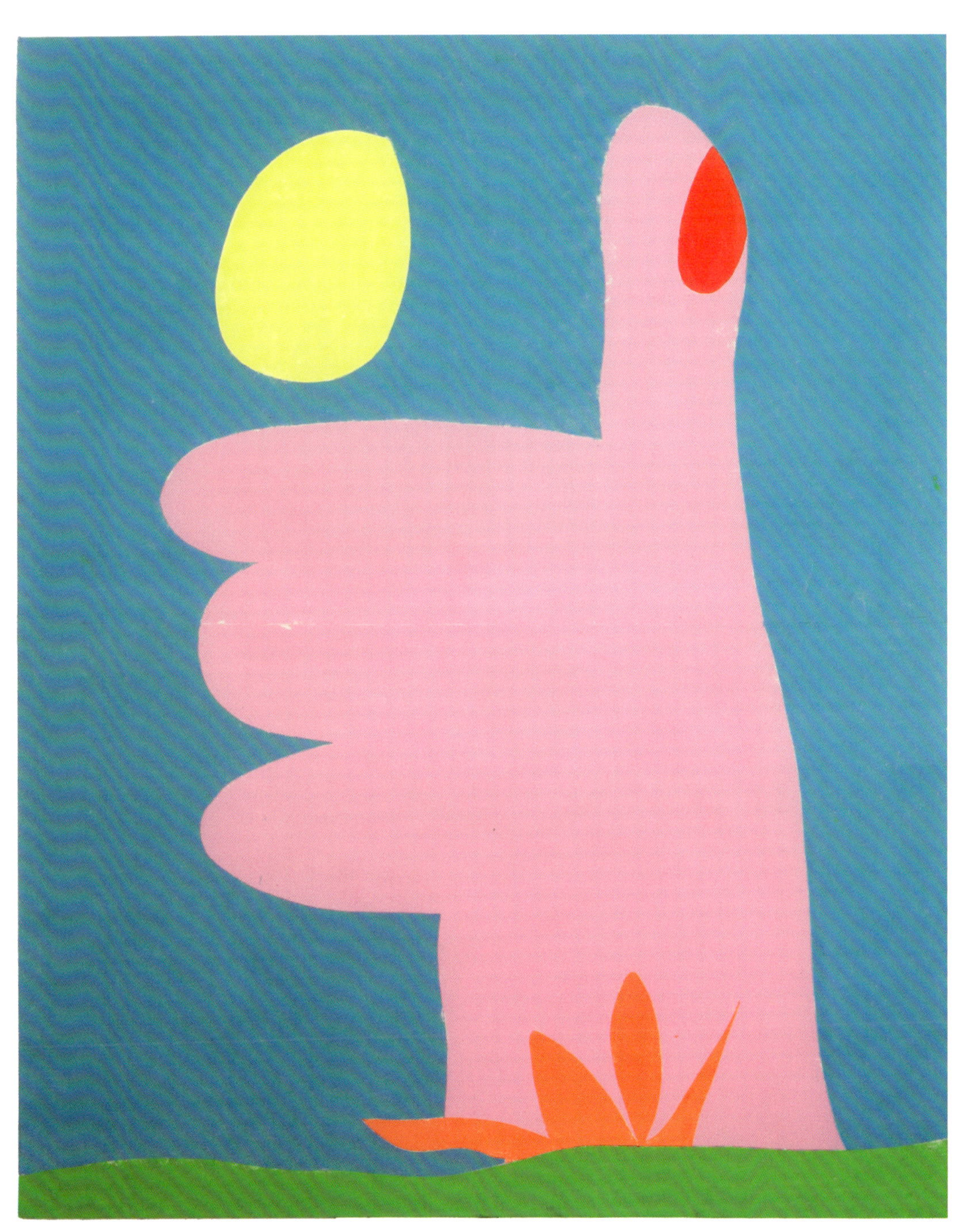

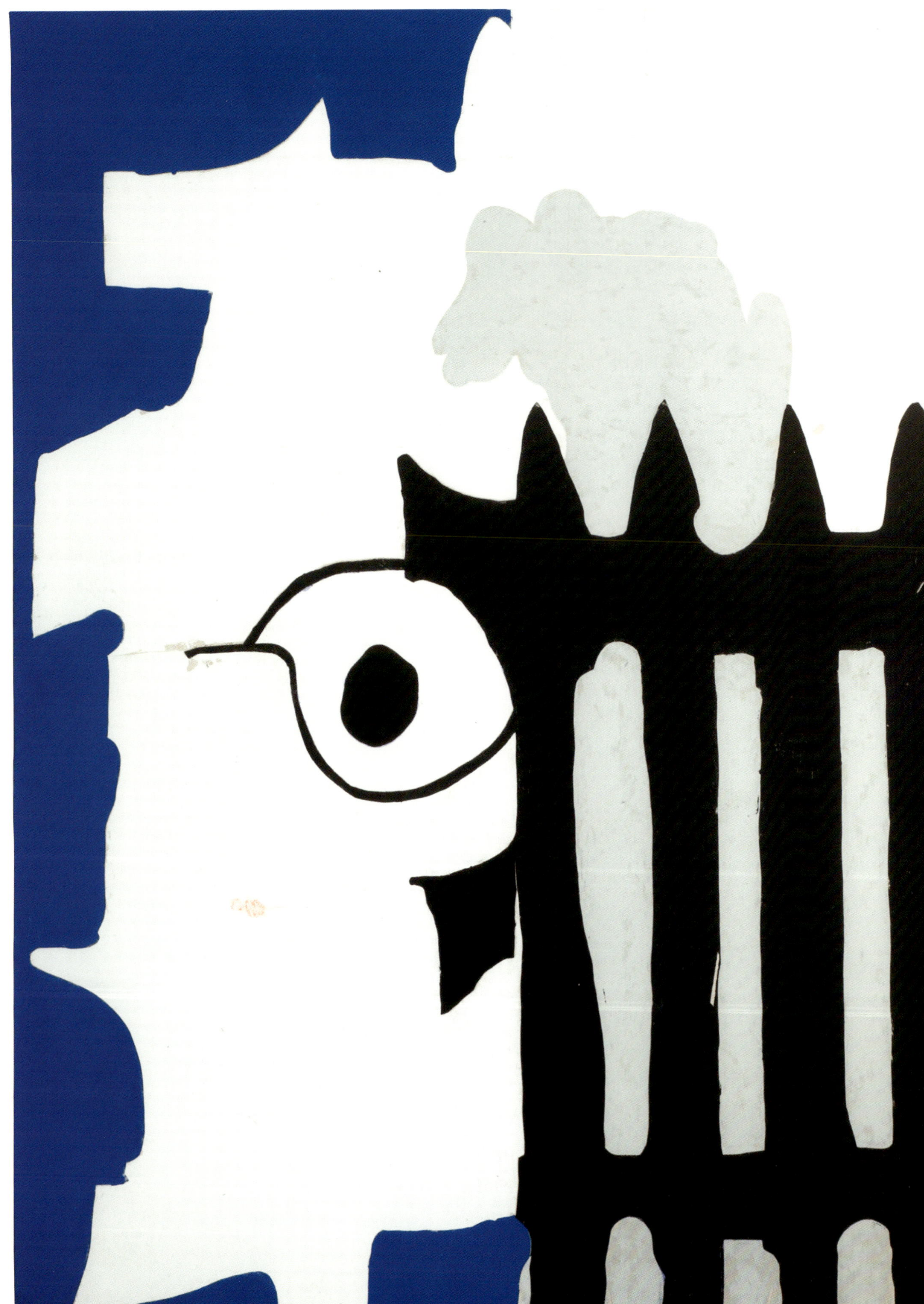

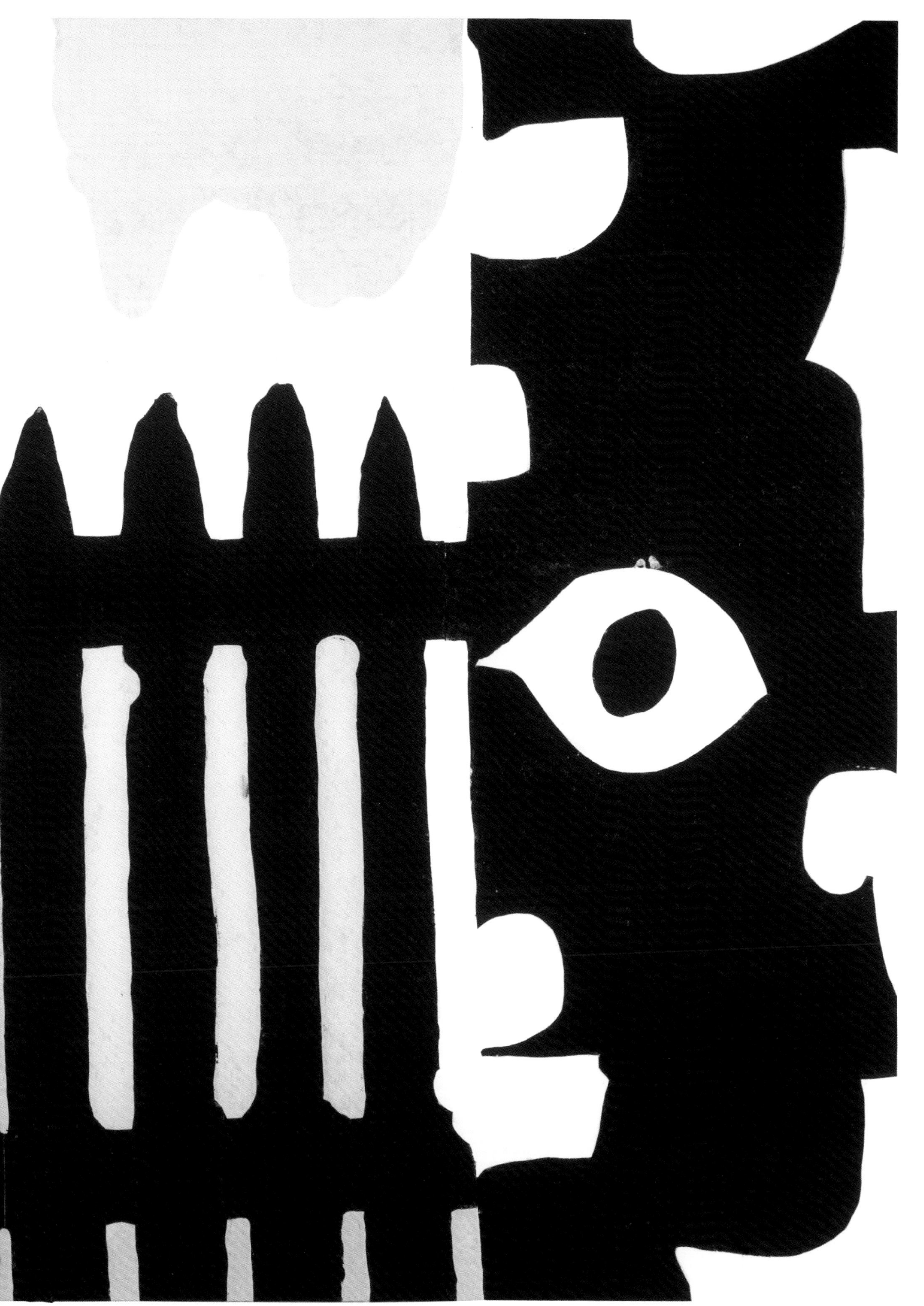

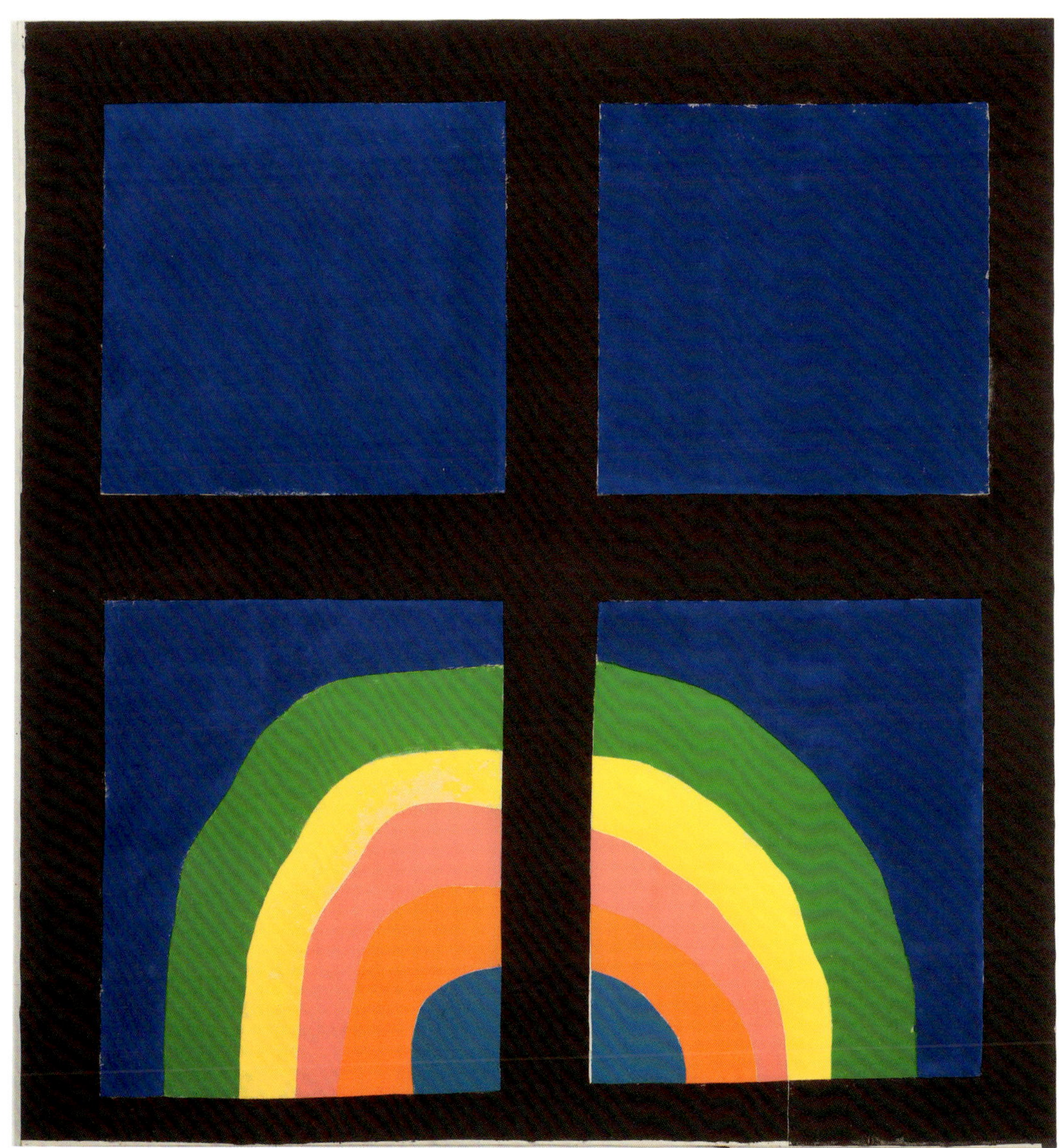

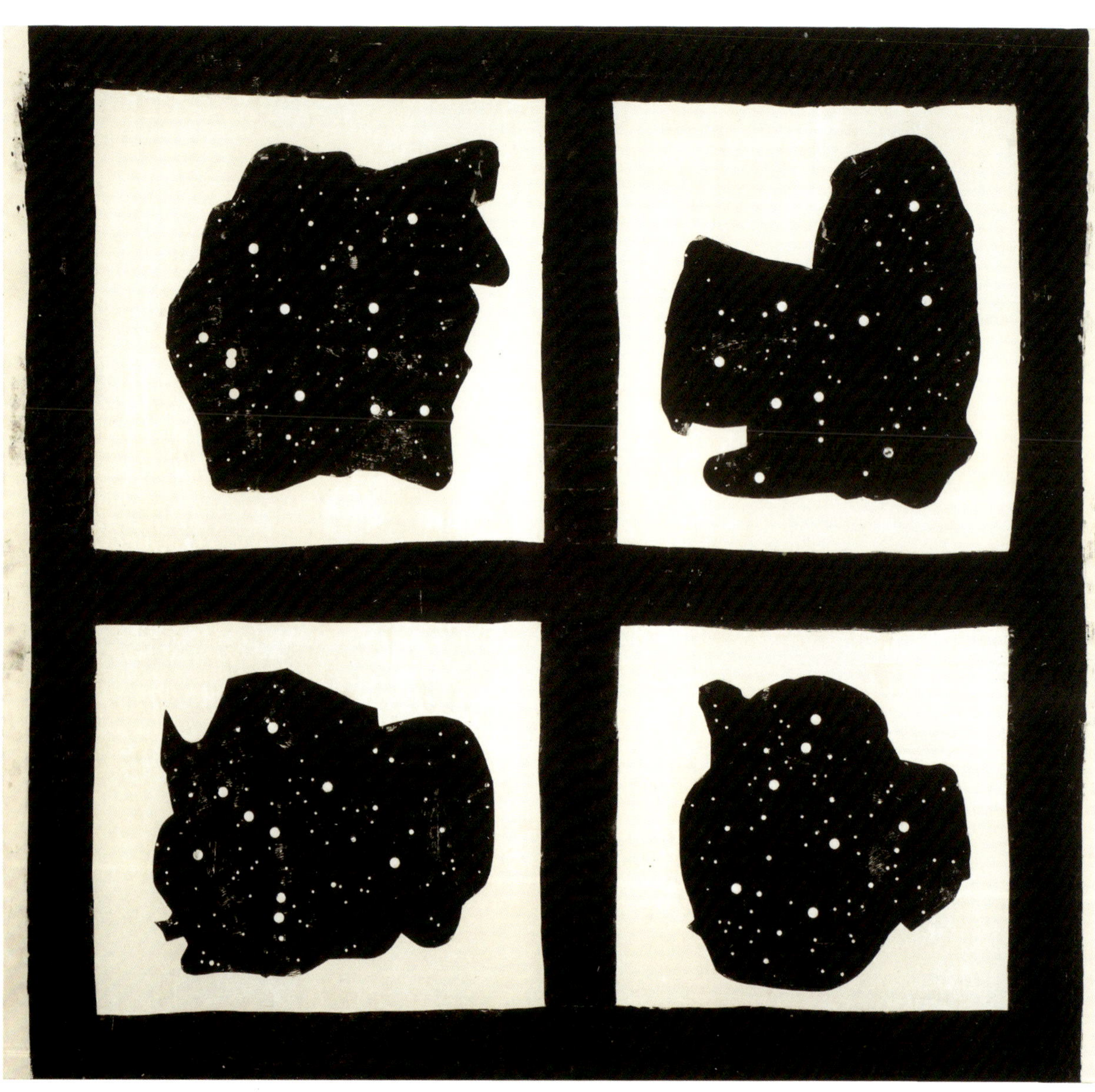

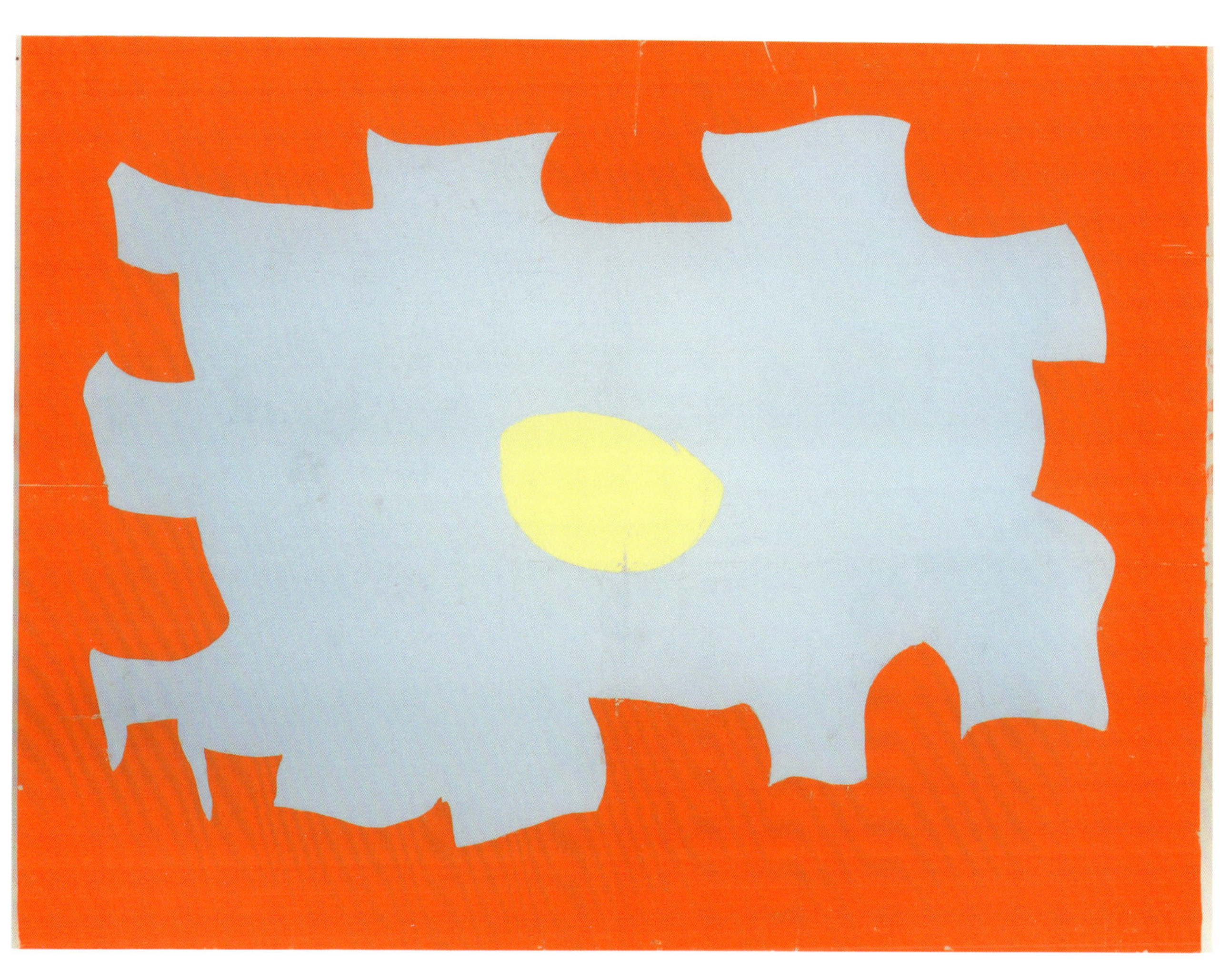

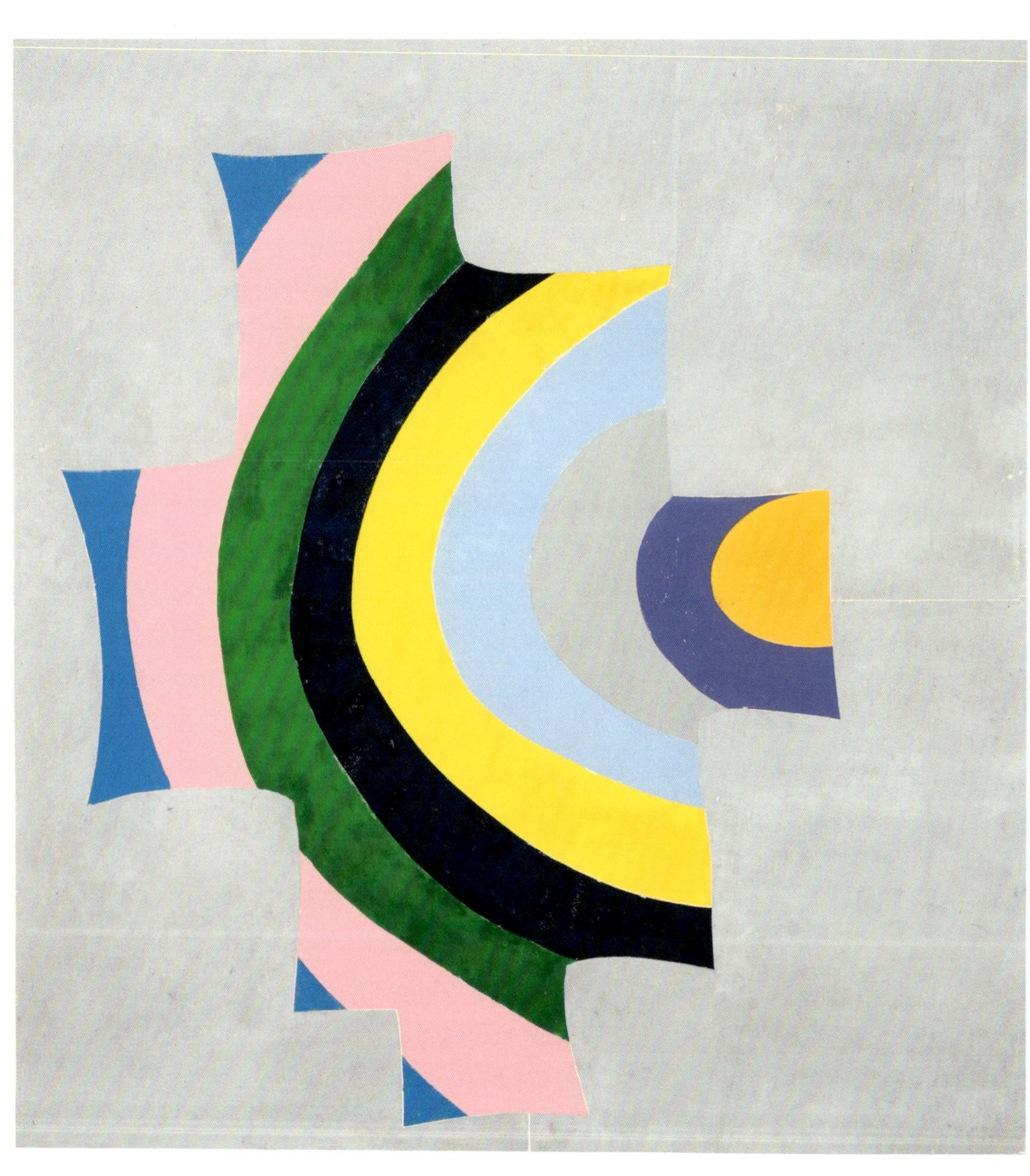

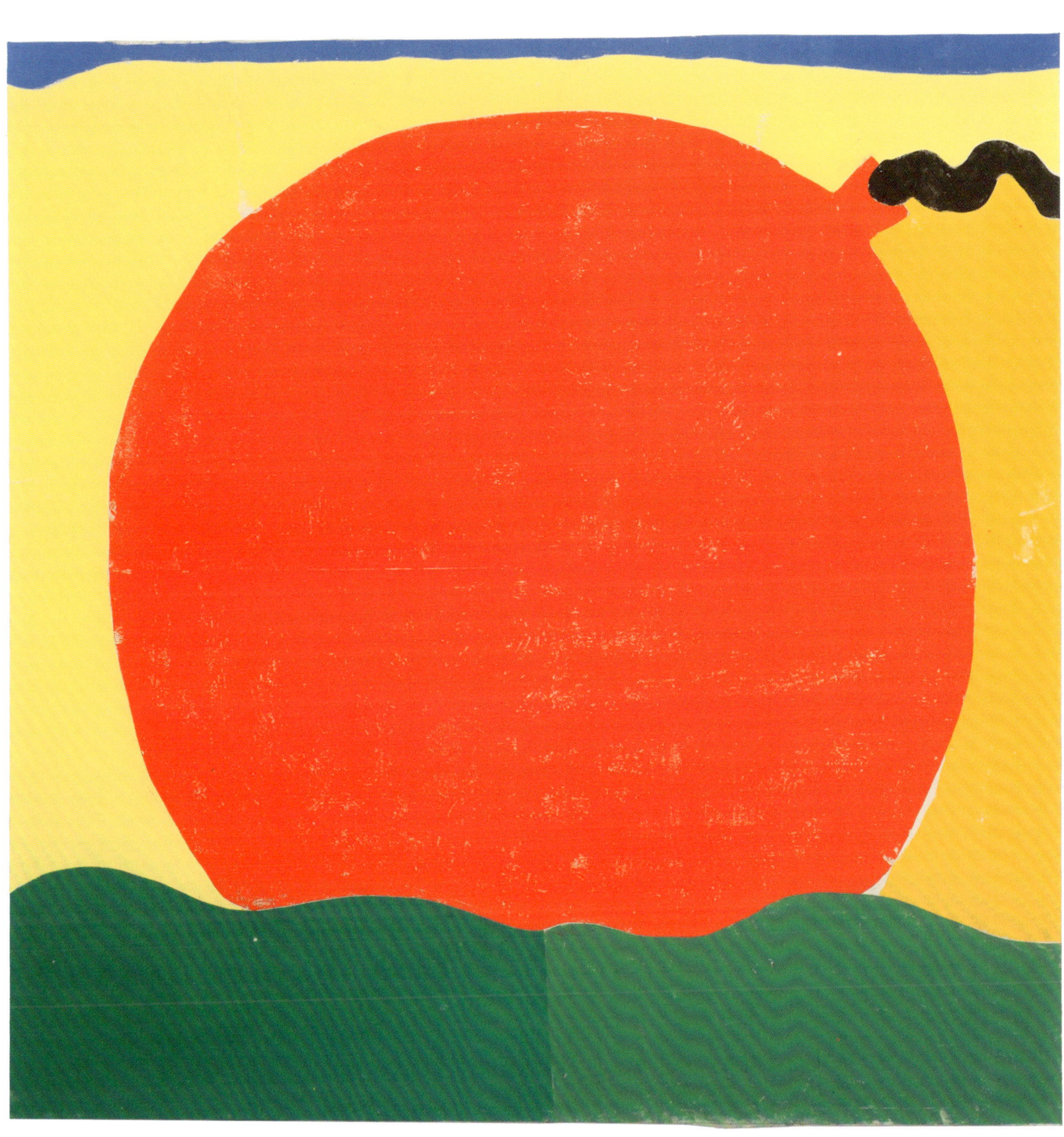

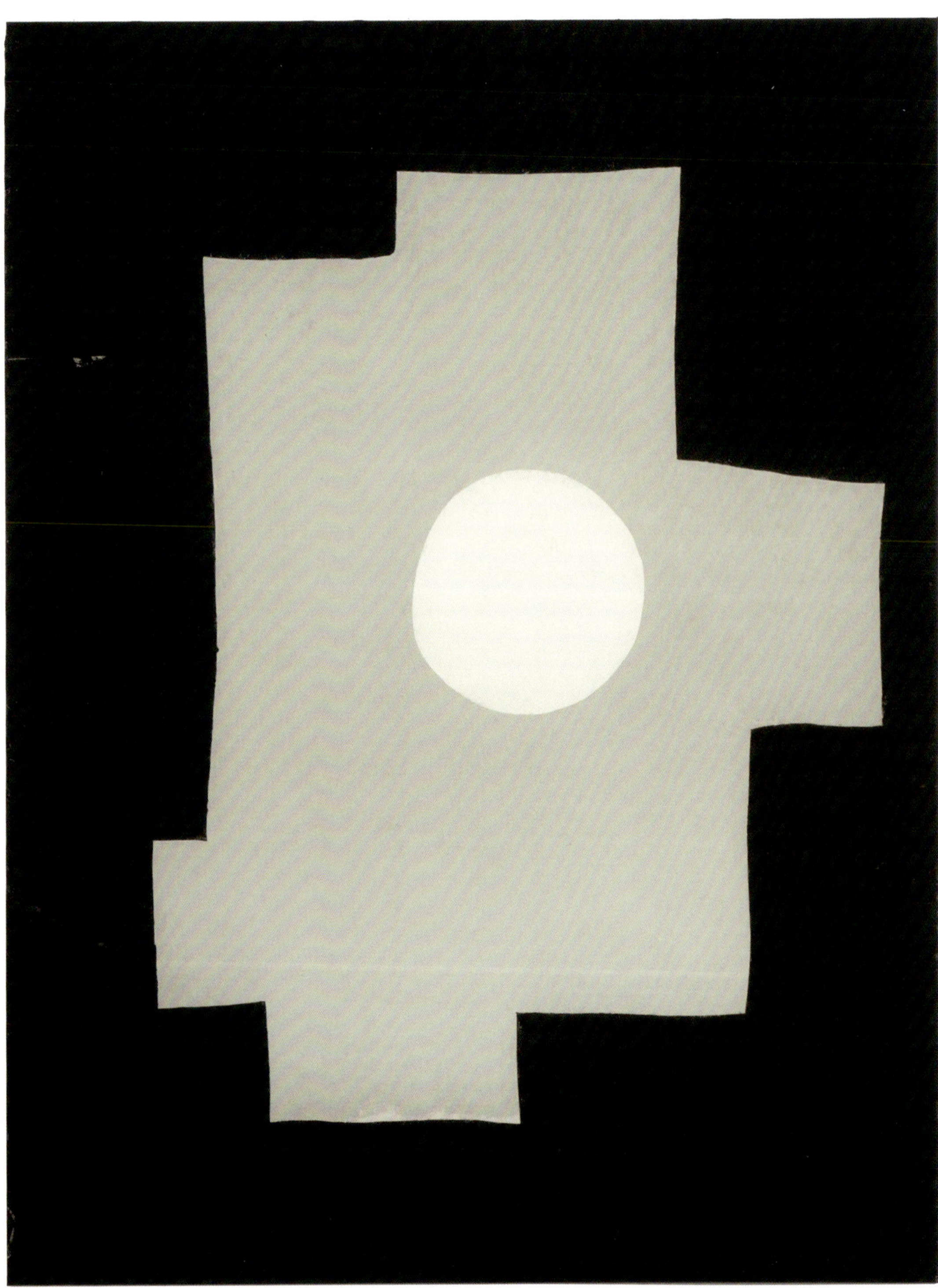

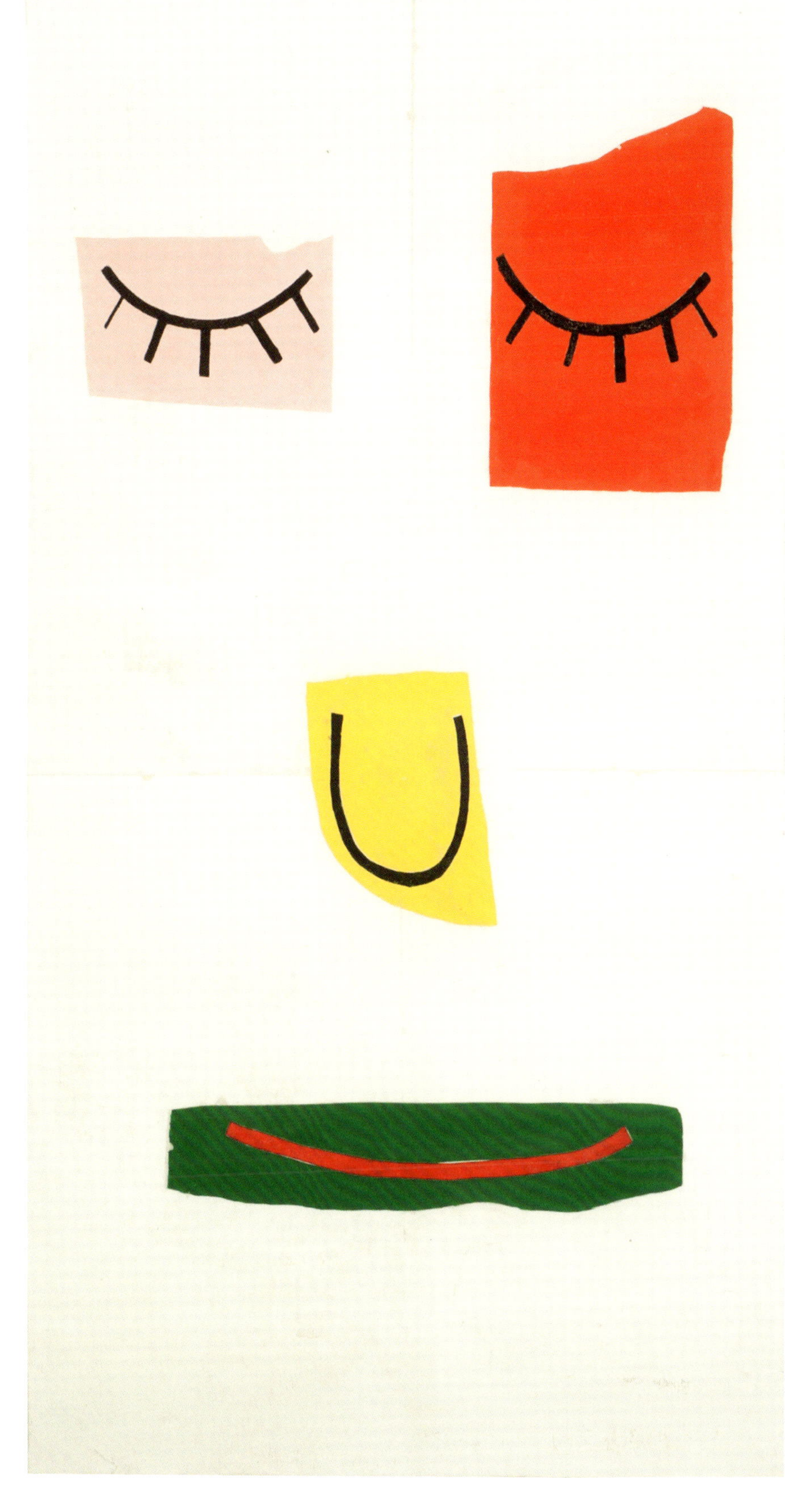

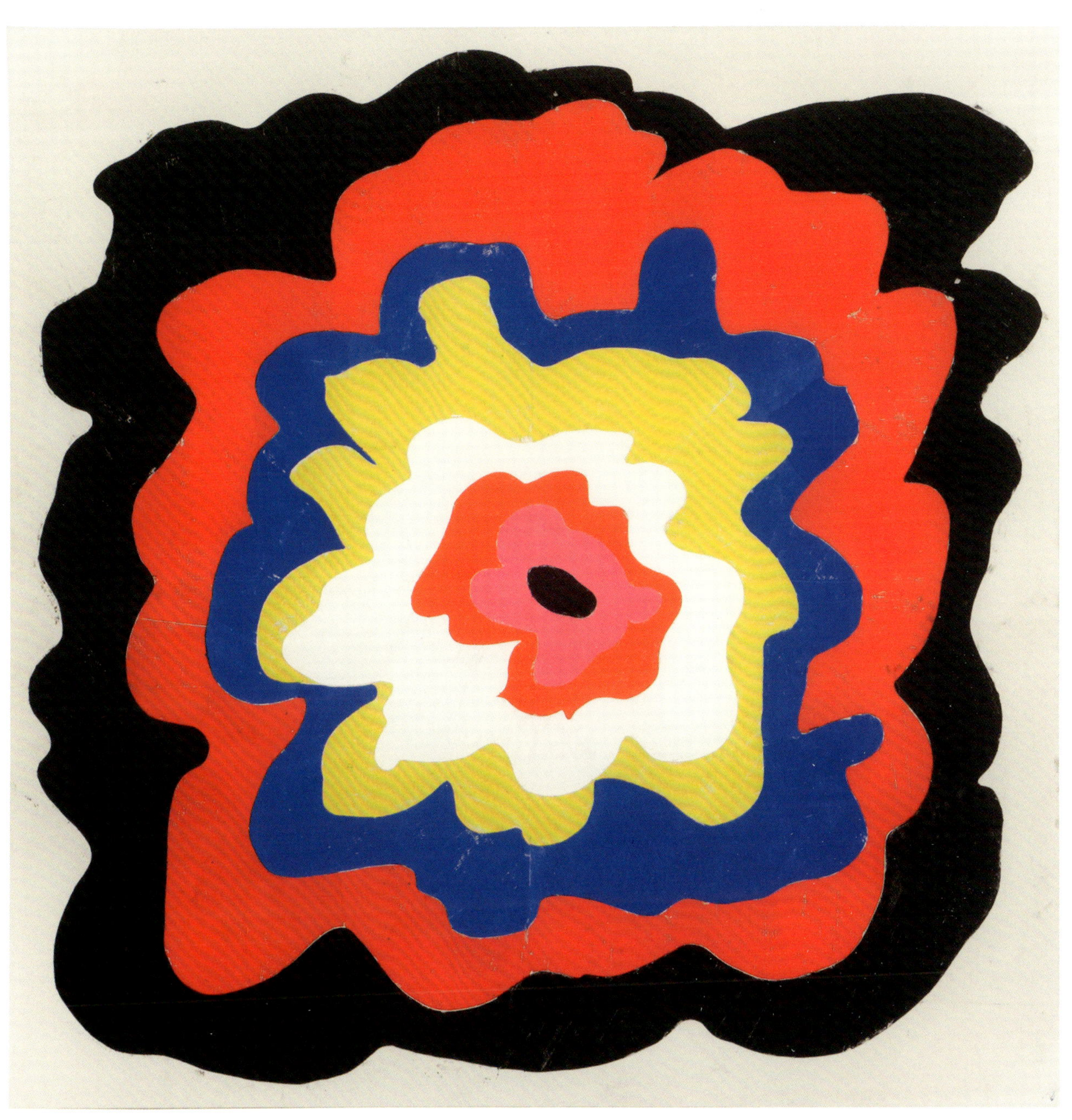

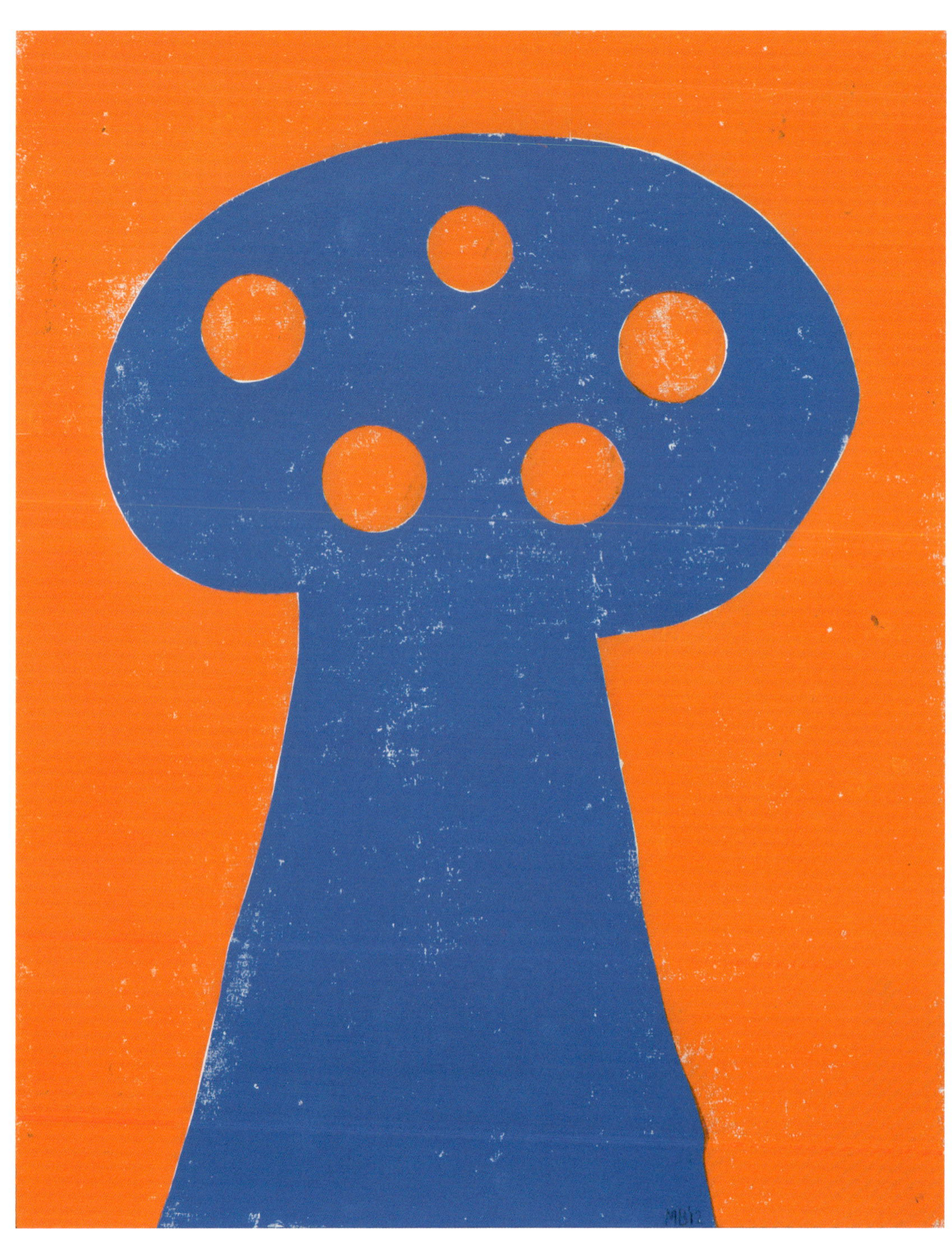

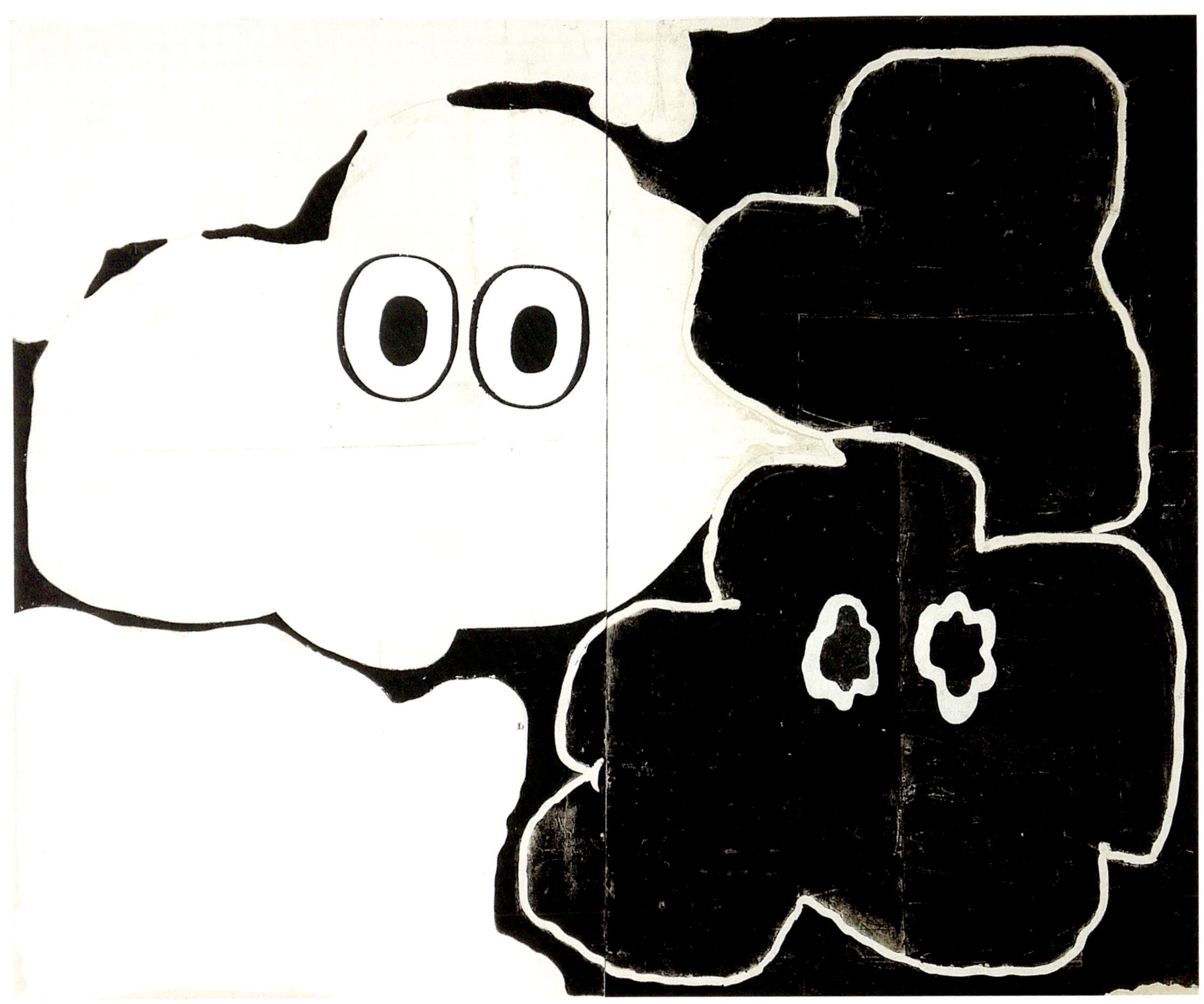

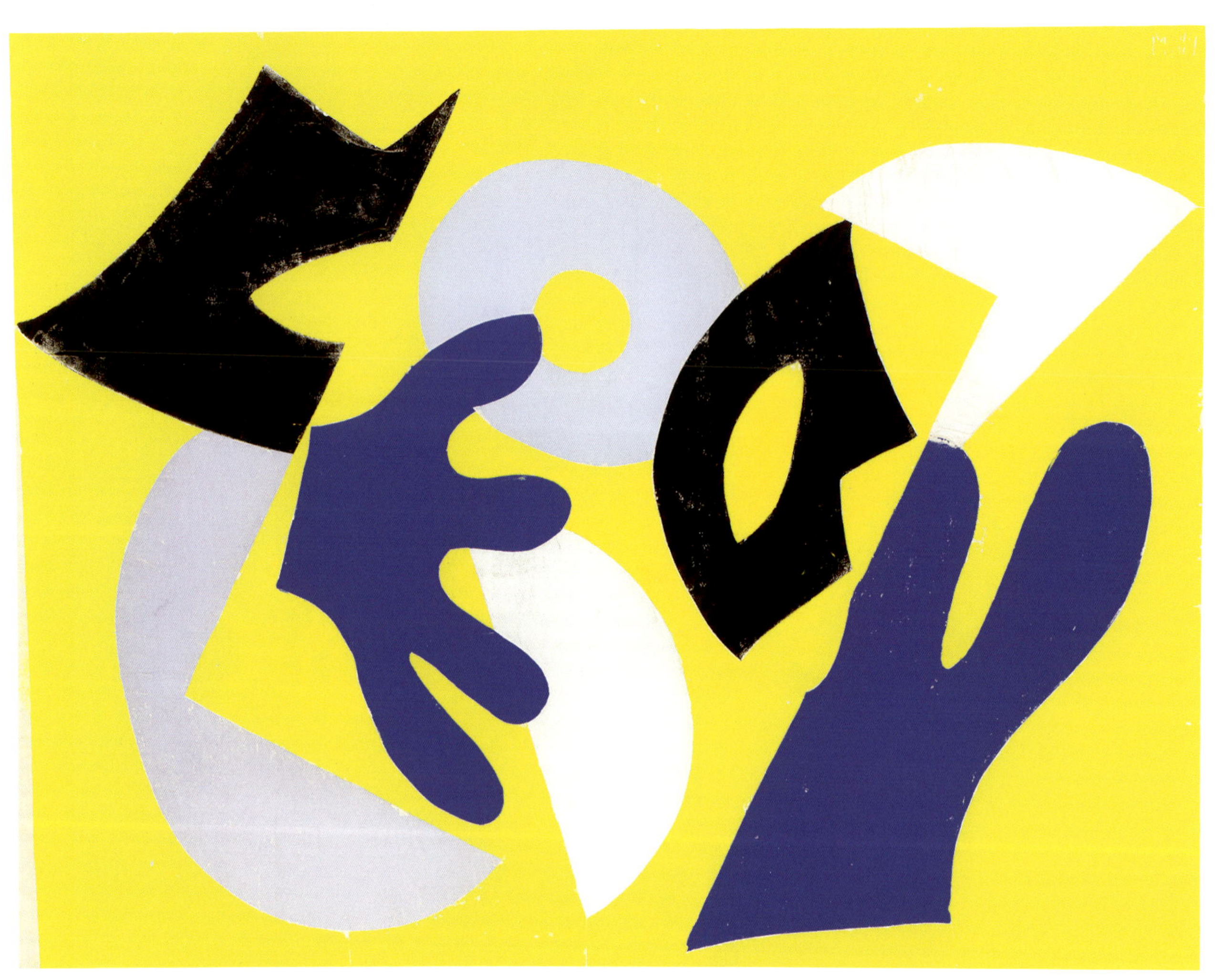

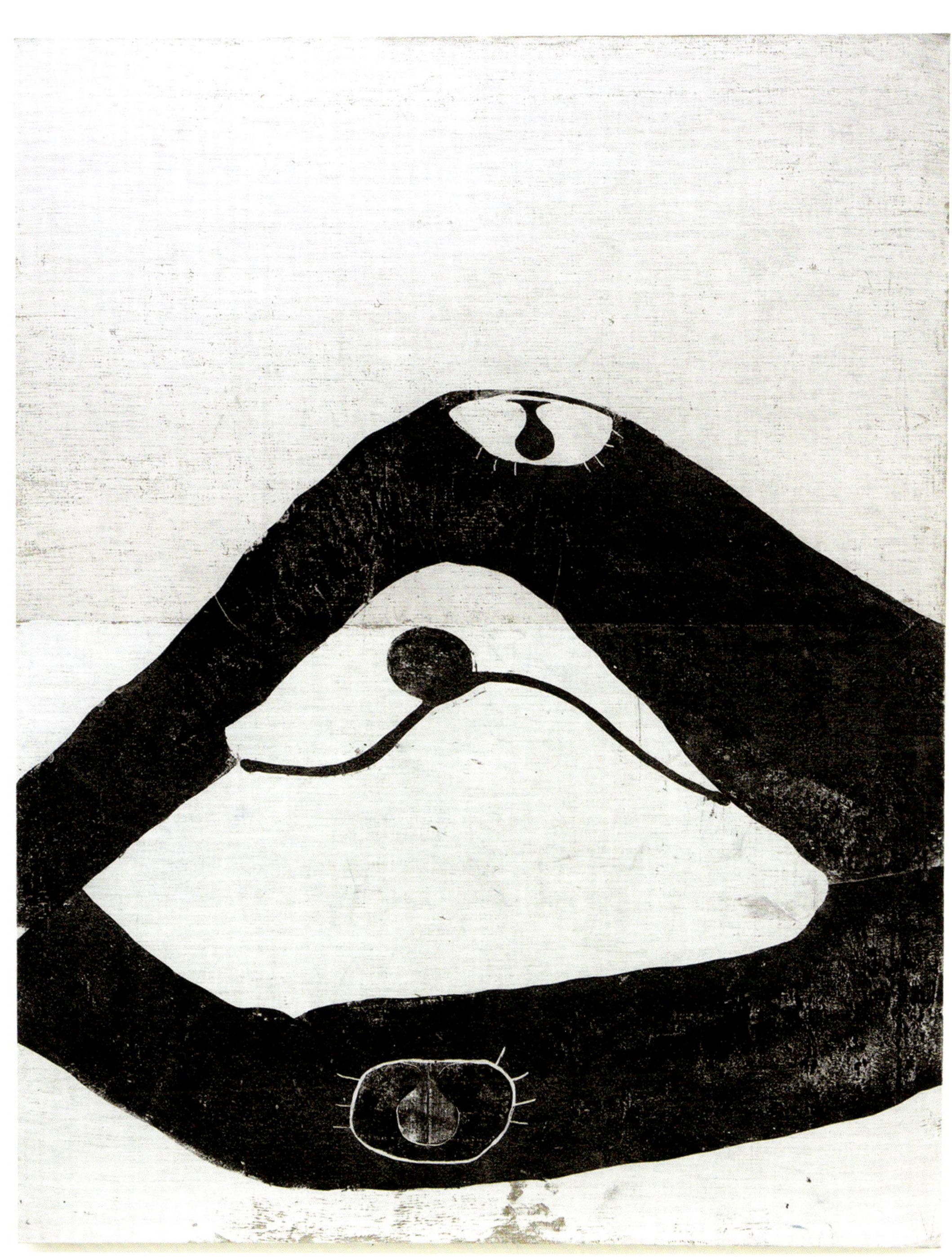

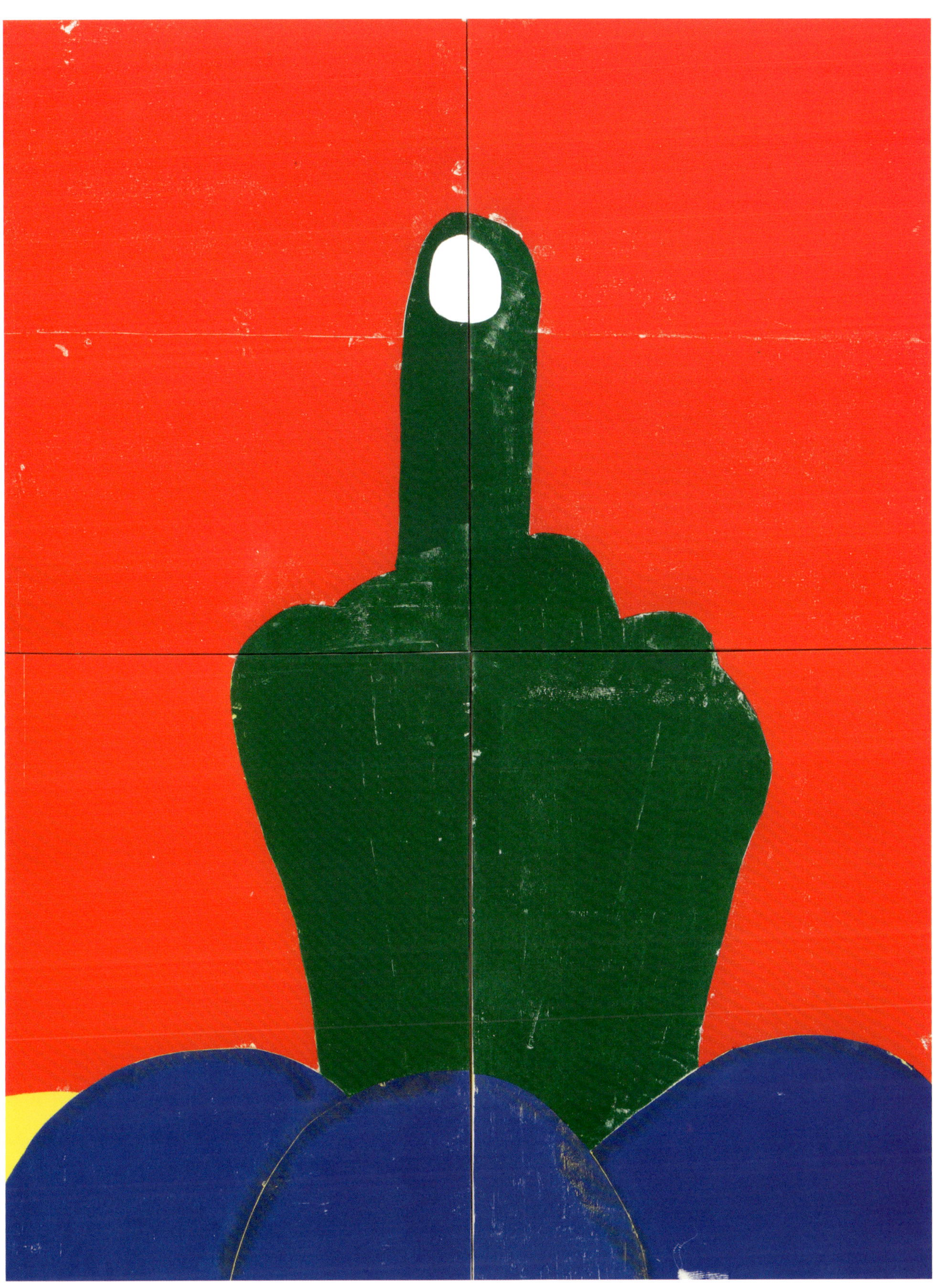

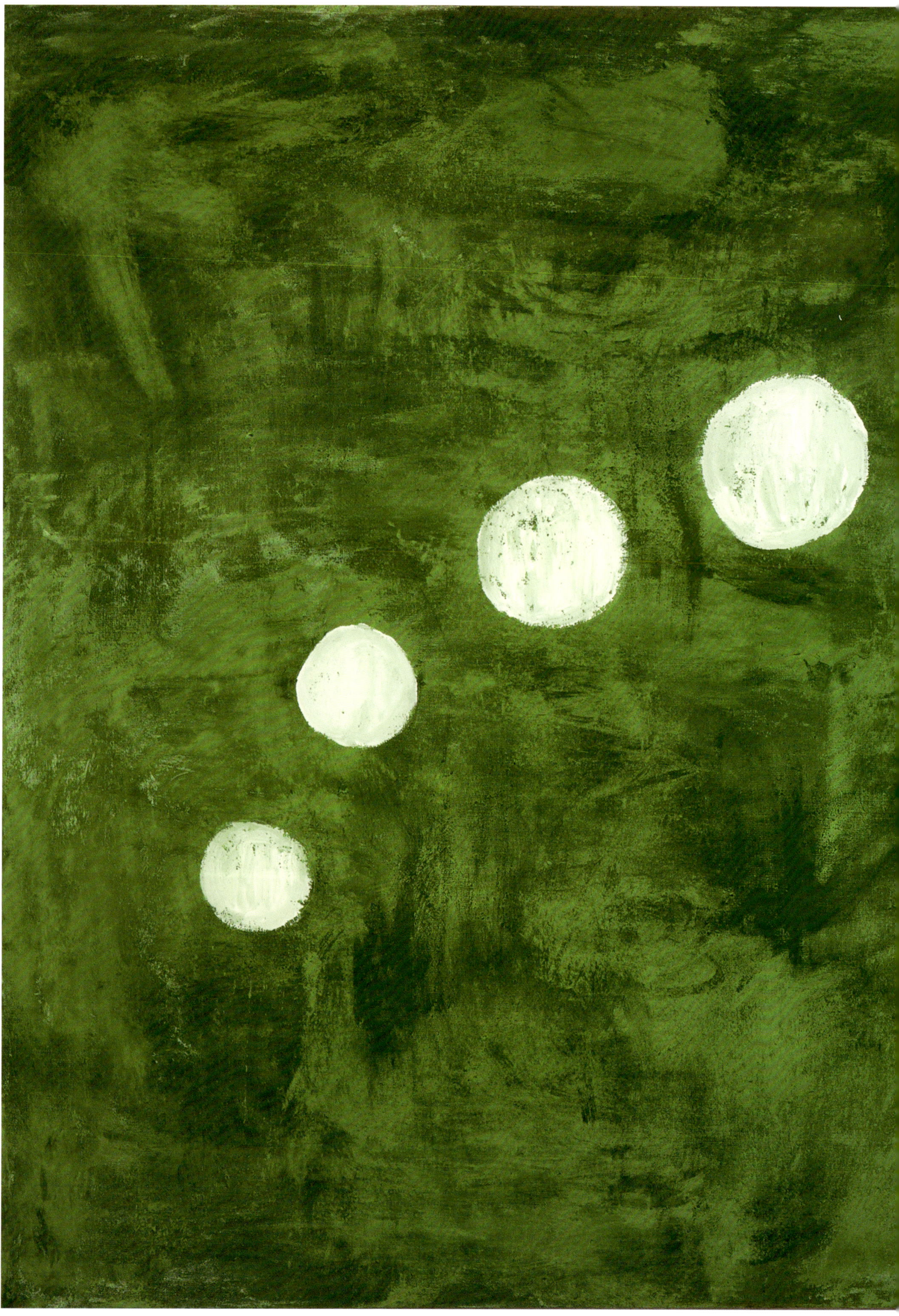

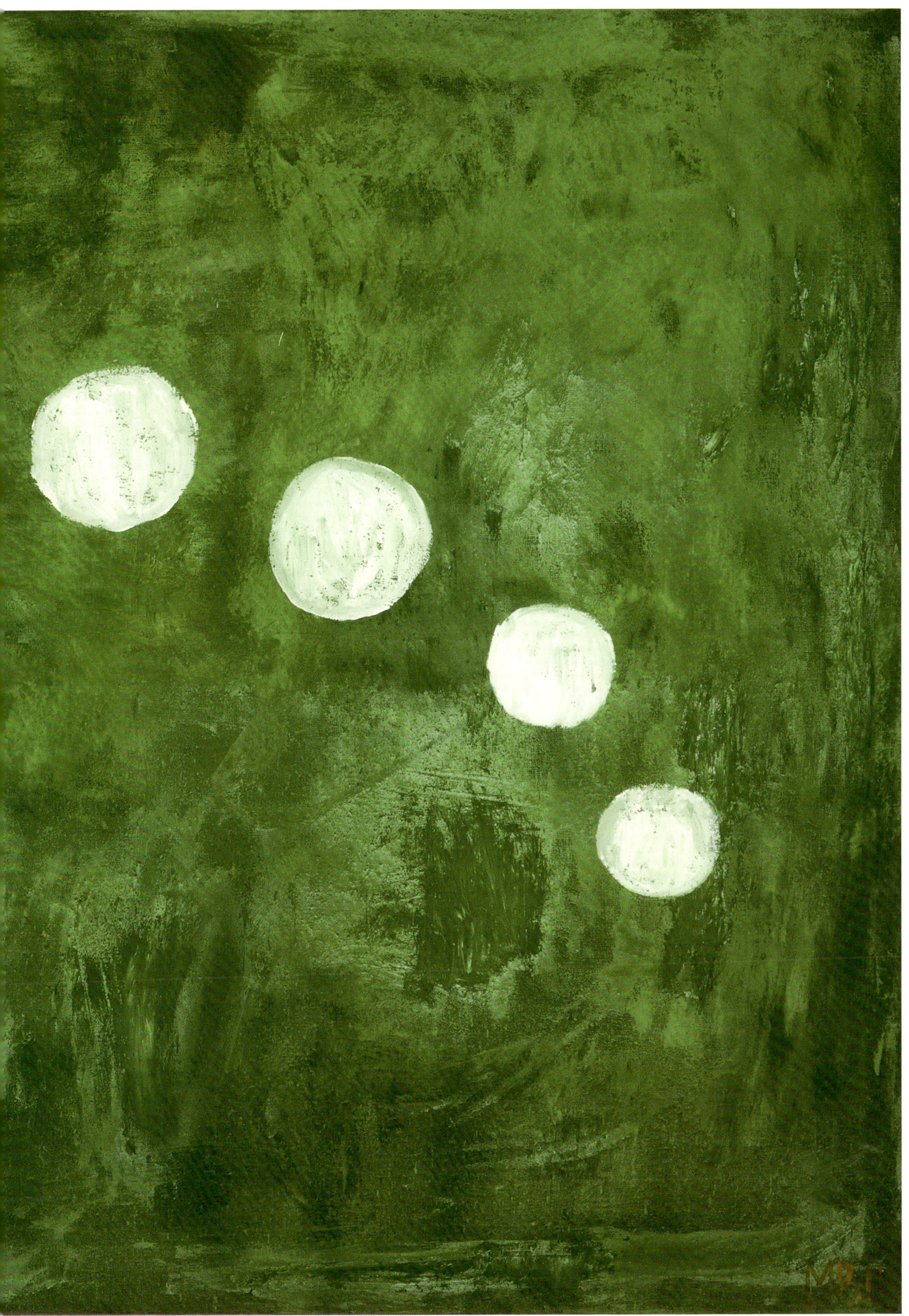

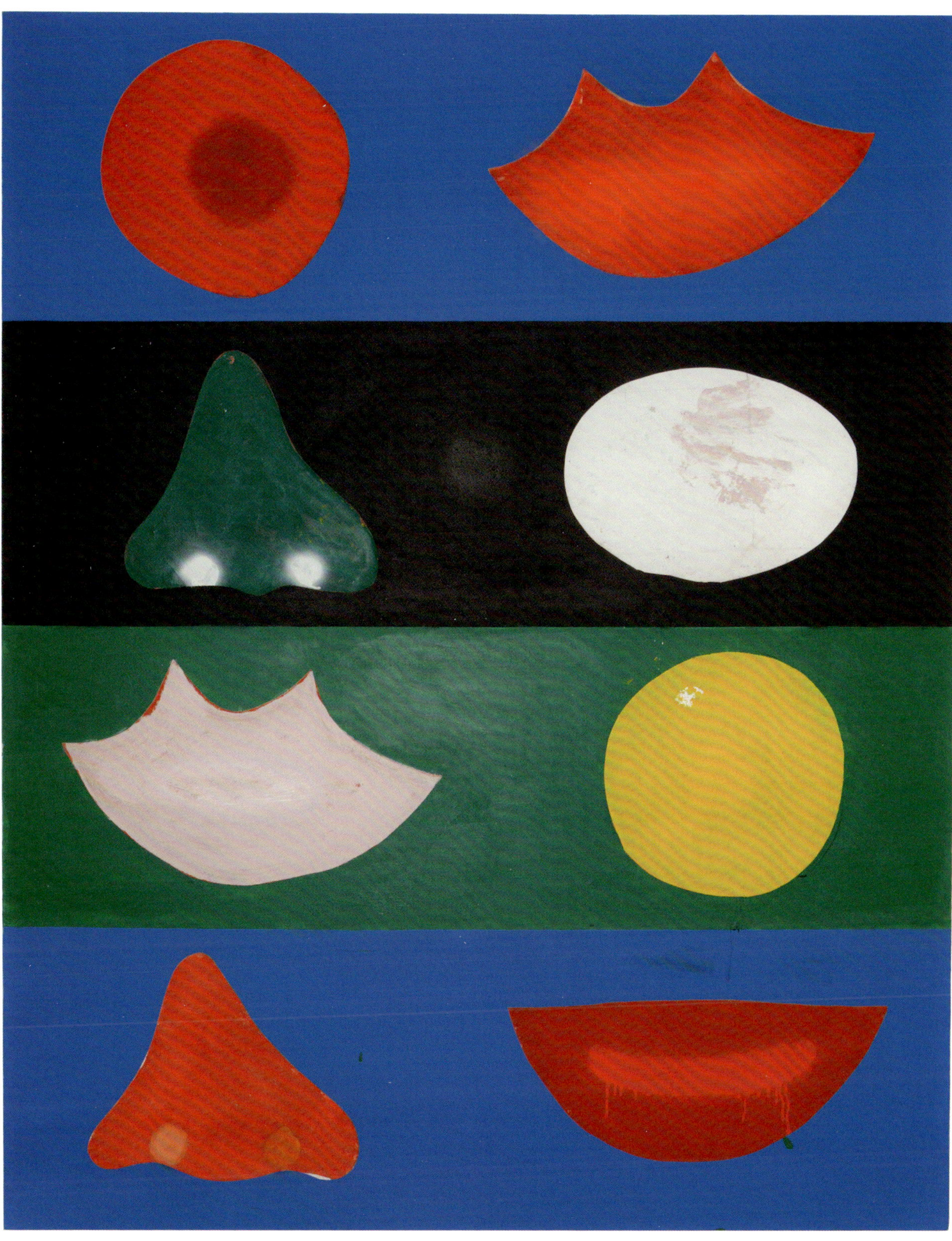

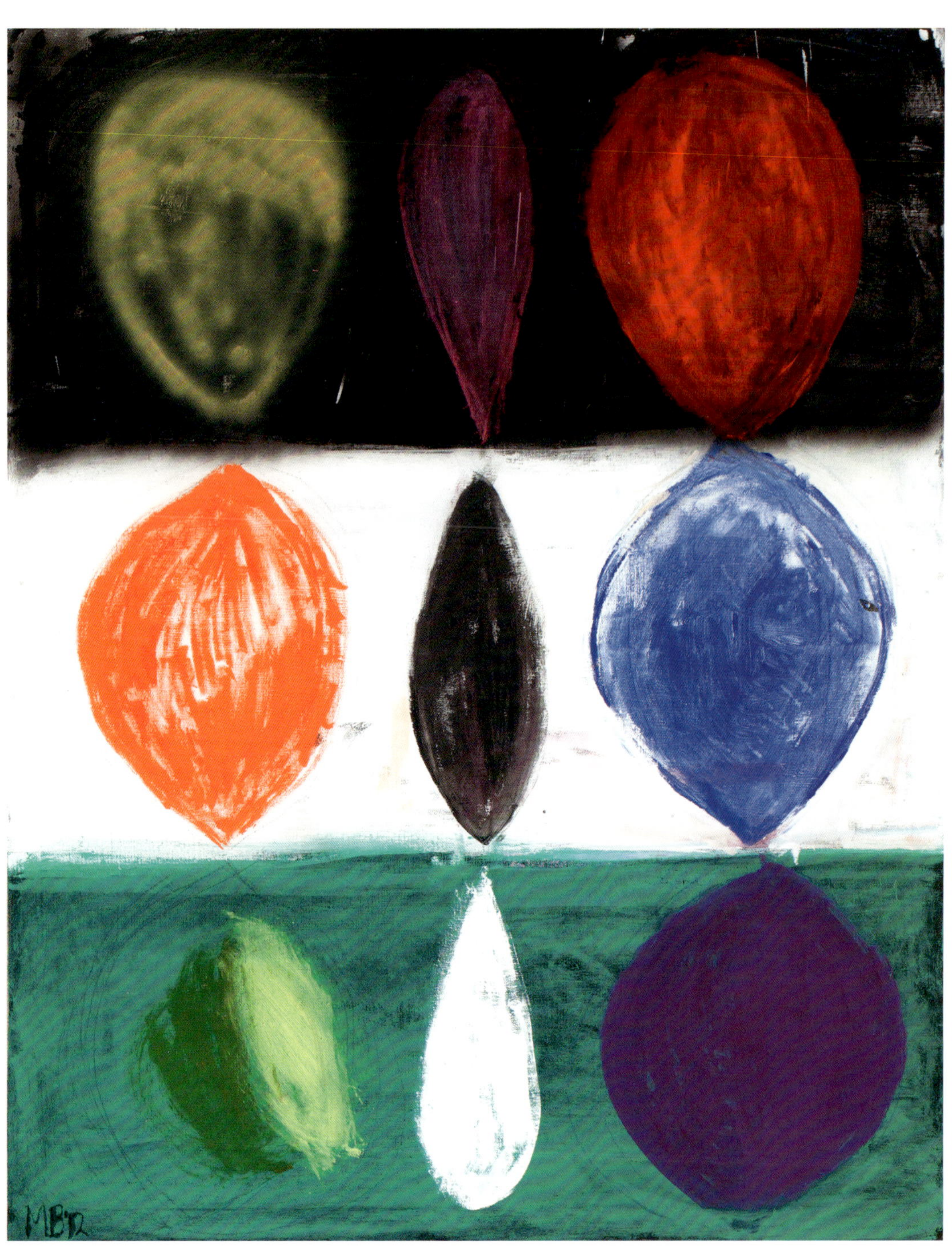

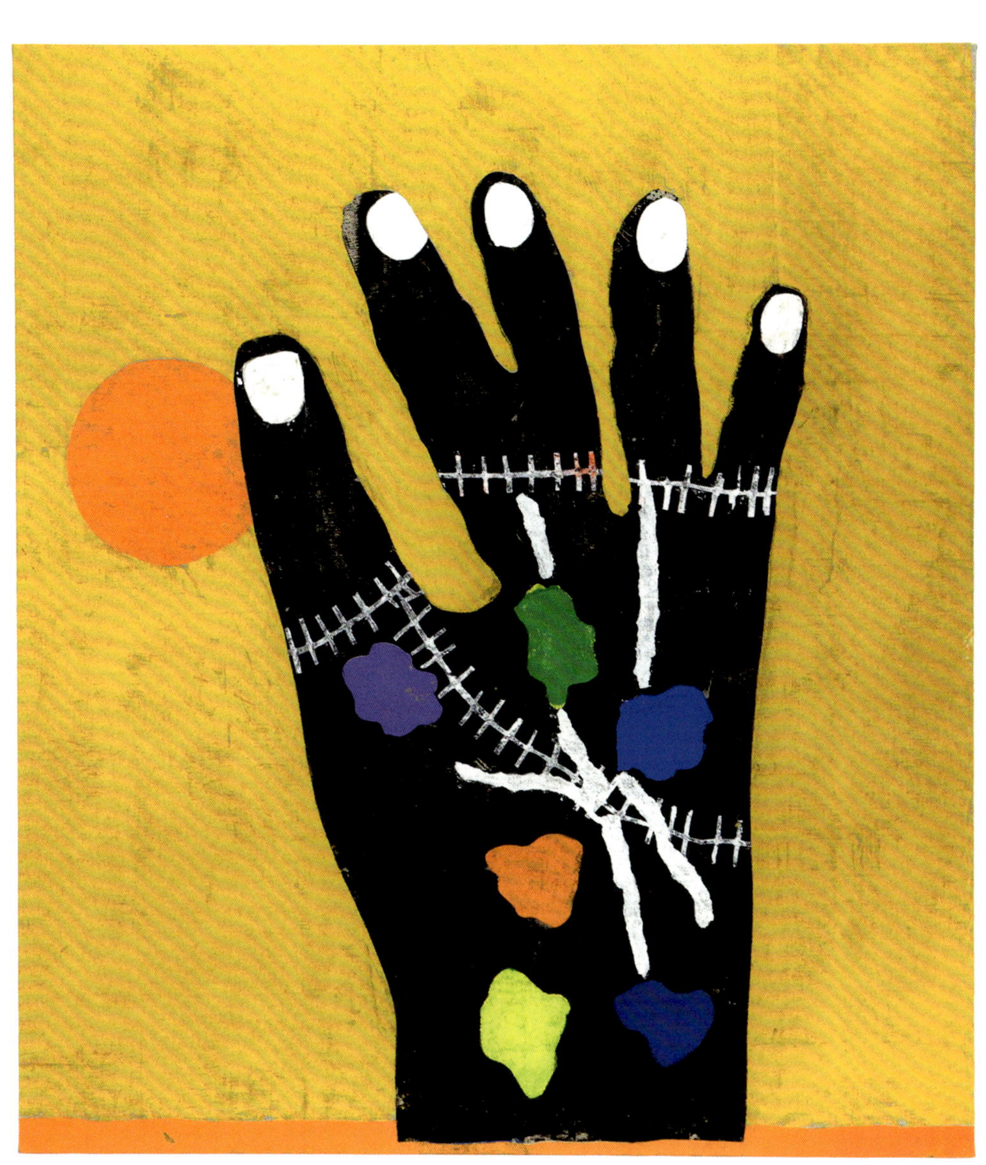

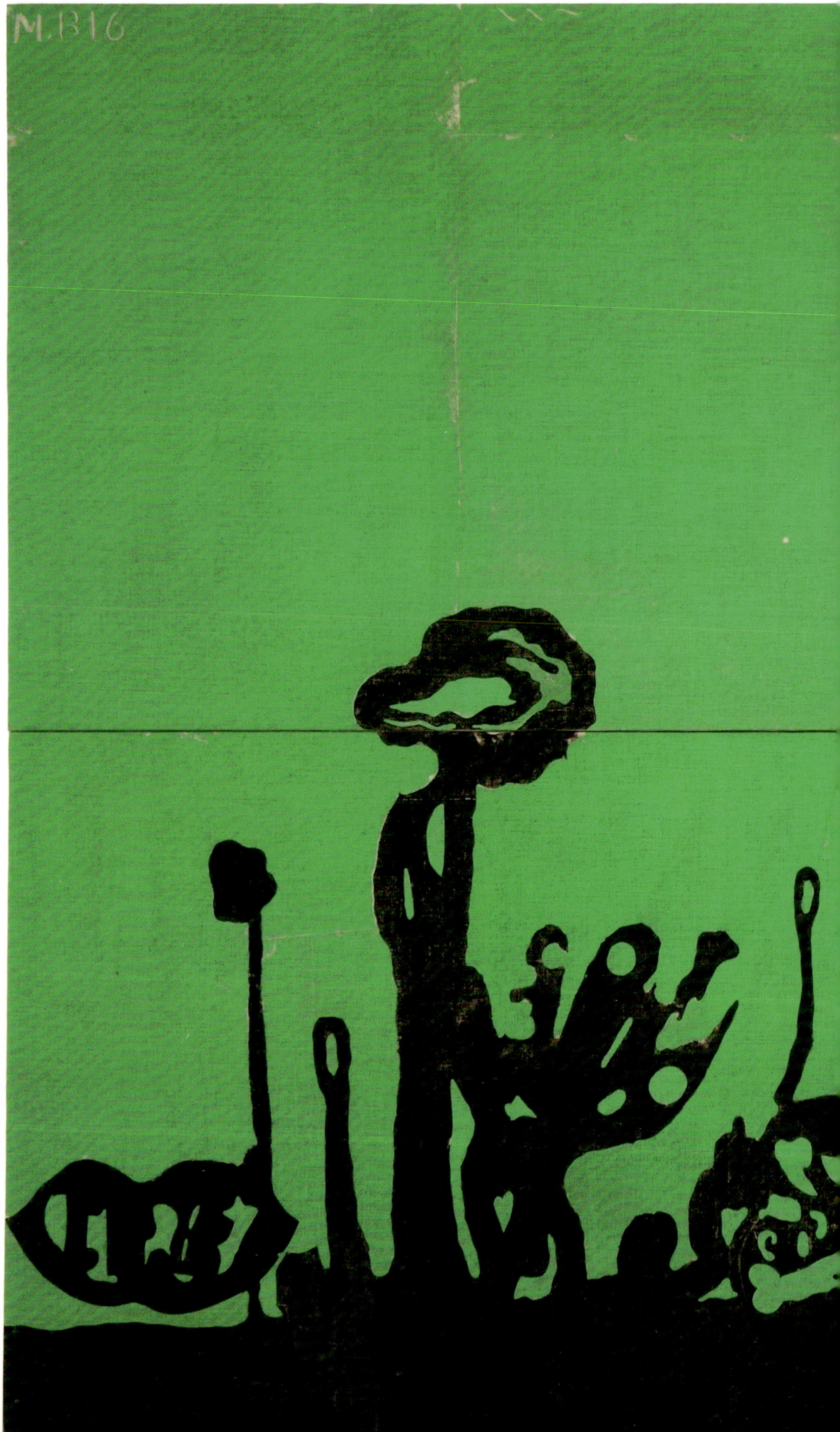

M.B16

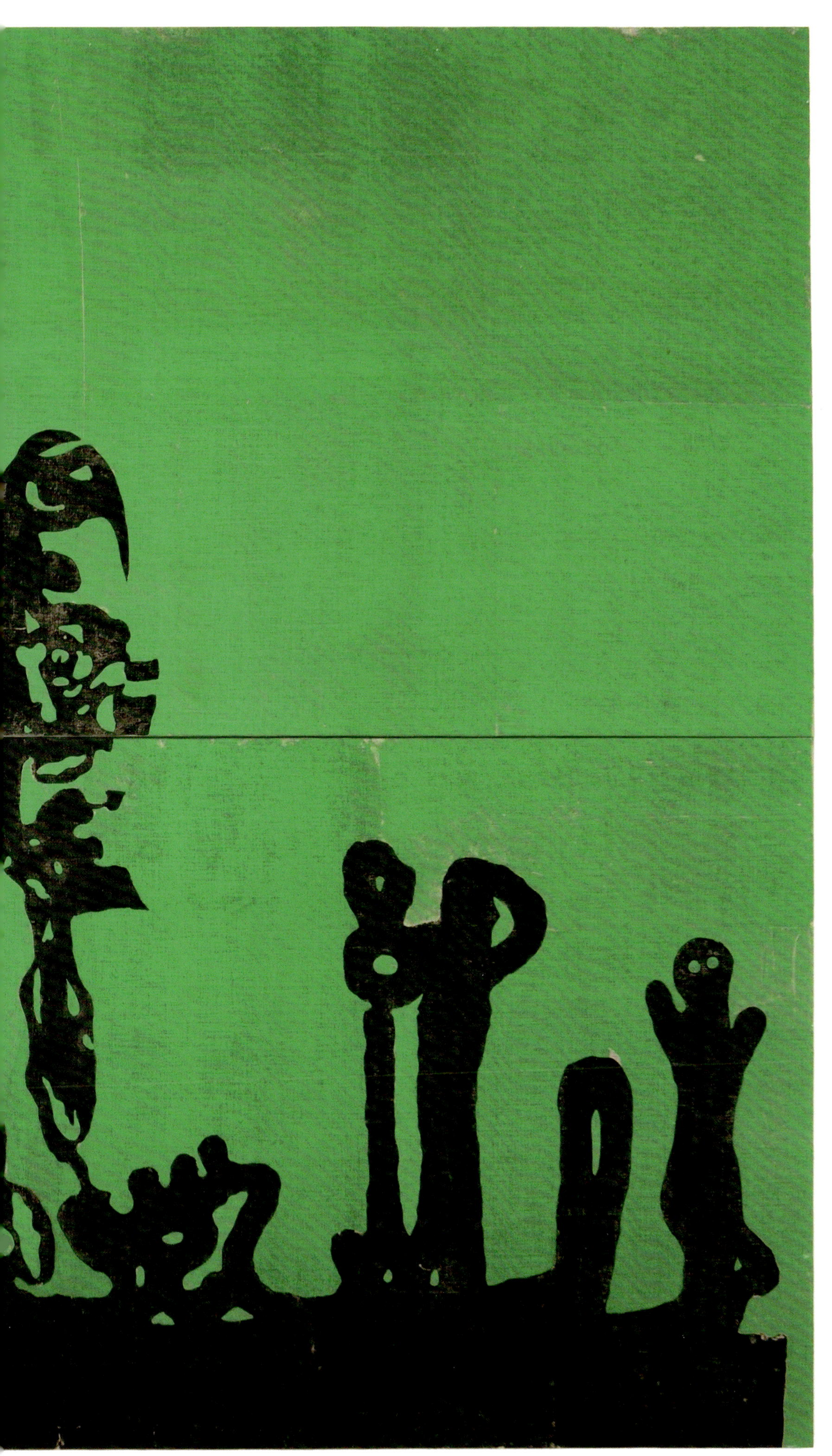

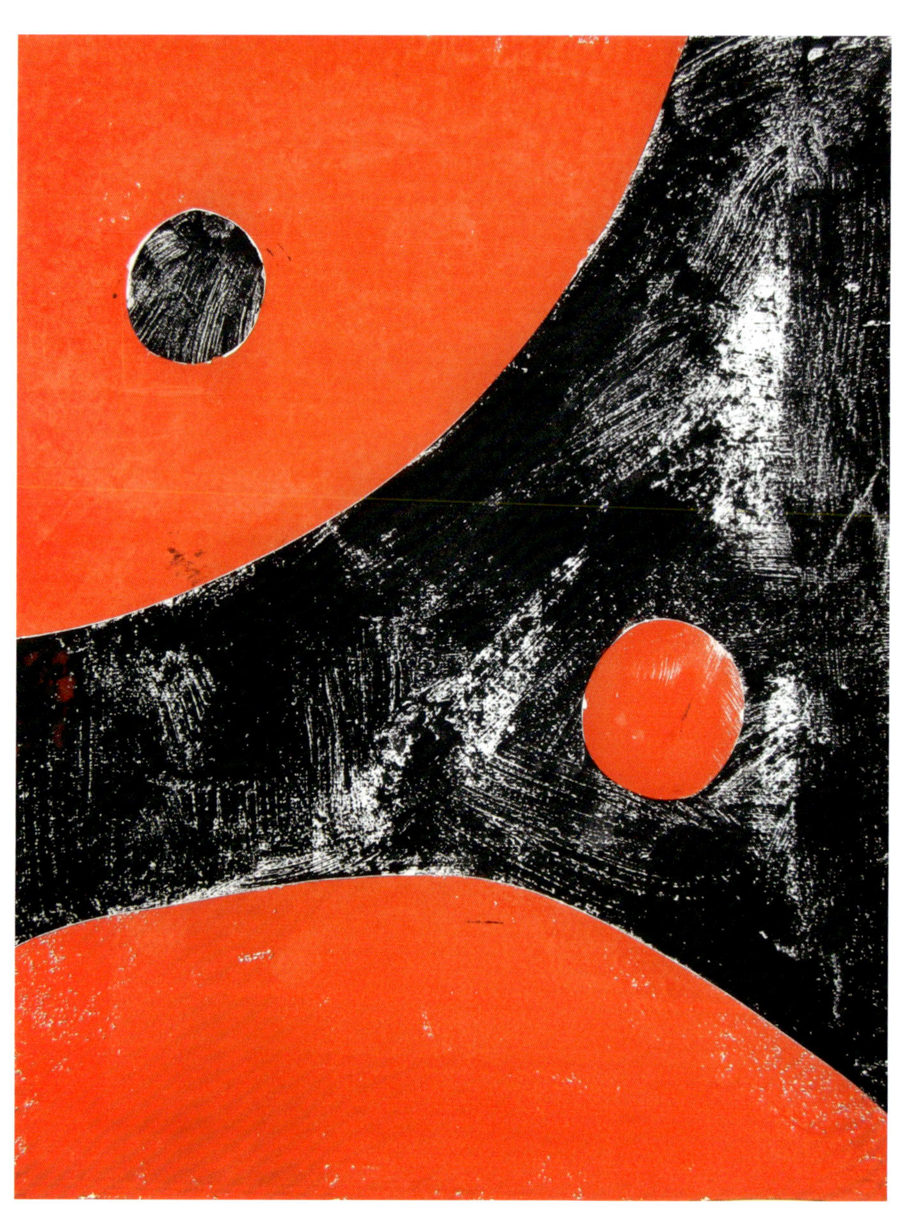

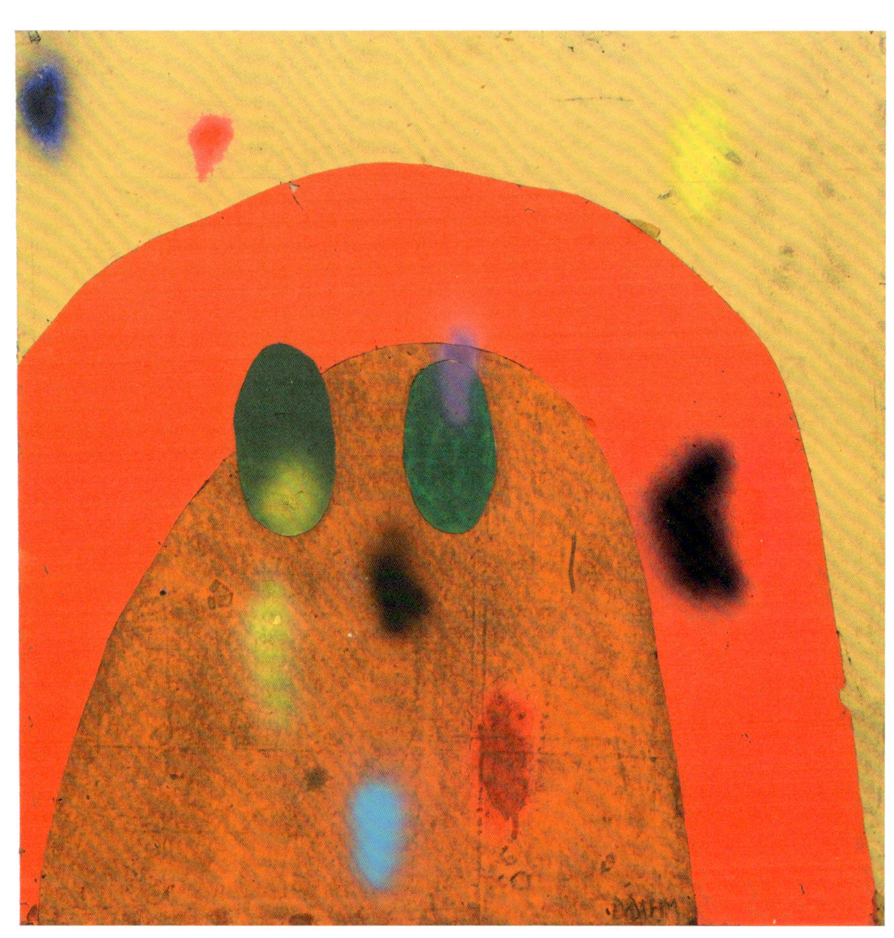

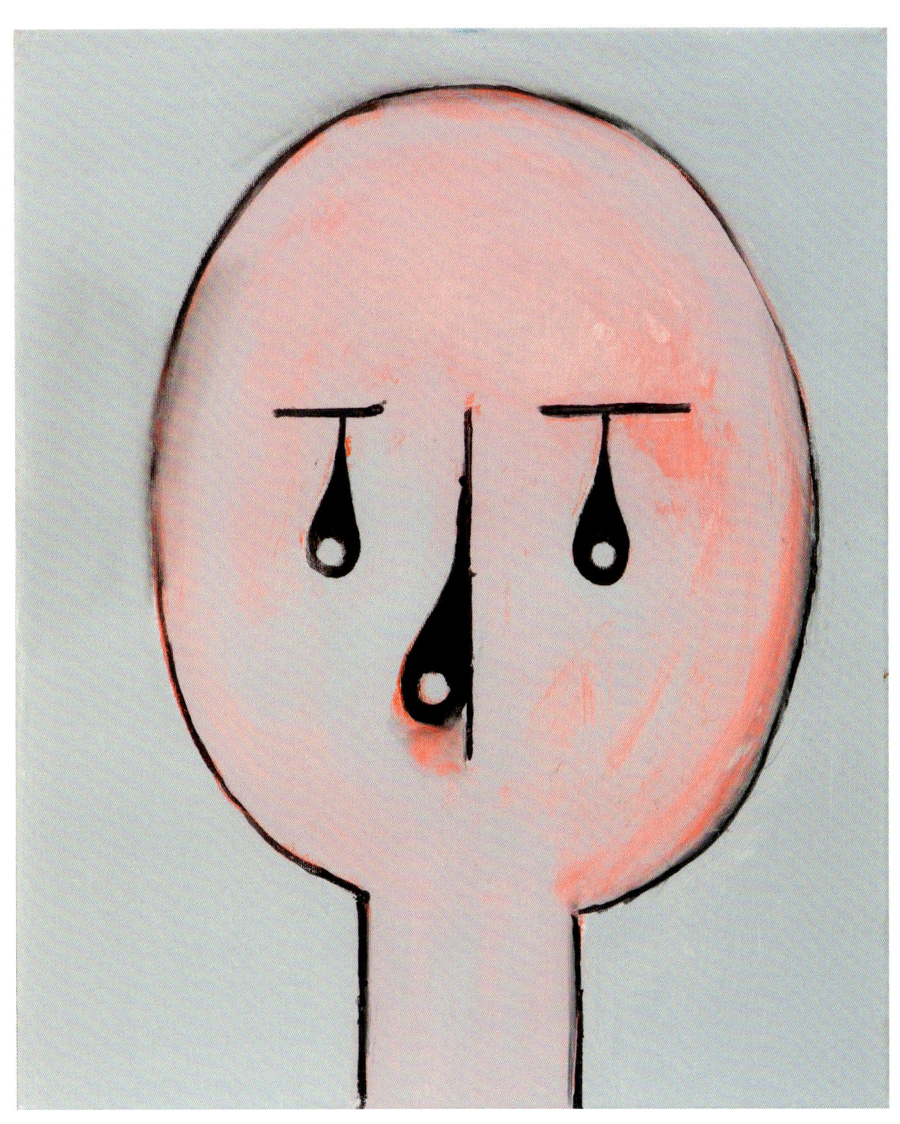

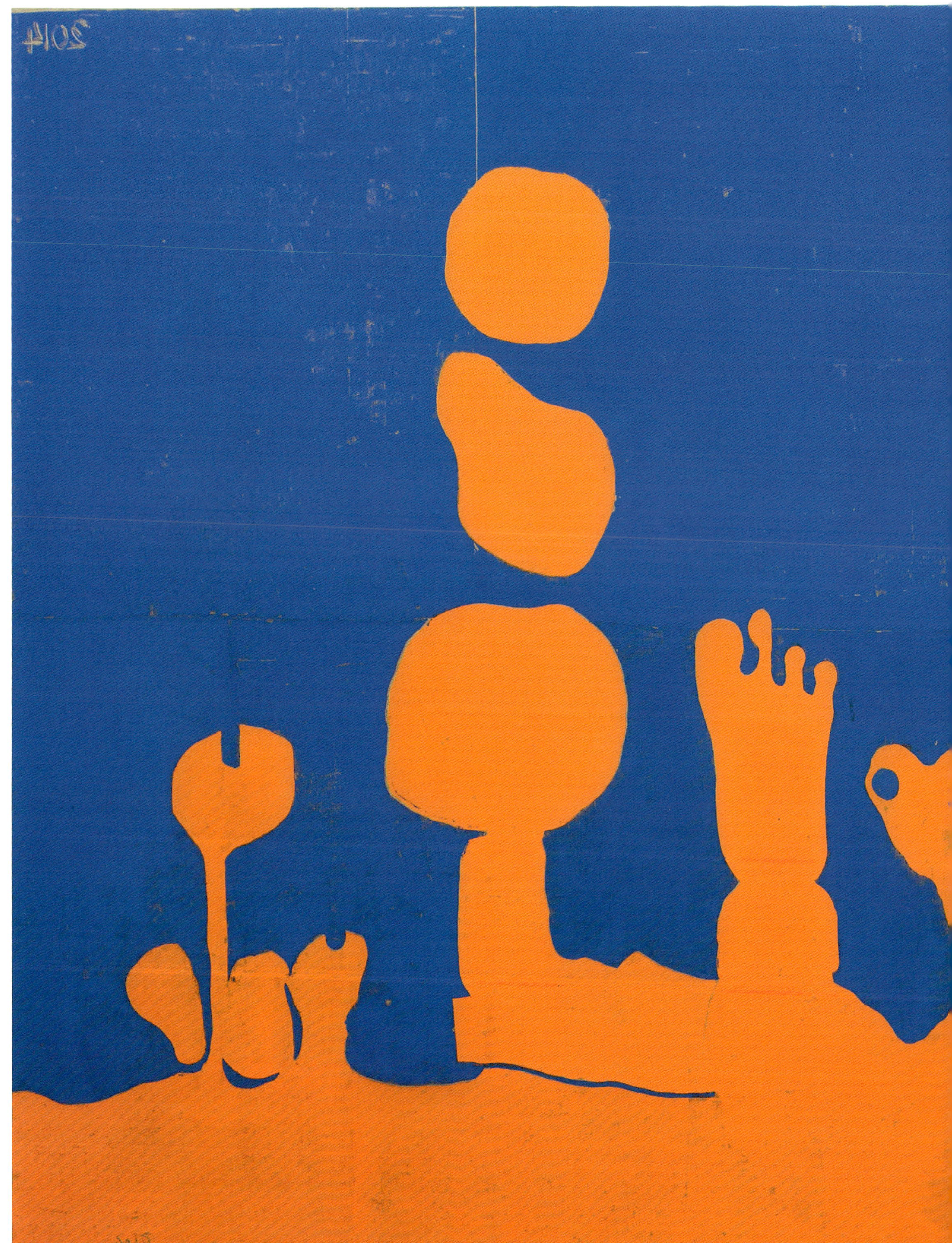

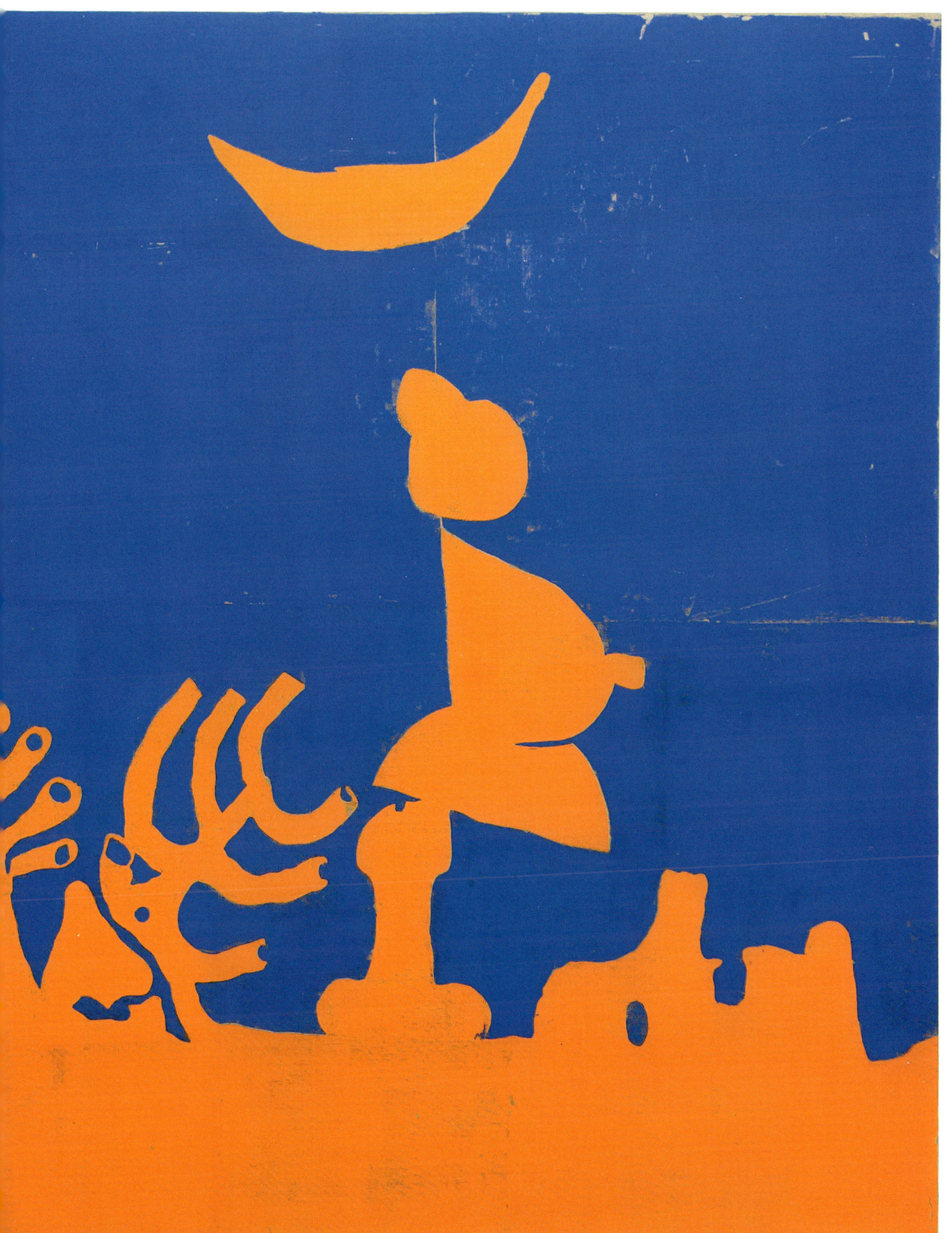

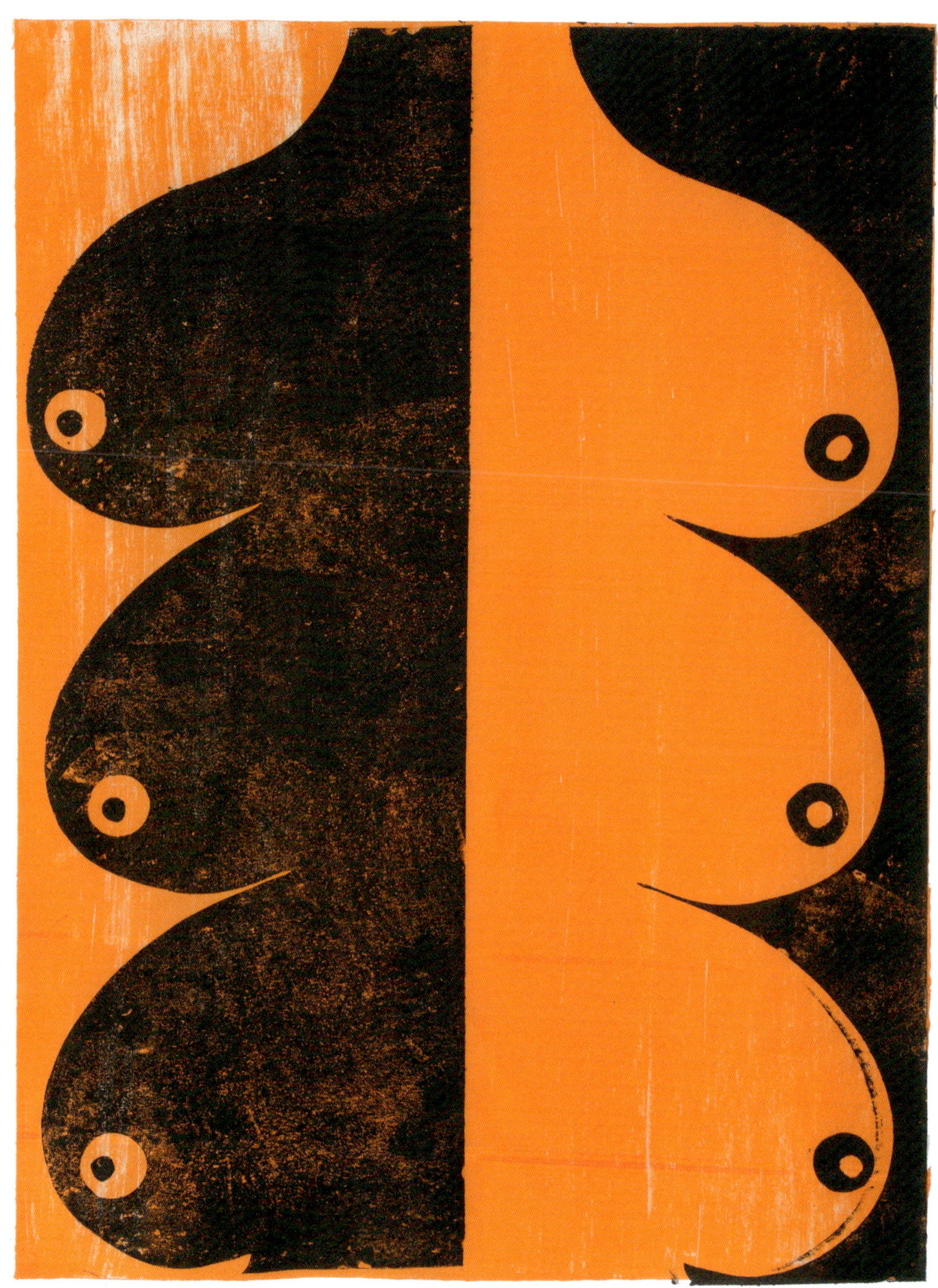

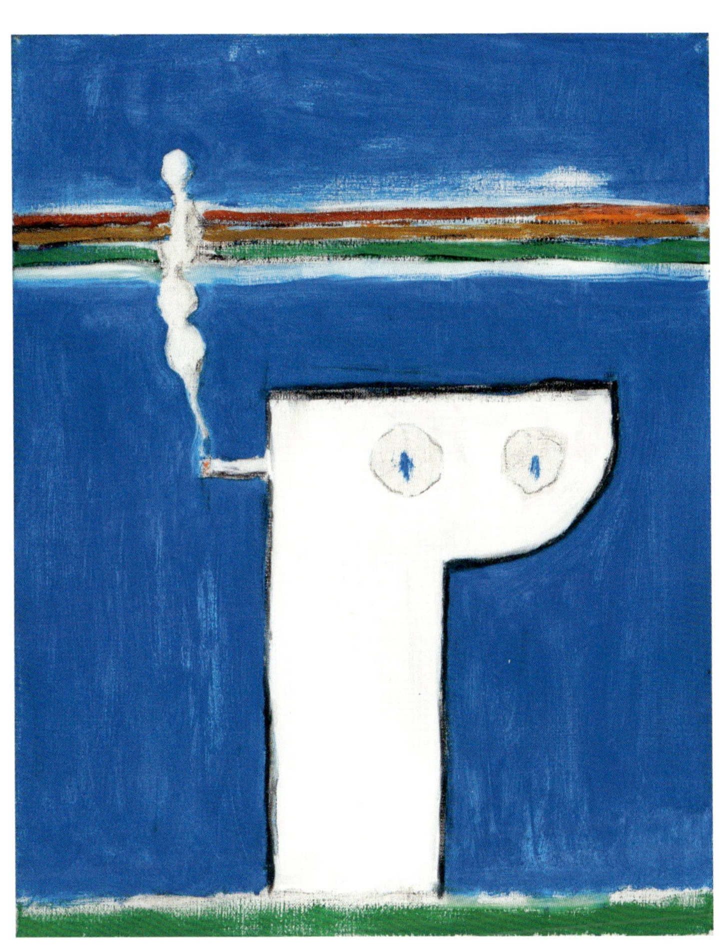

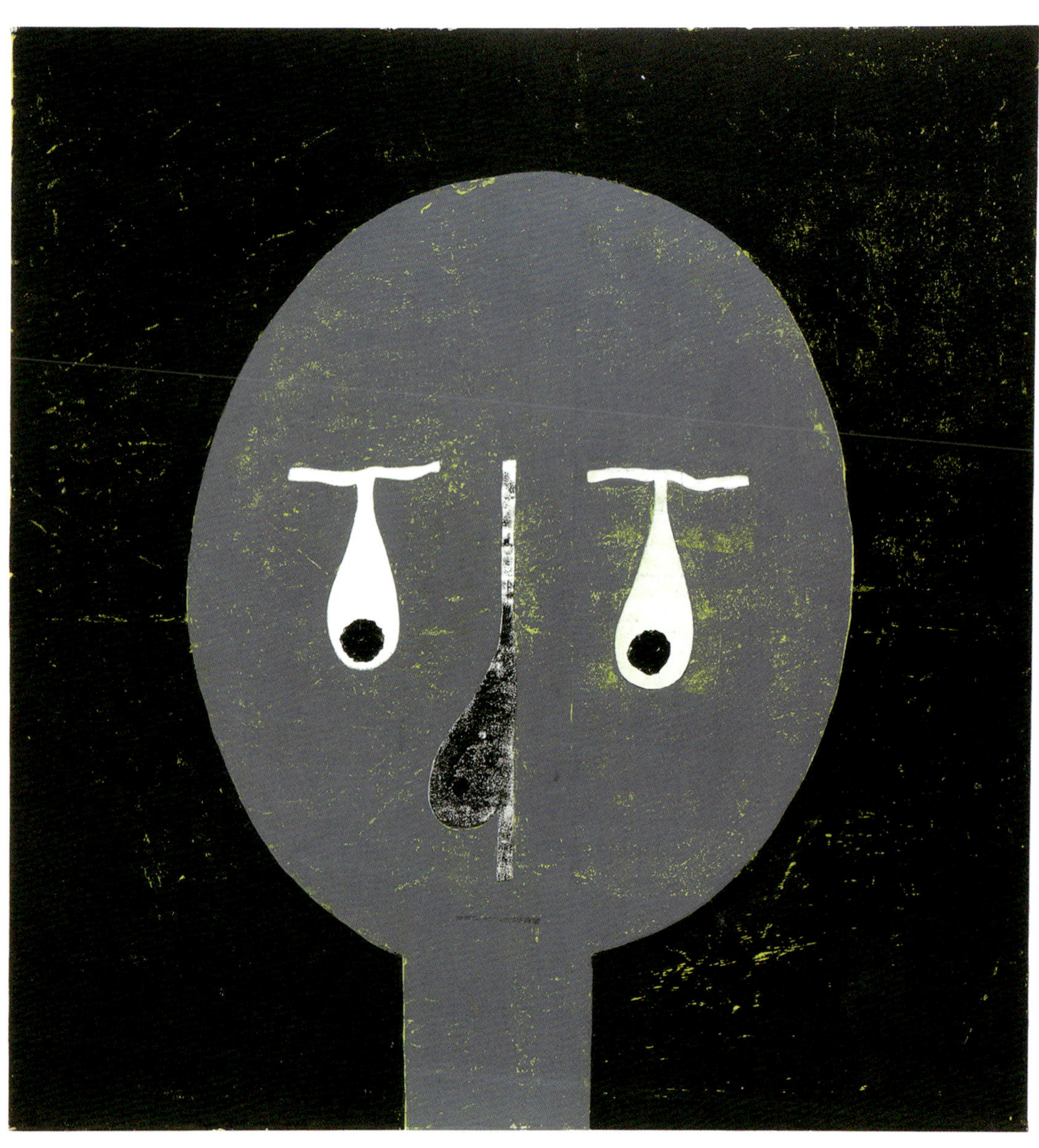

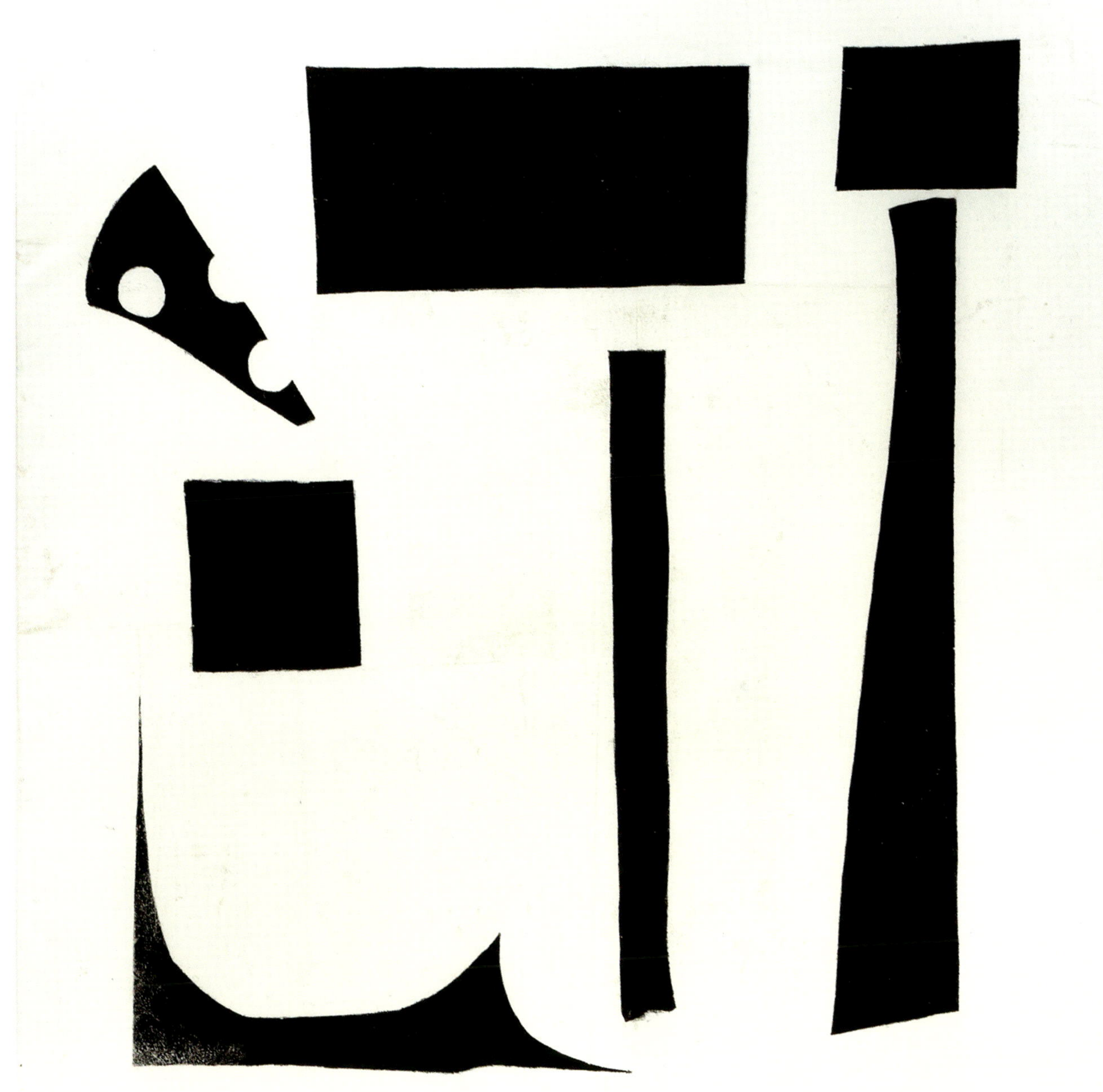

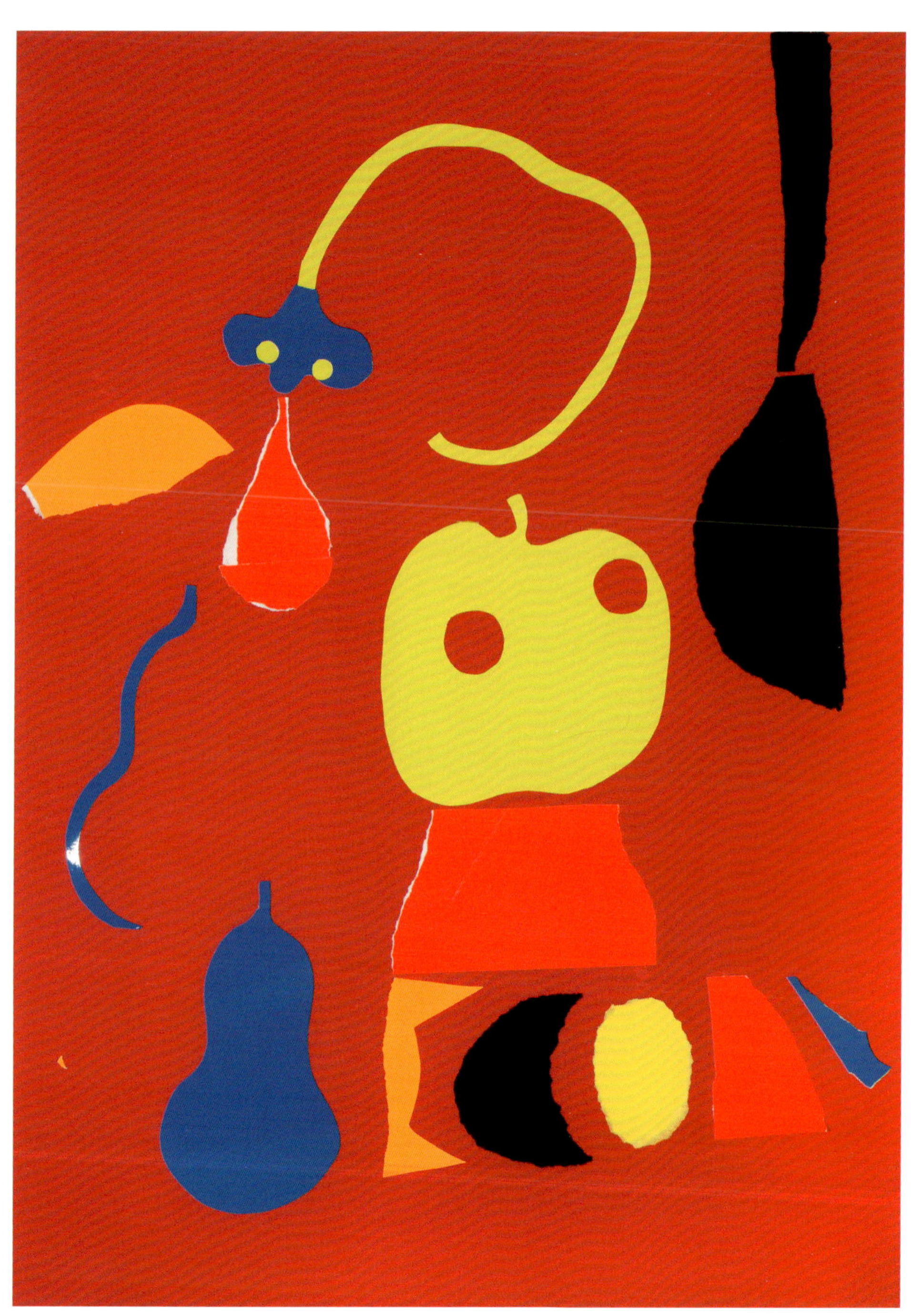

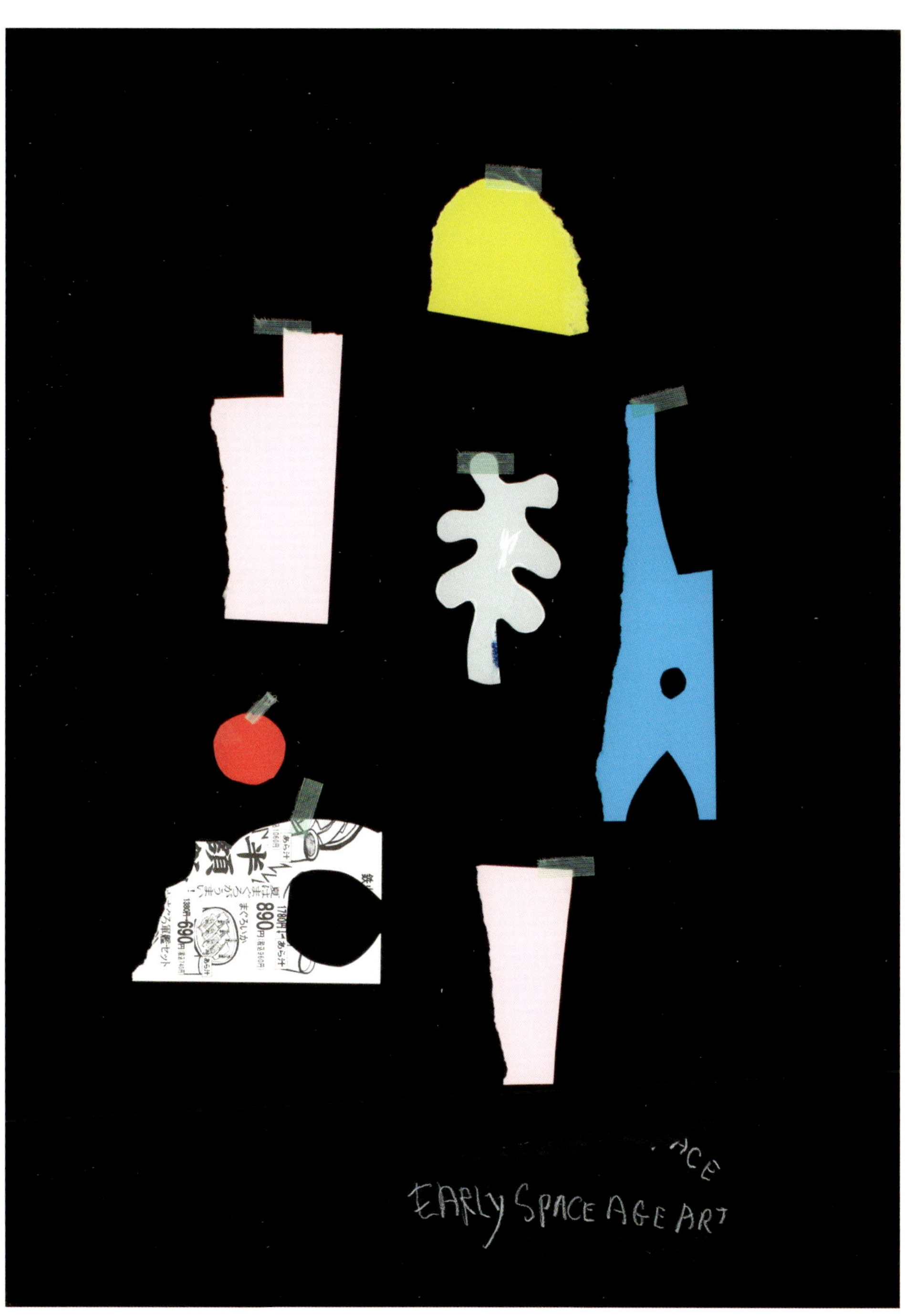
EARLY SPACE AGE ART

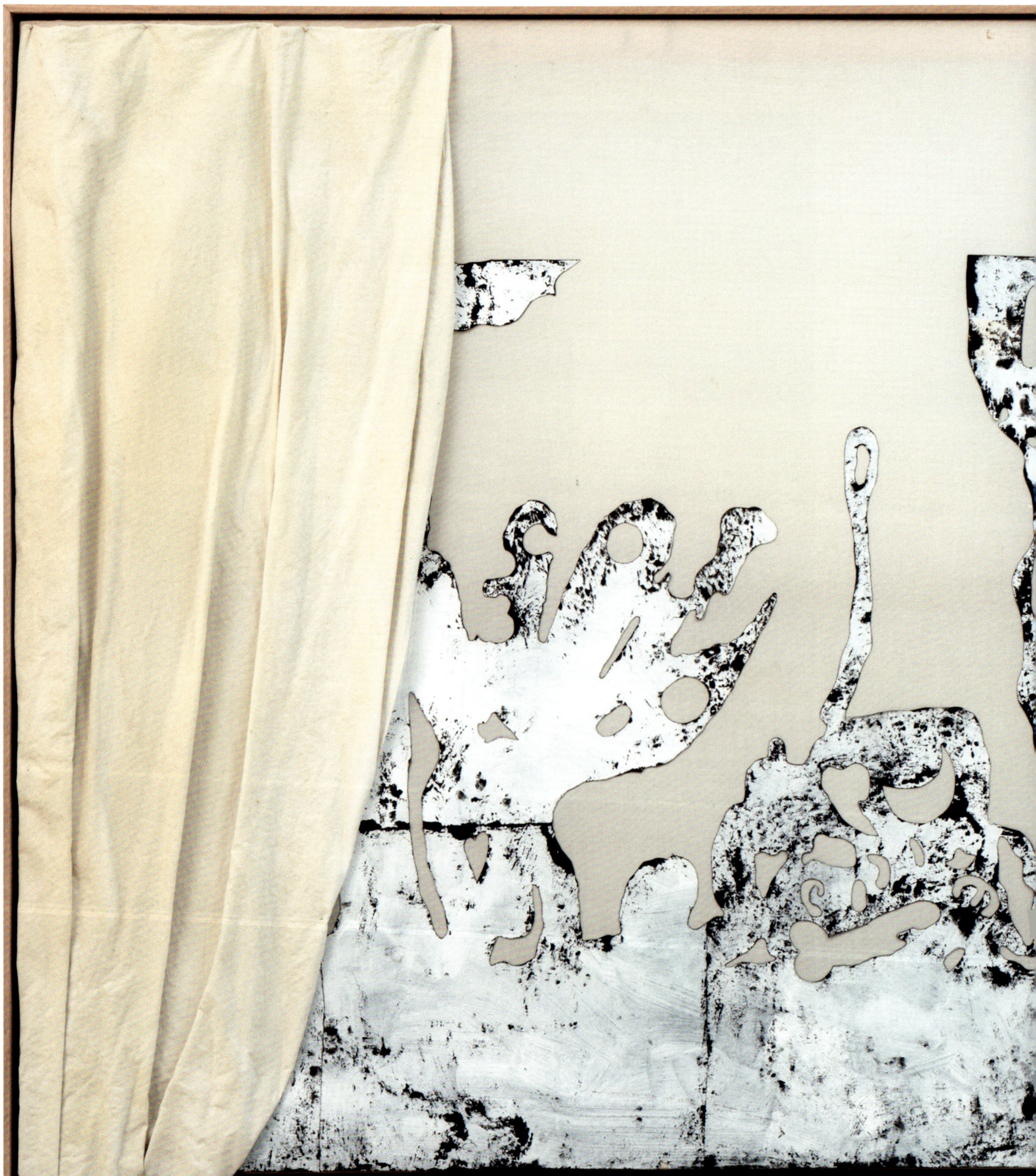

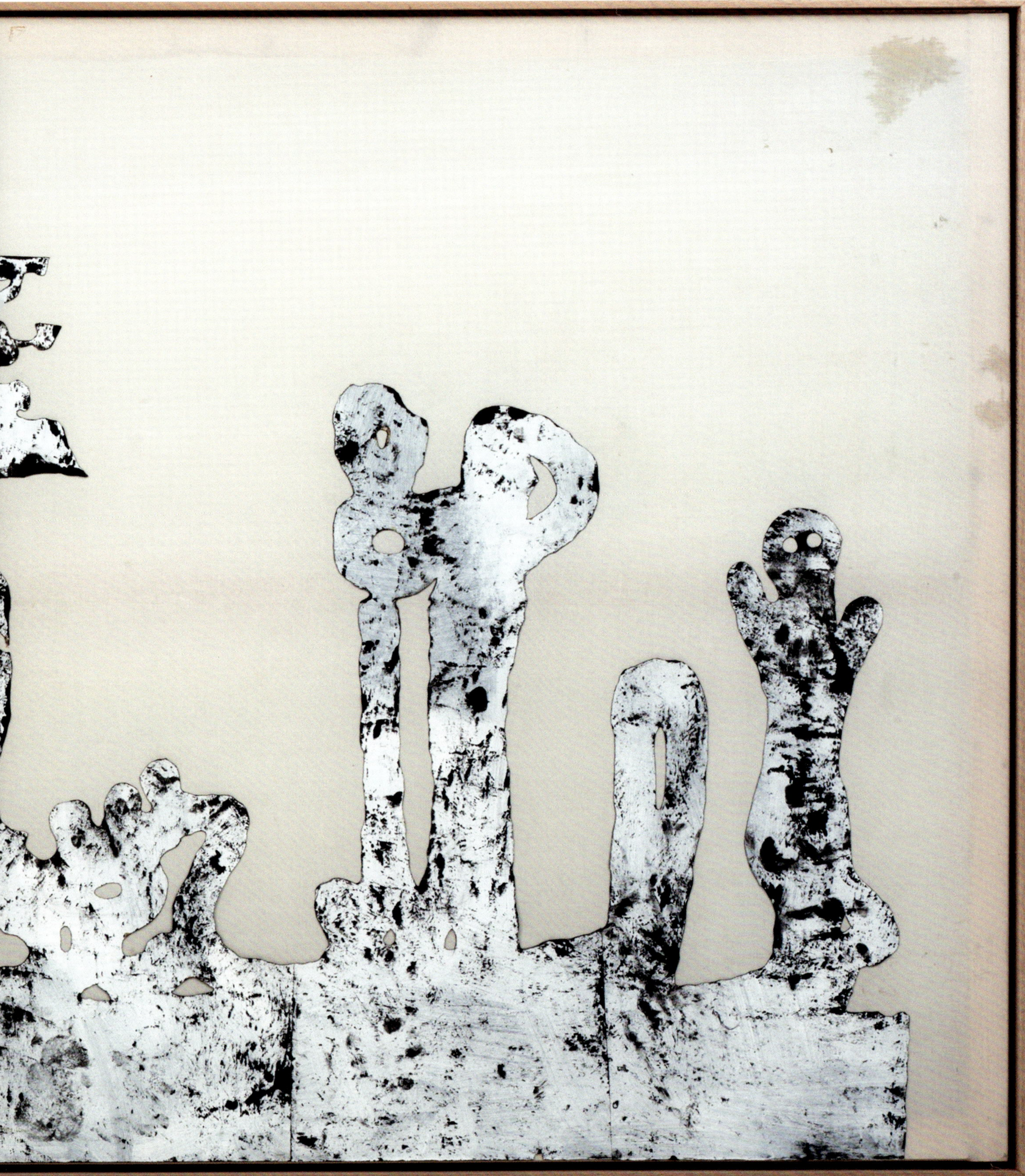

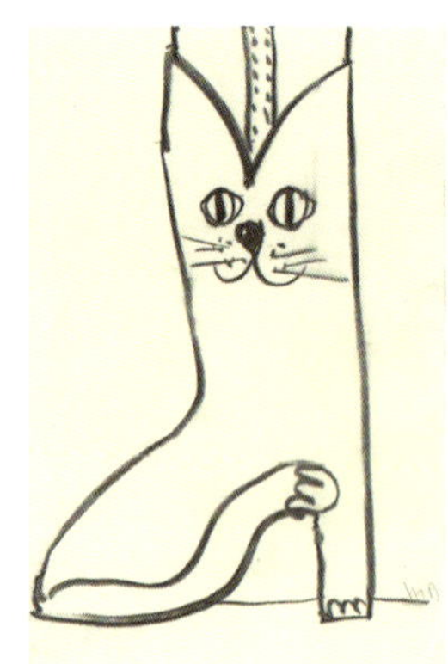
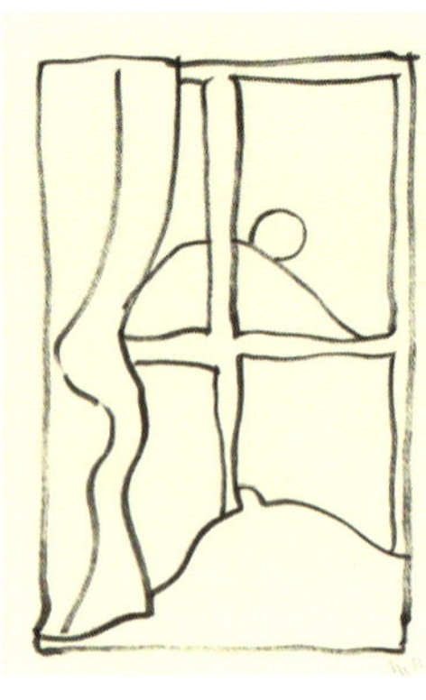
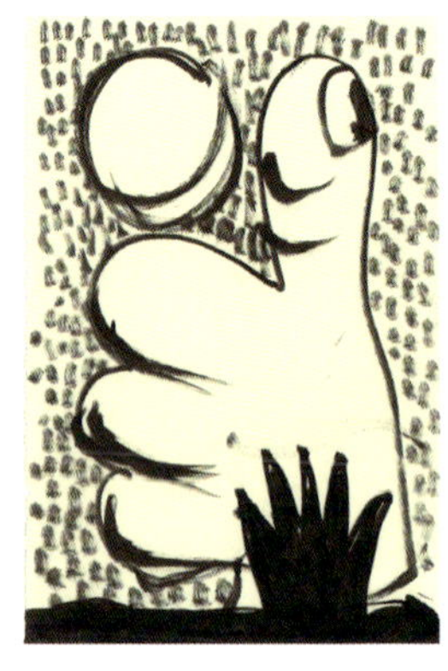
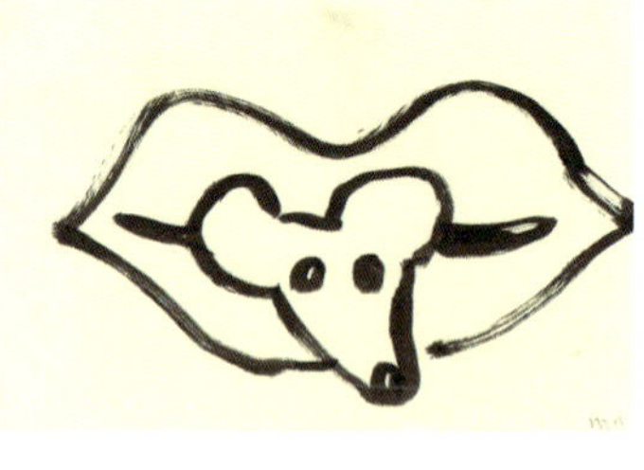
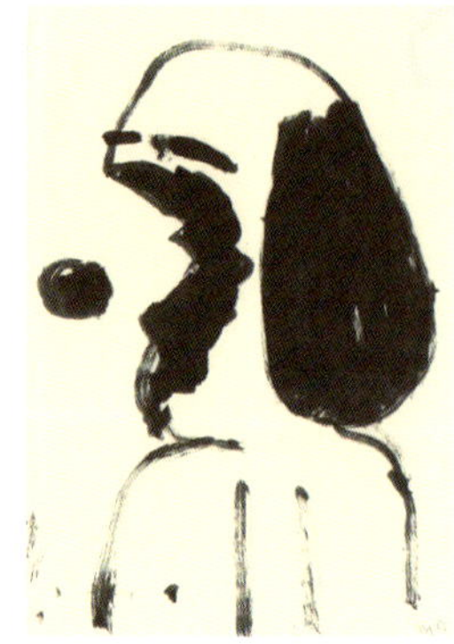
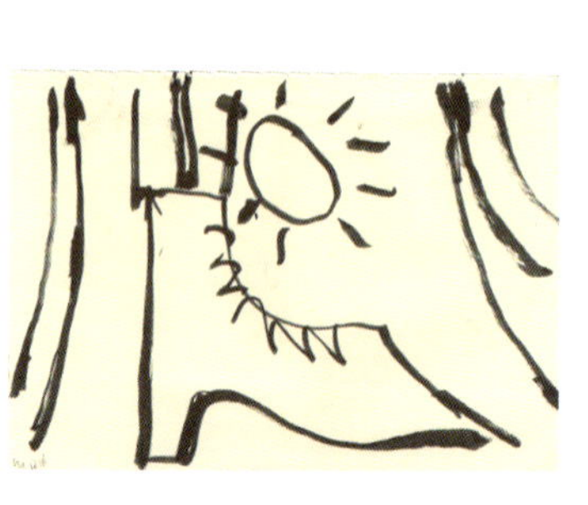
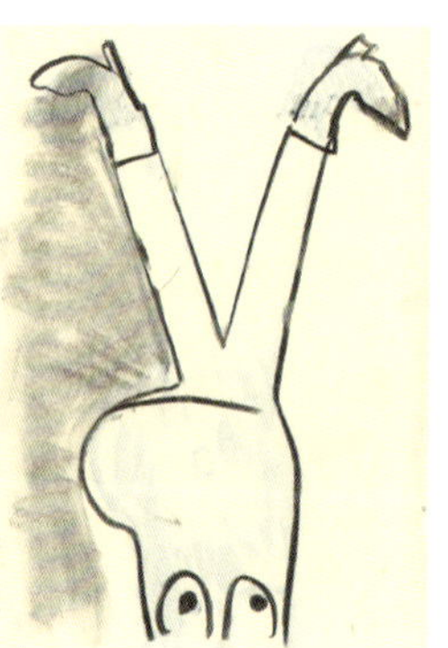
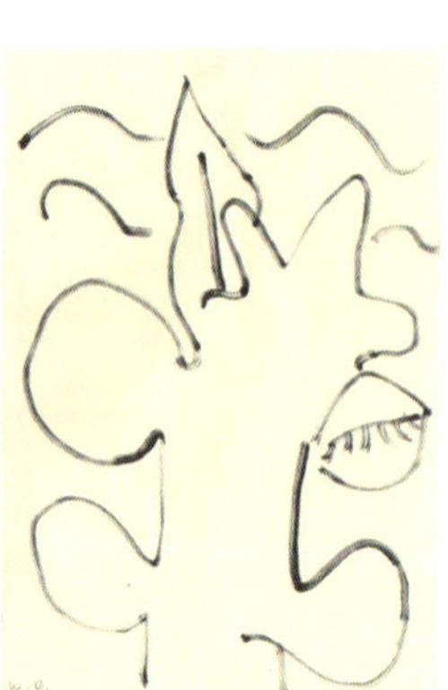
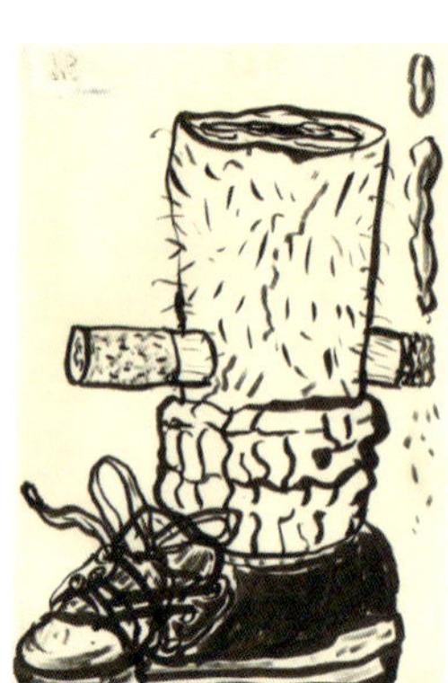

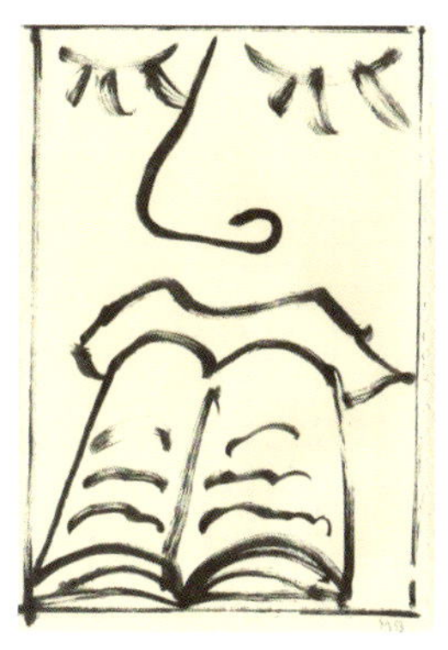
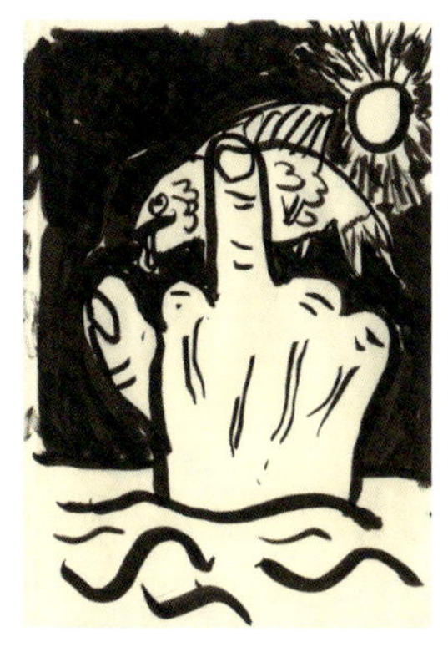
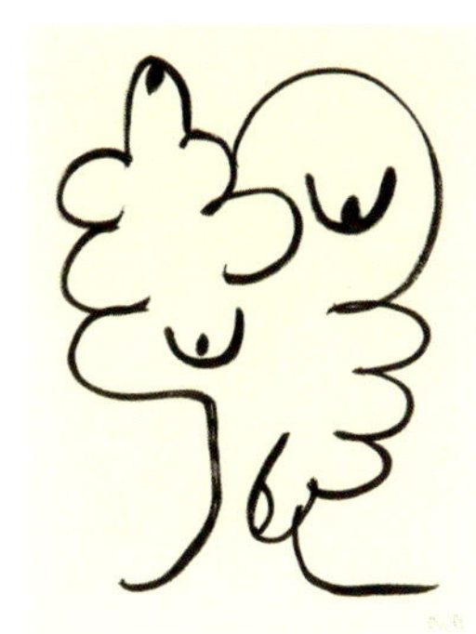
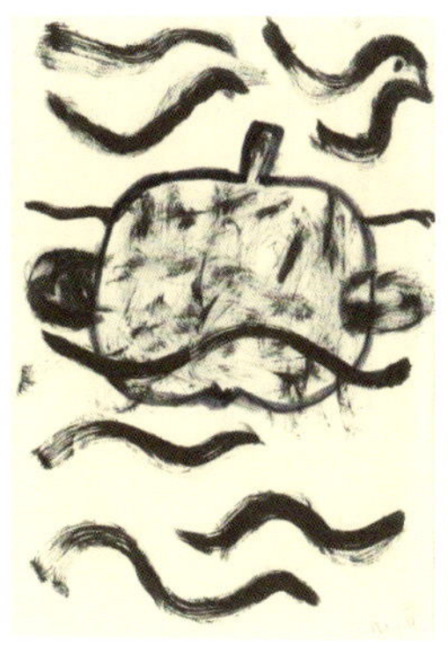
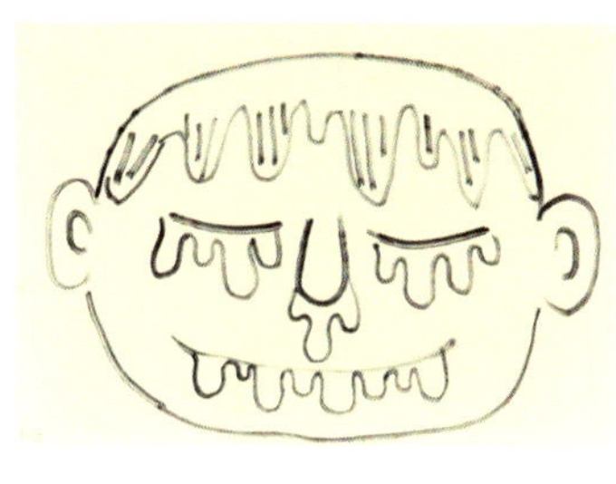
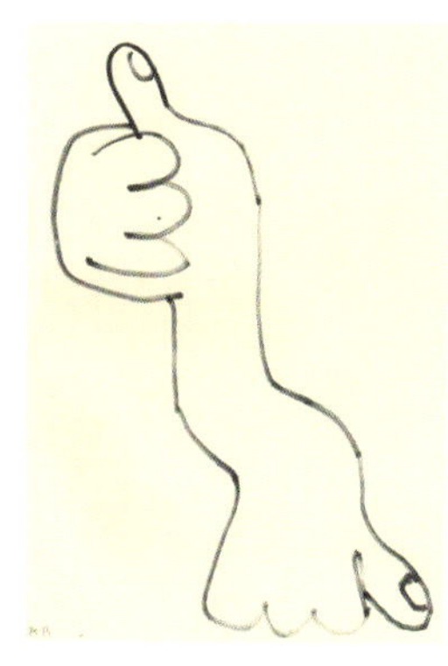
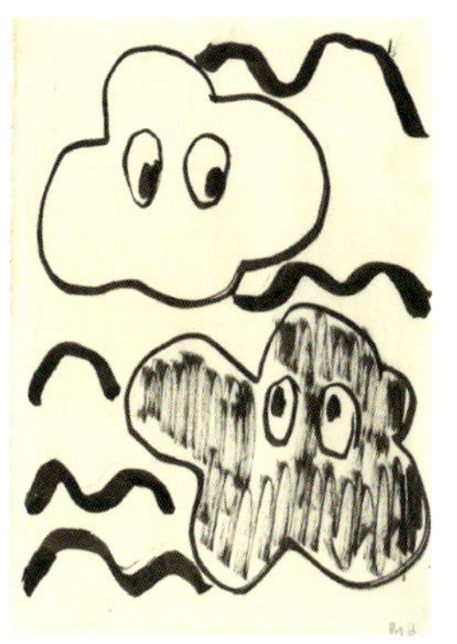
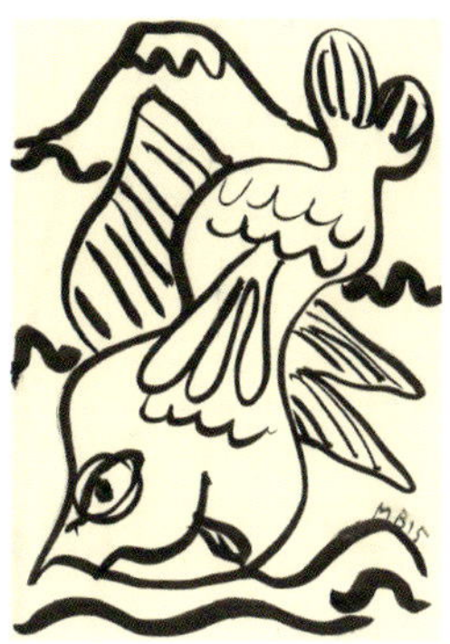
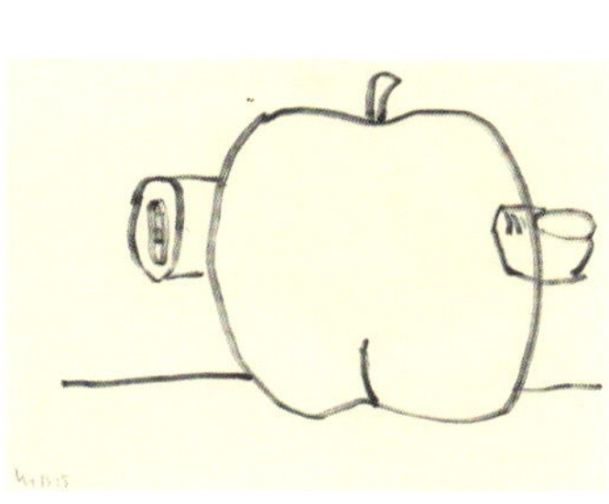
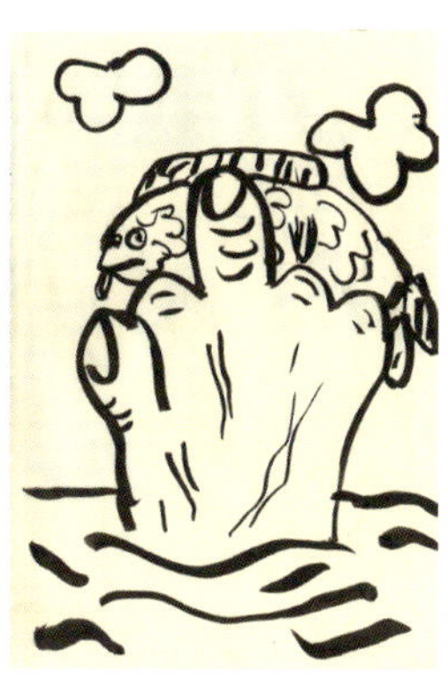

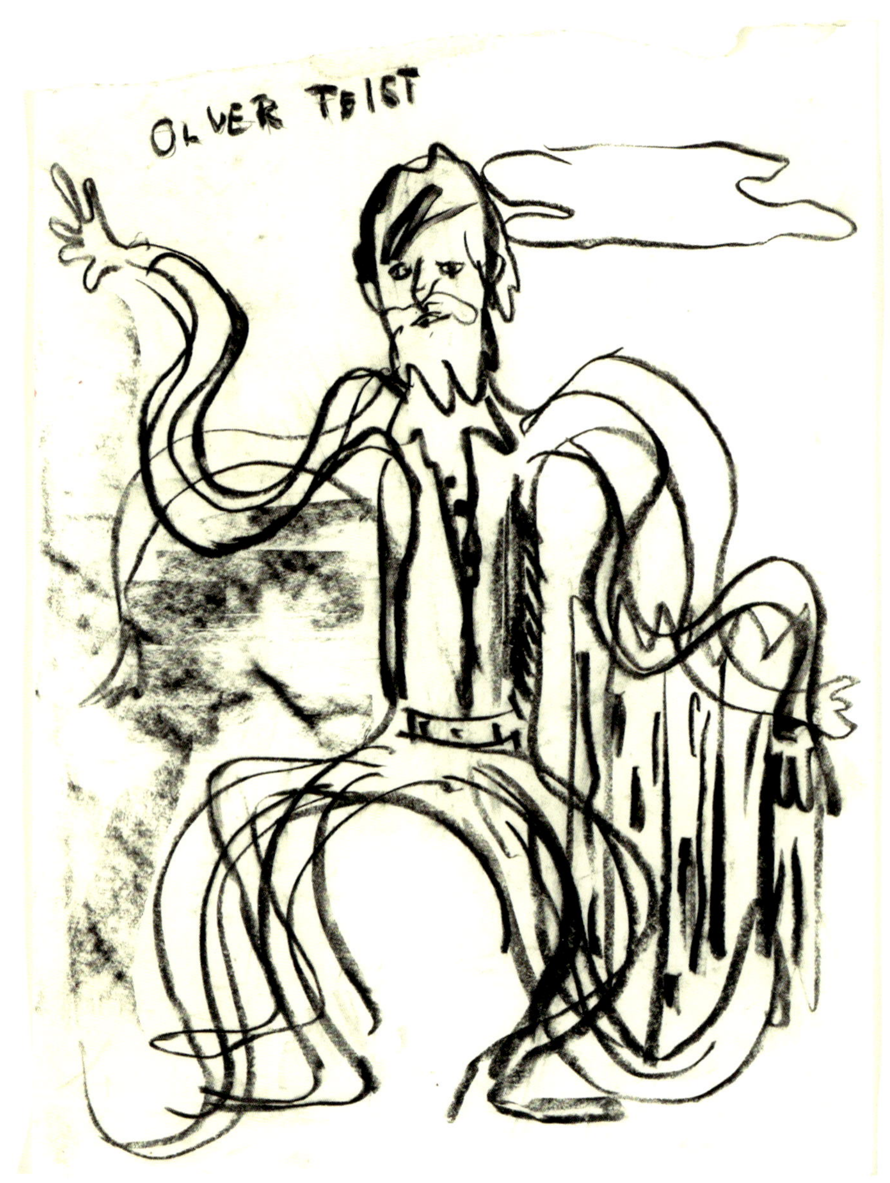
OLVER TBIST

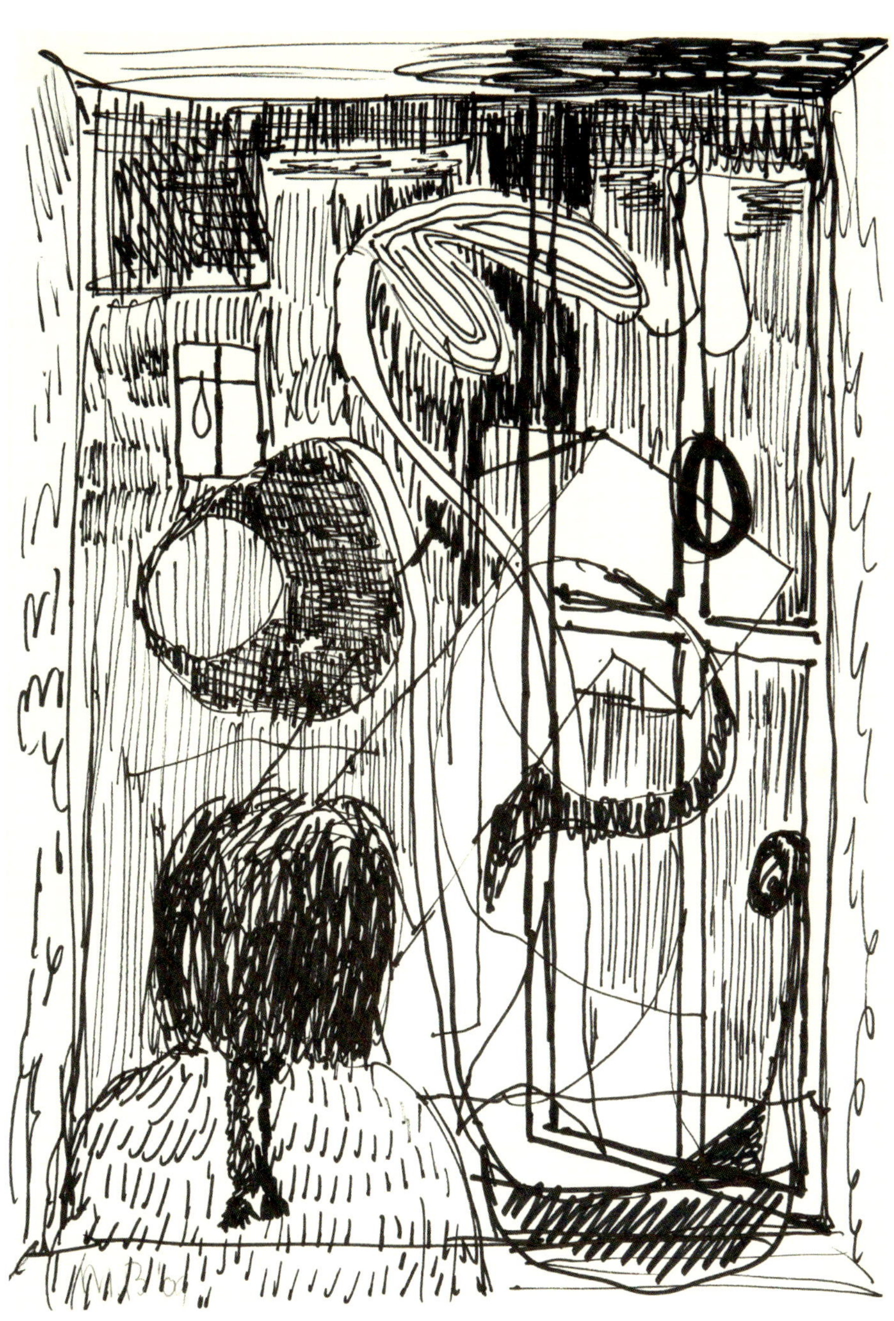

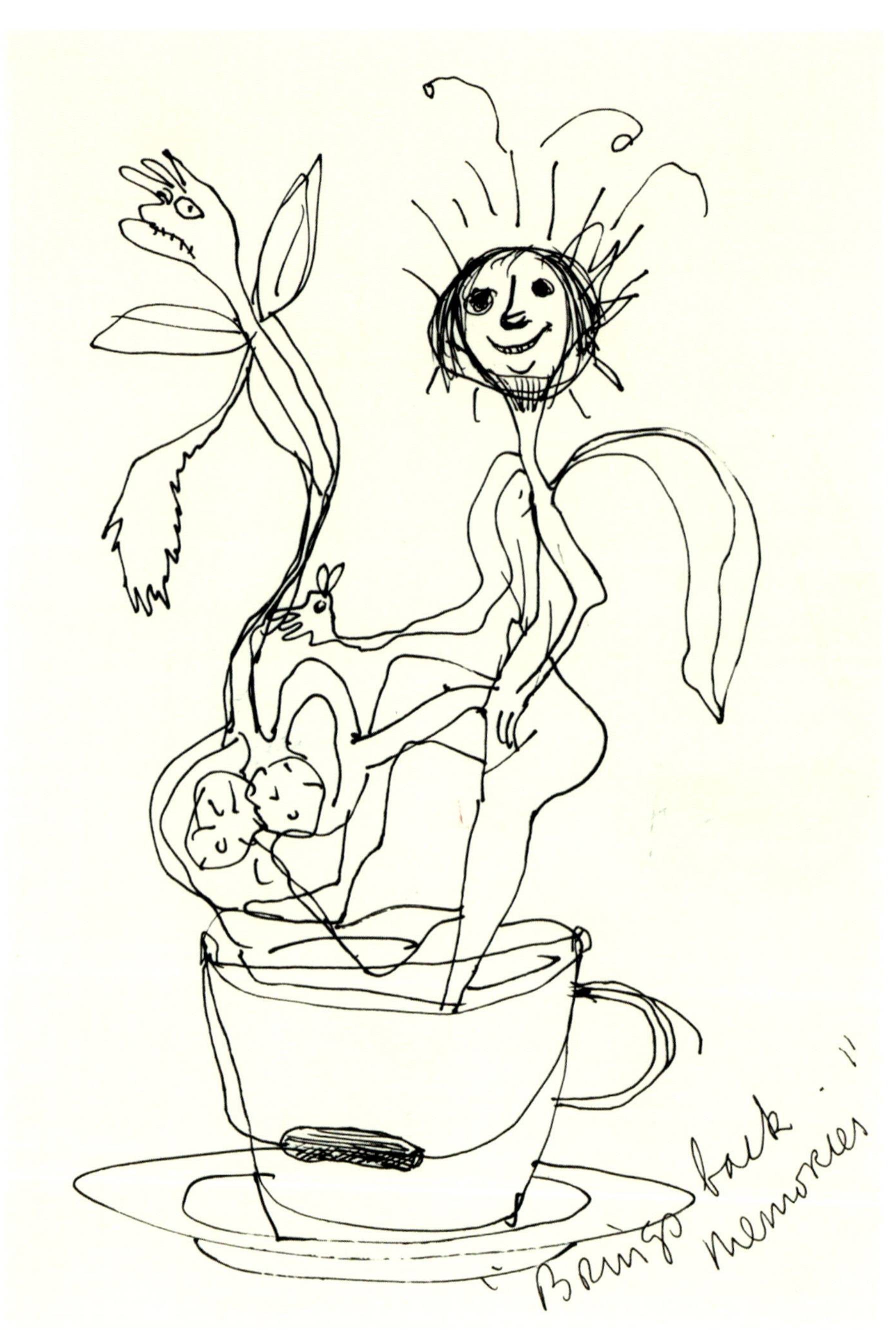
Brings back memories!

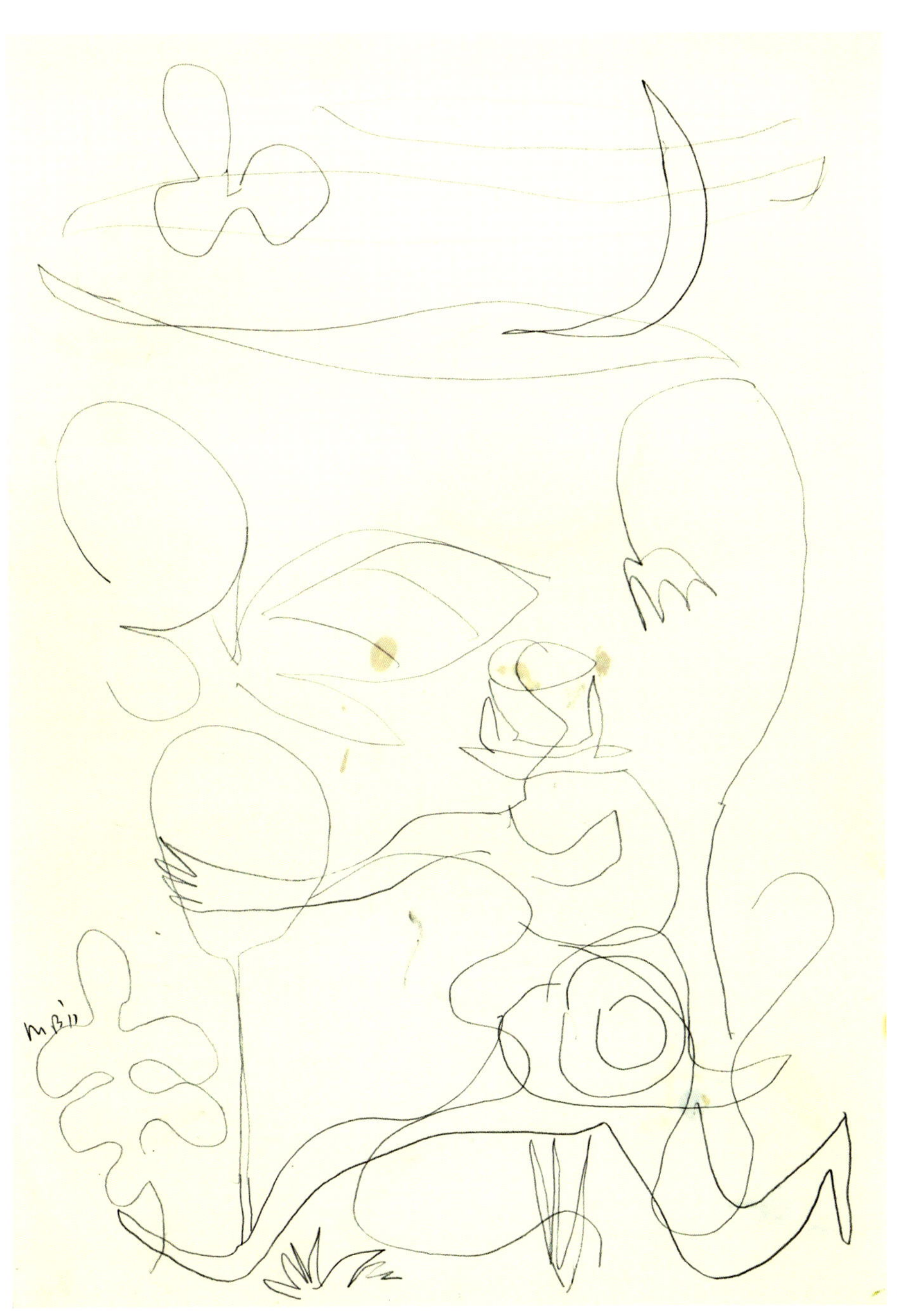

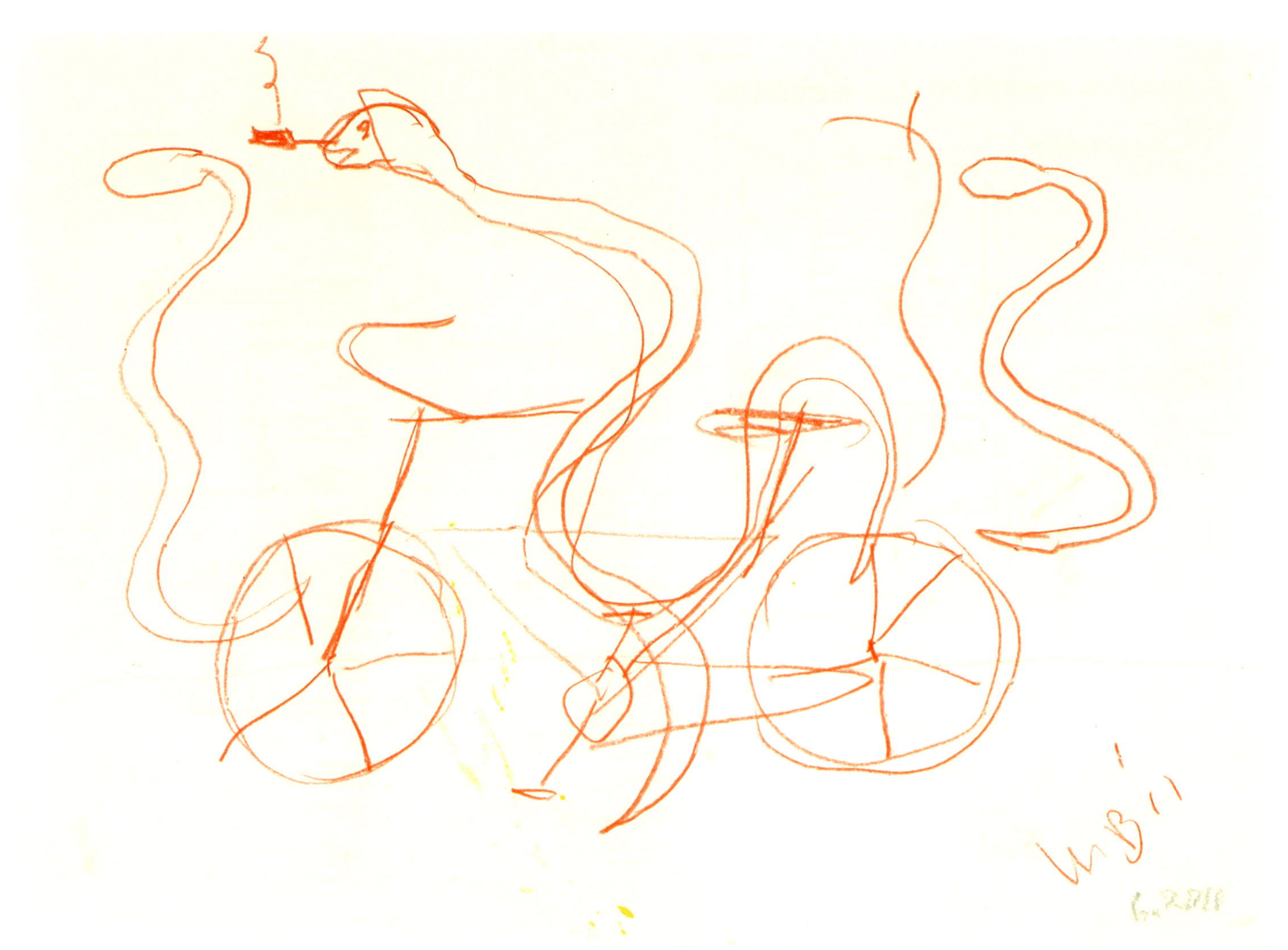

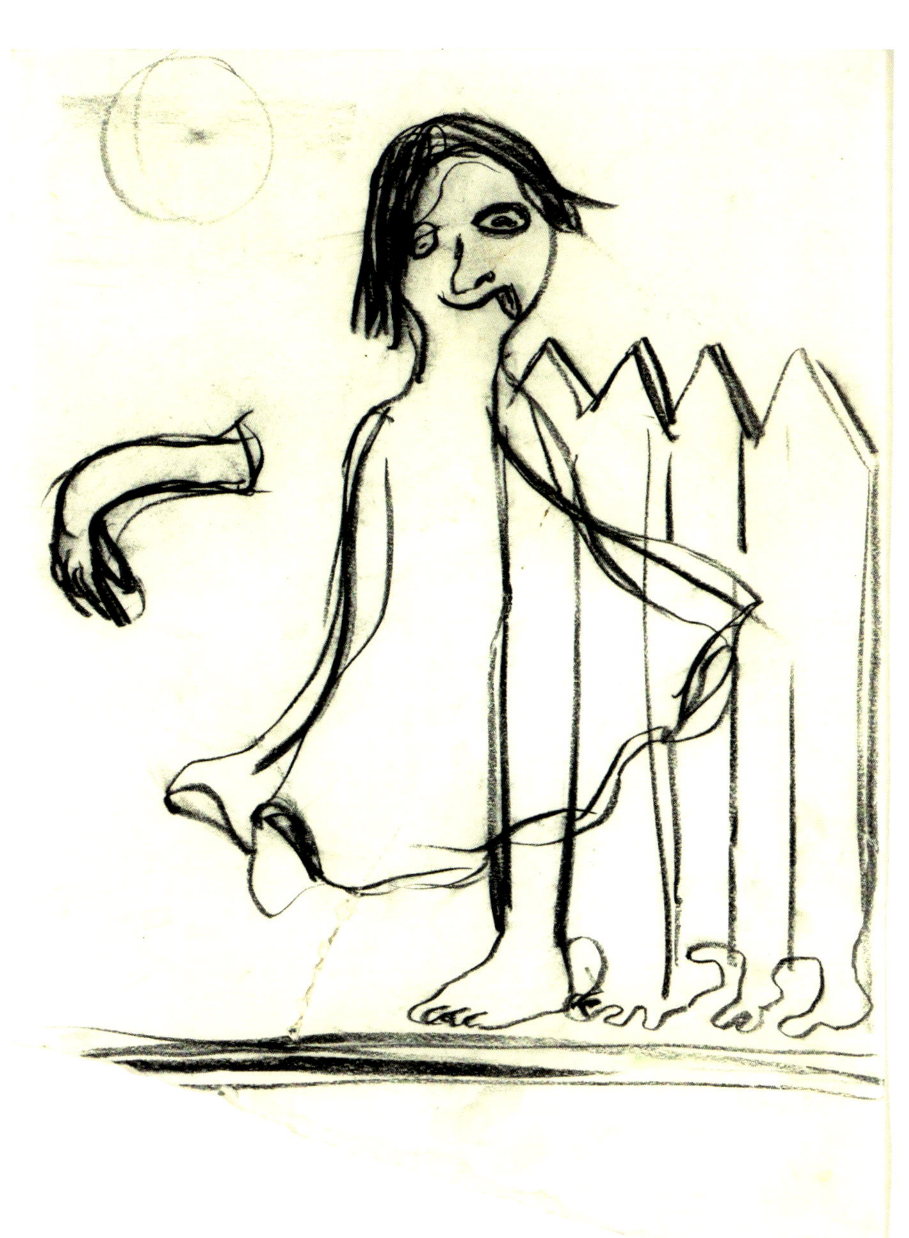

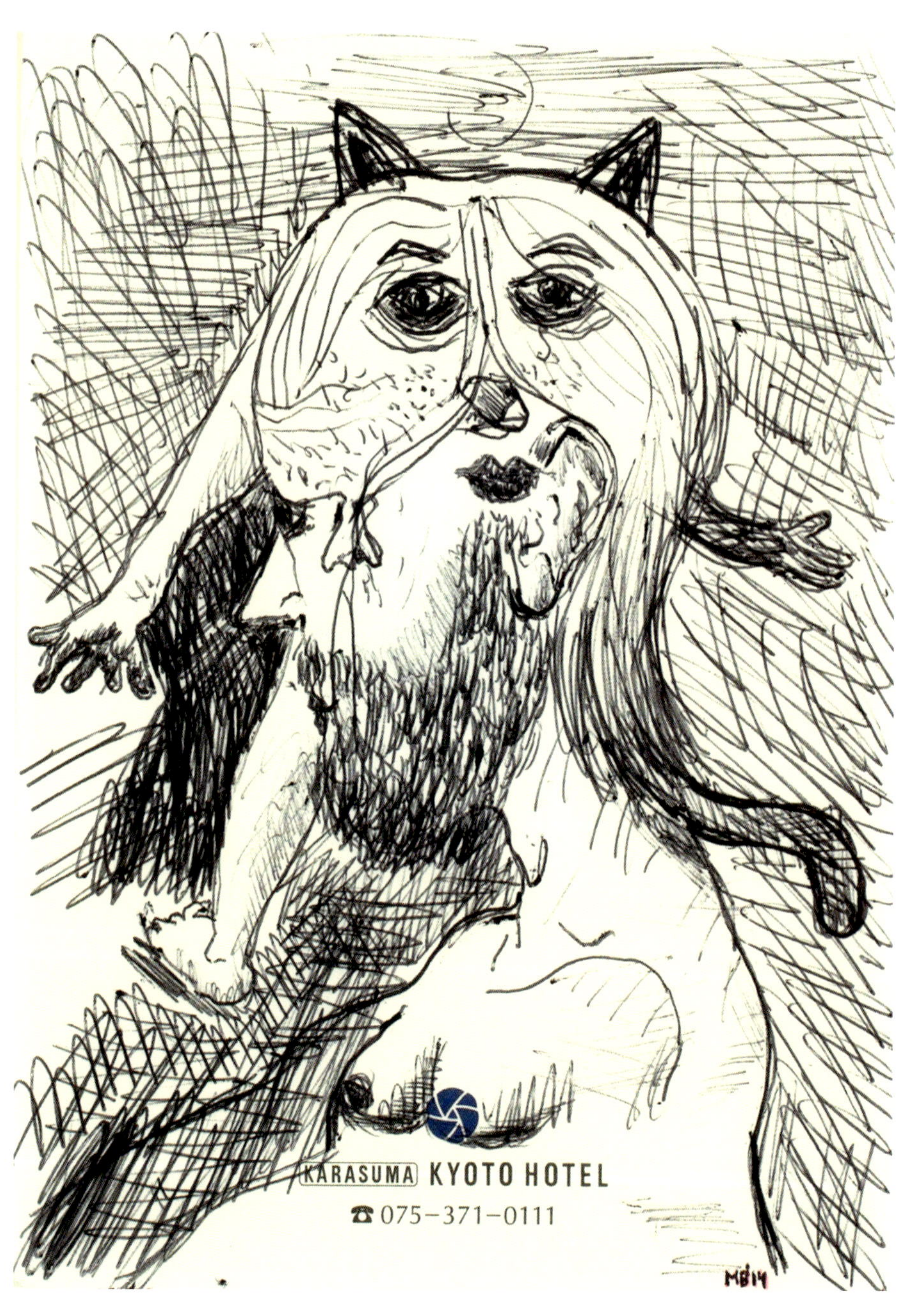
KARASUMA KYOTO HOTEL
☎ 075-371-0111
MB14

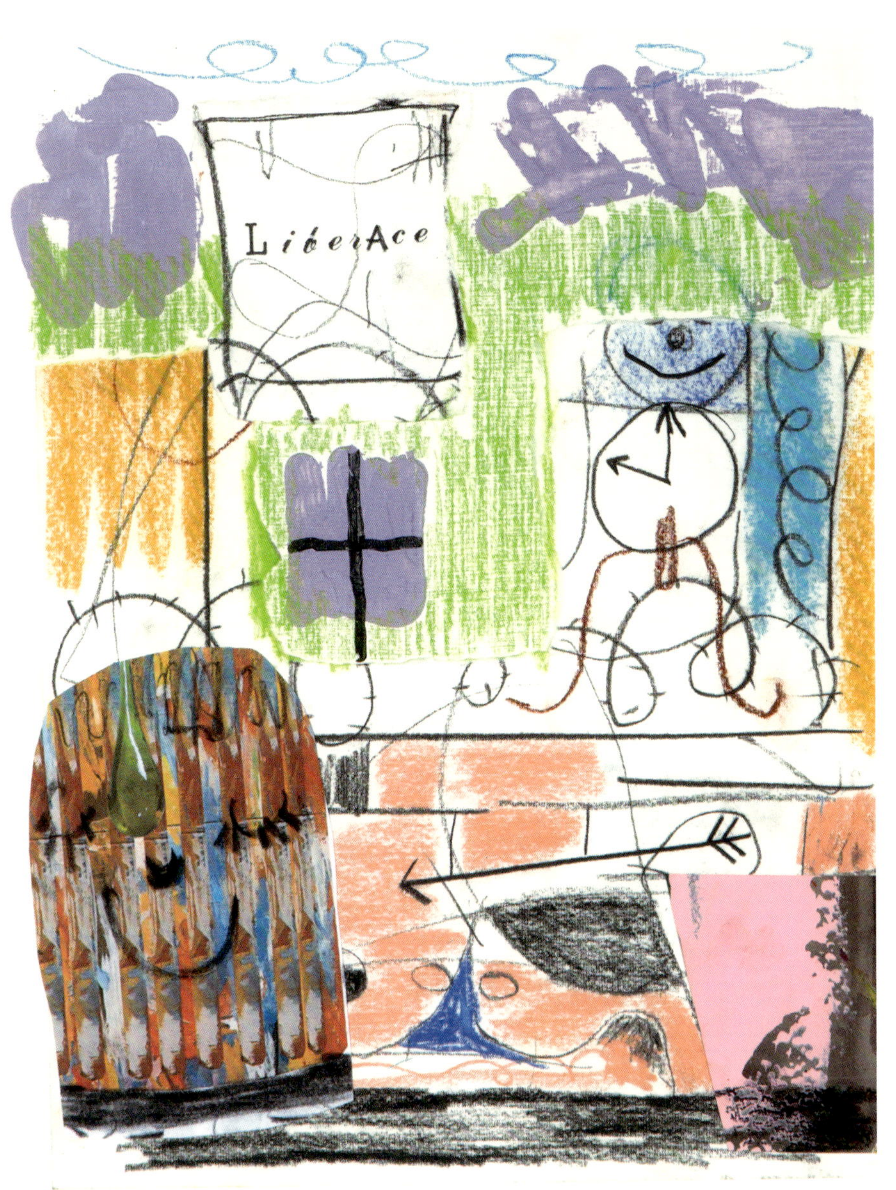
LiberAce

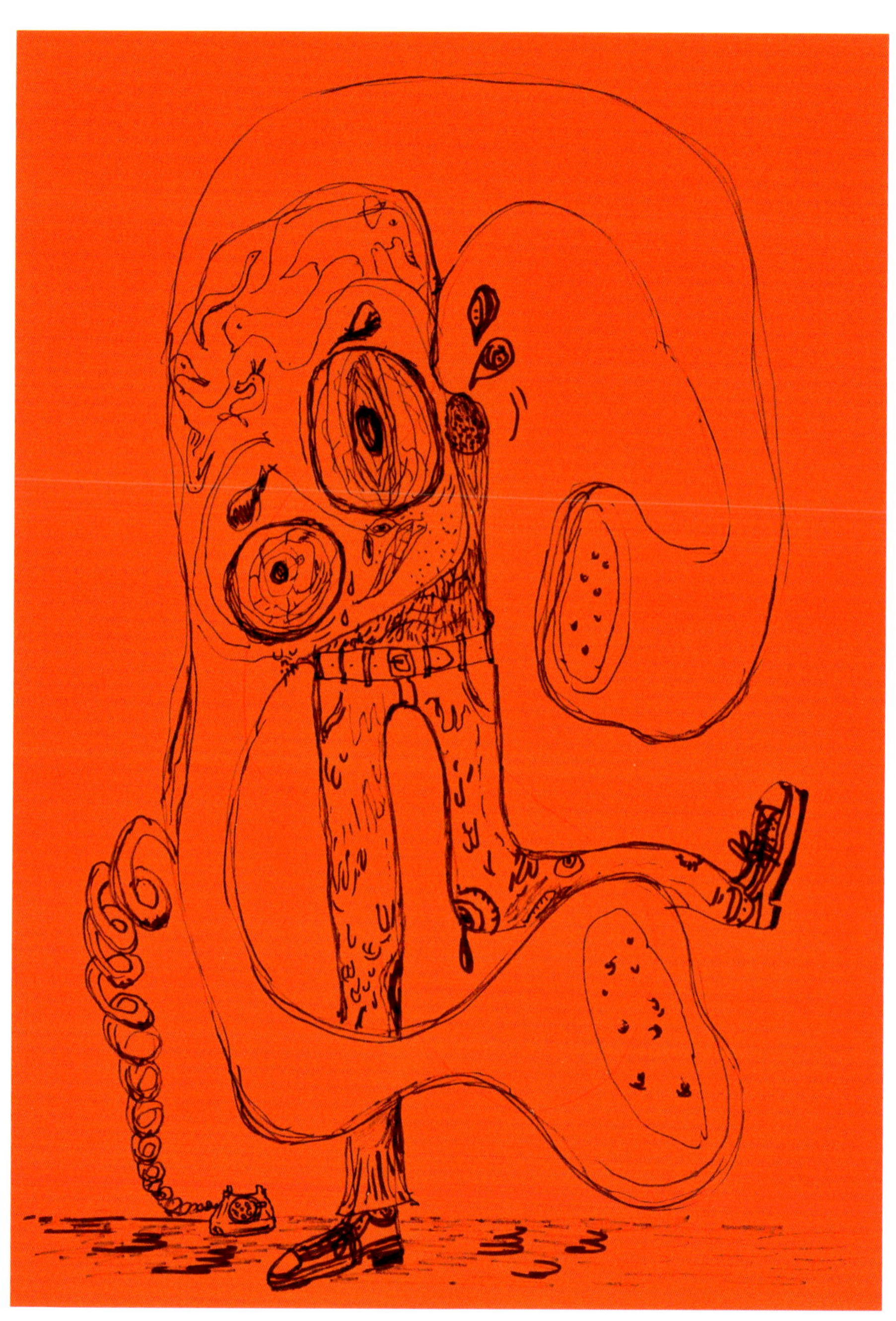

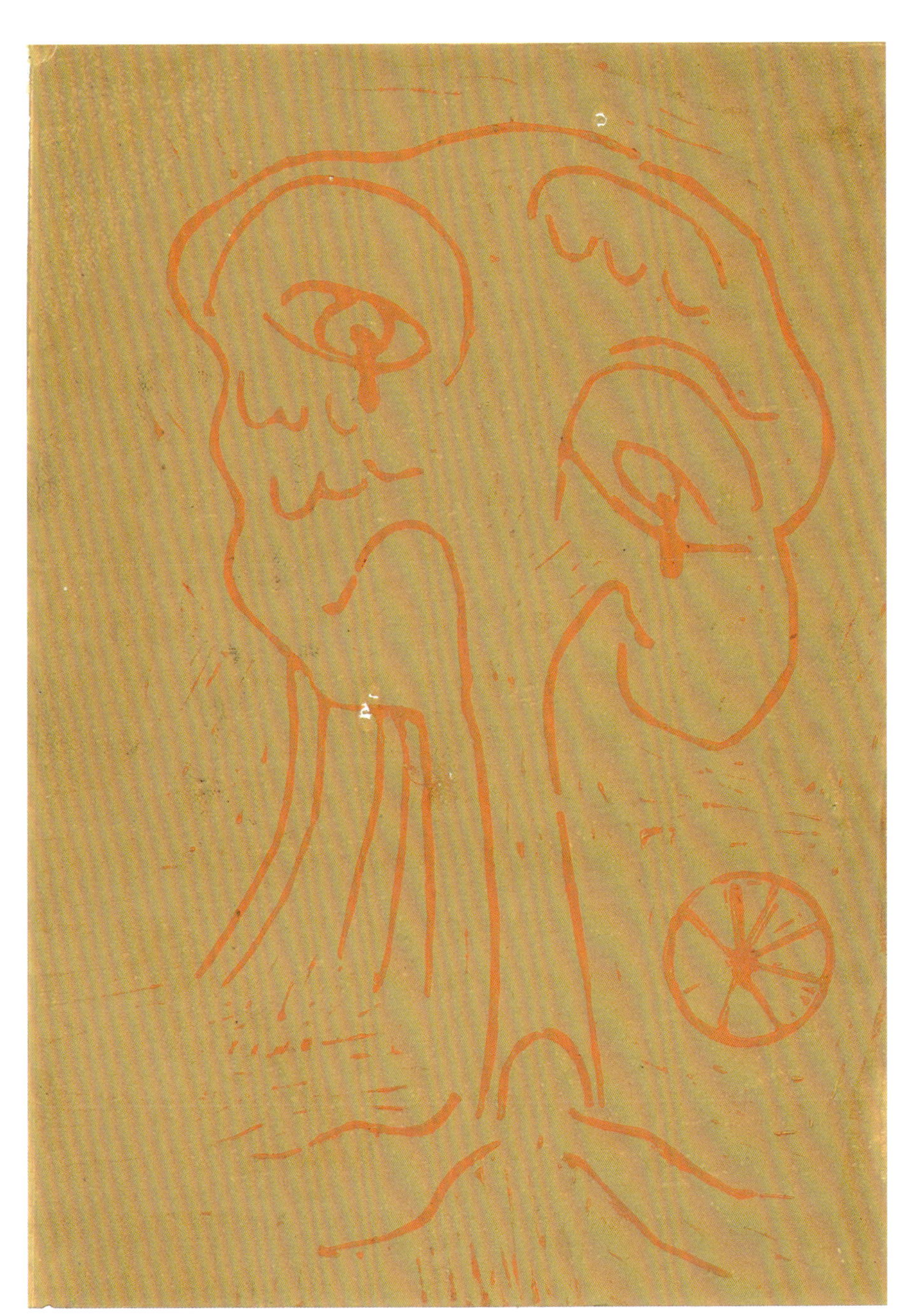

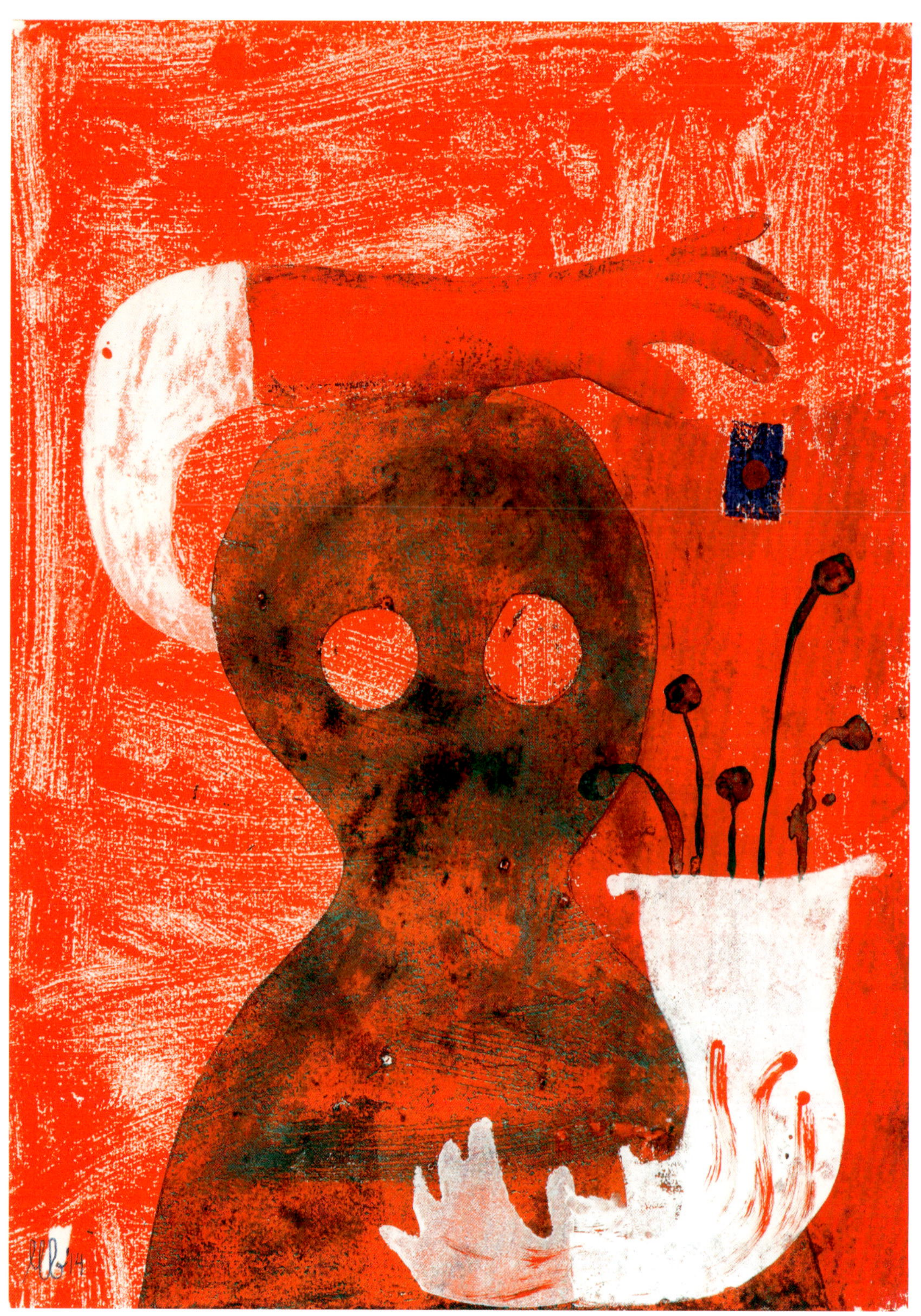

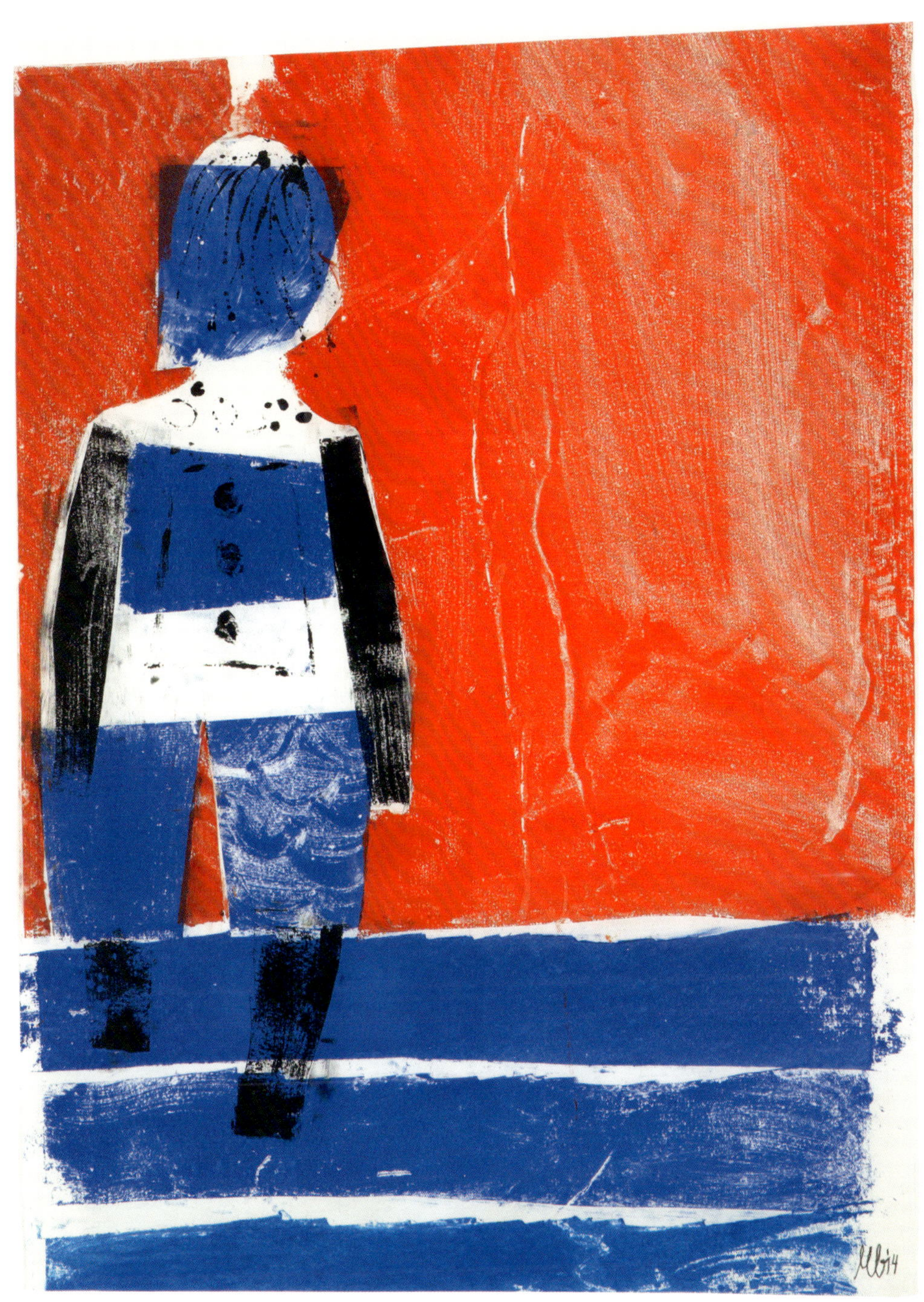

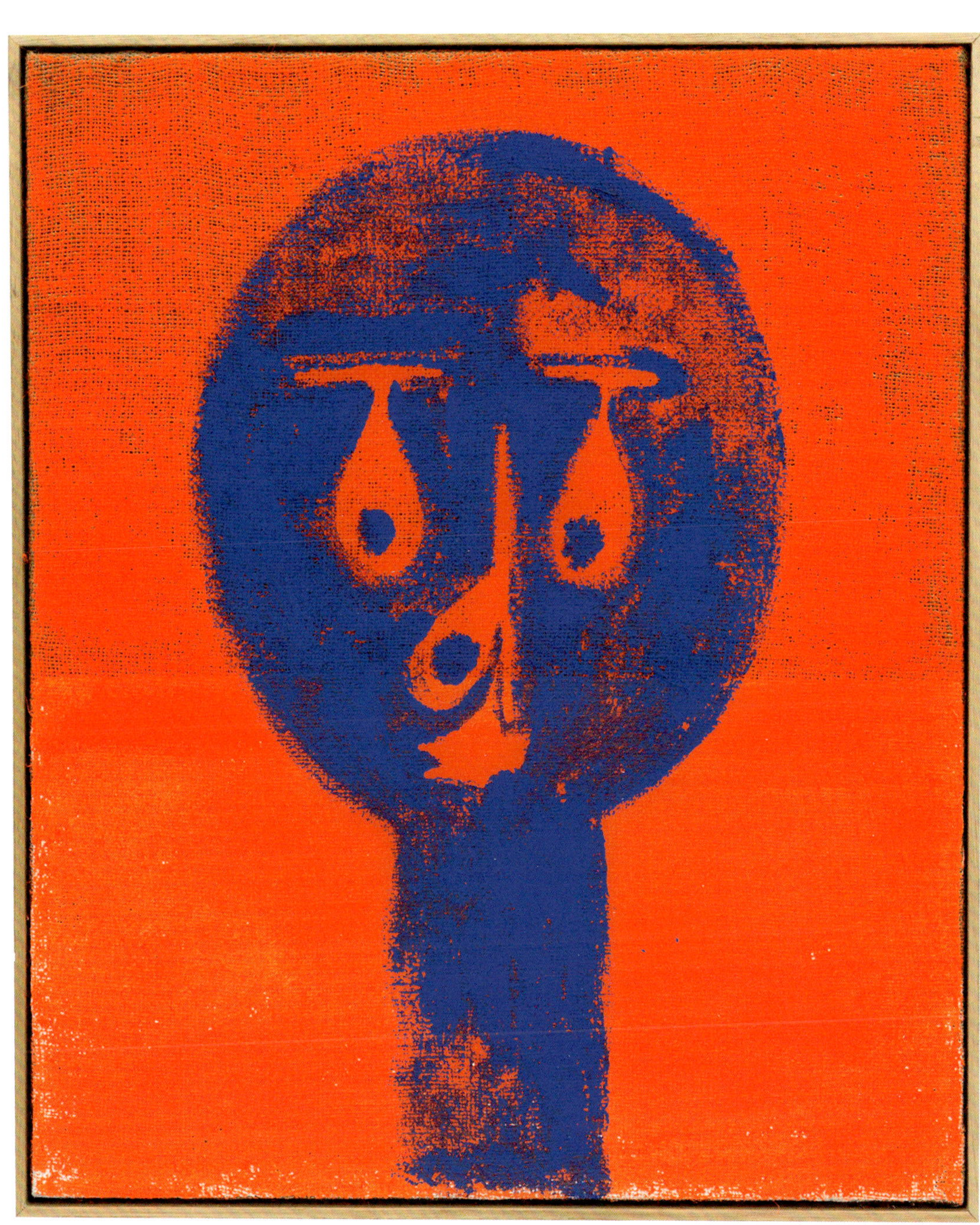

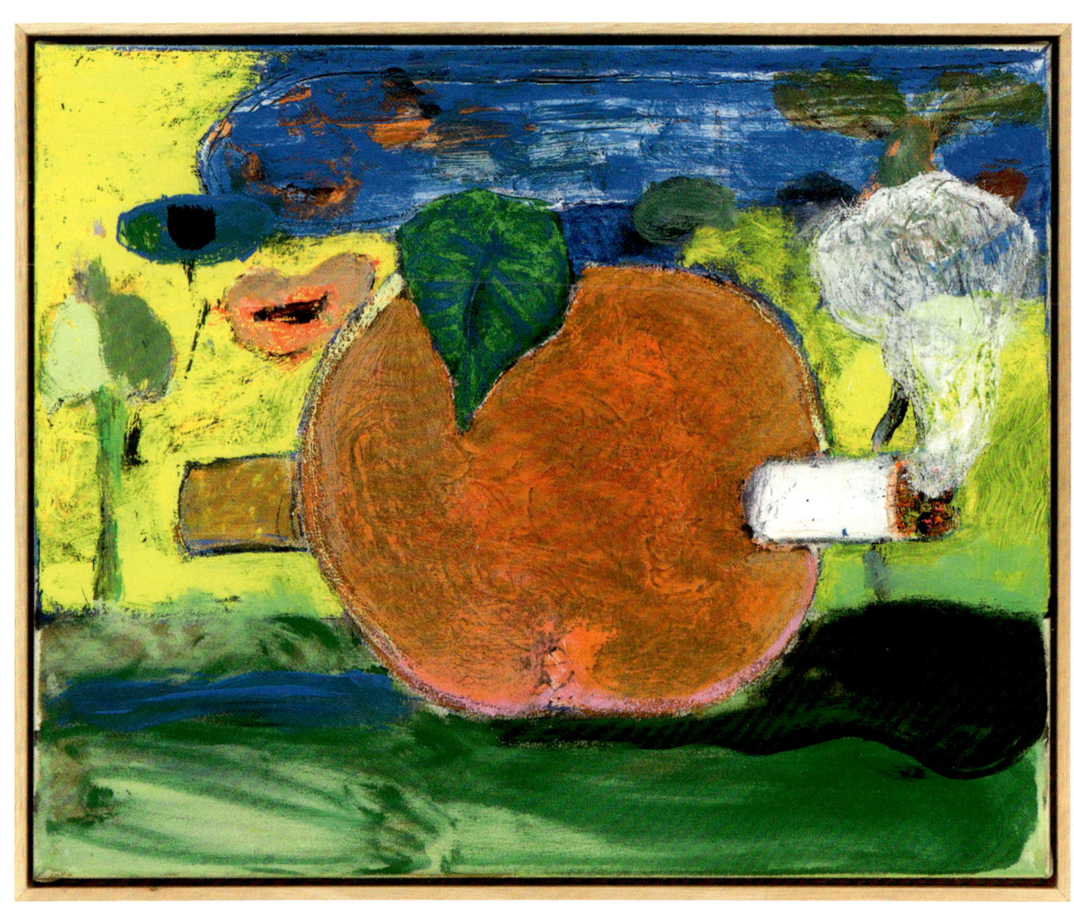

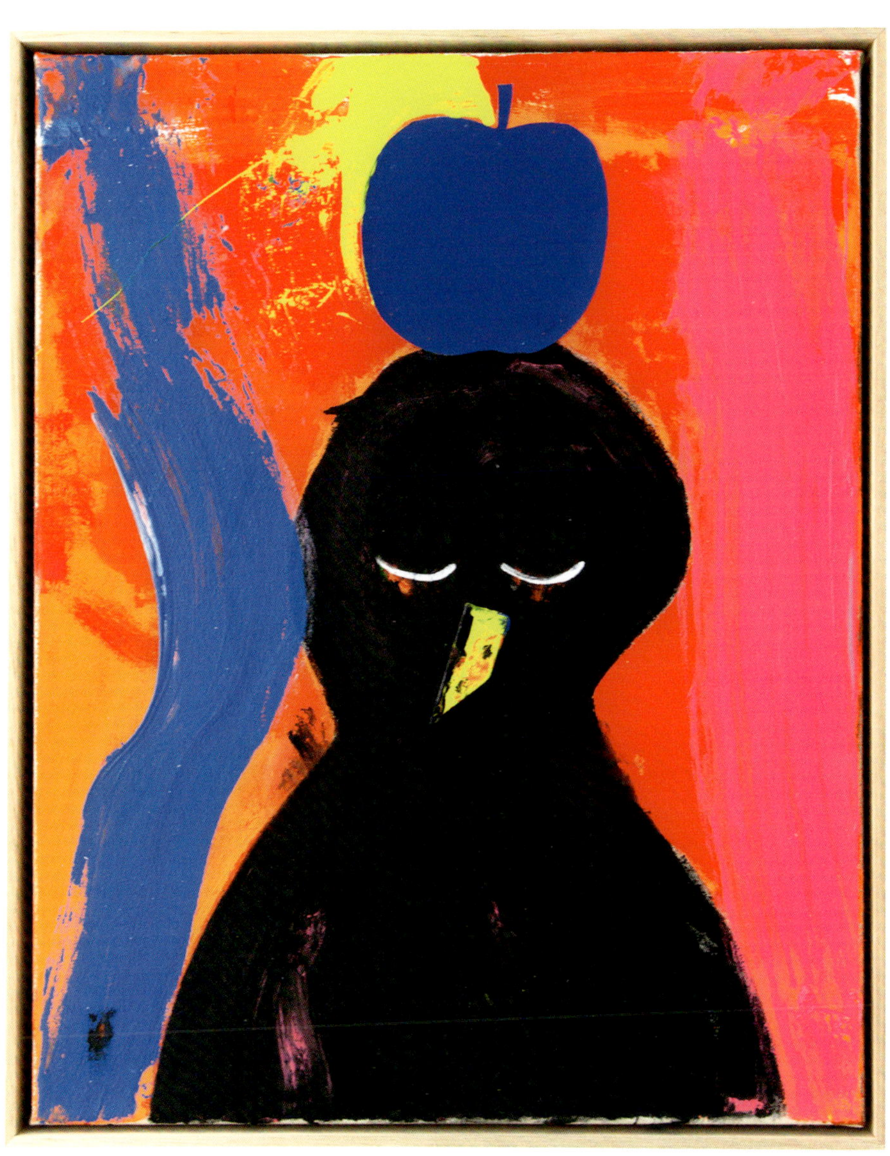

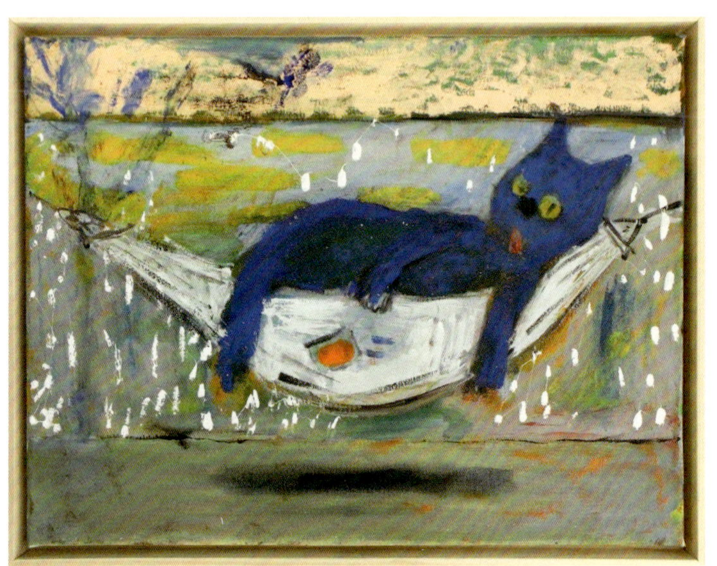

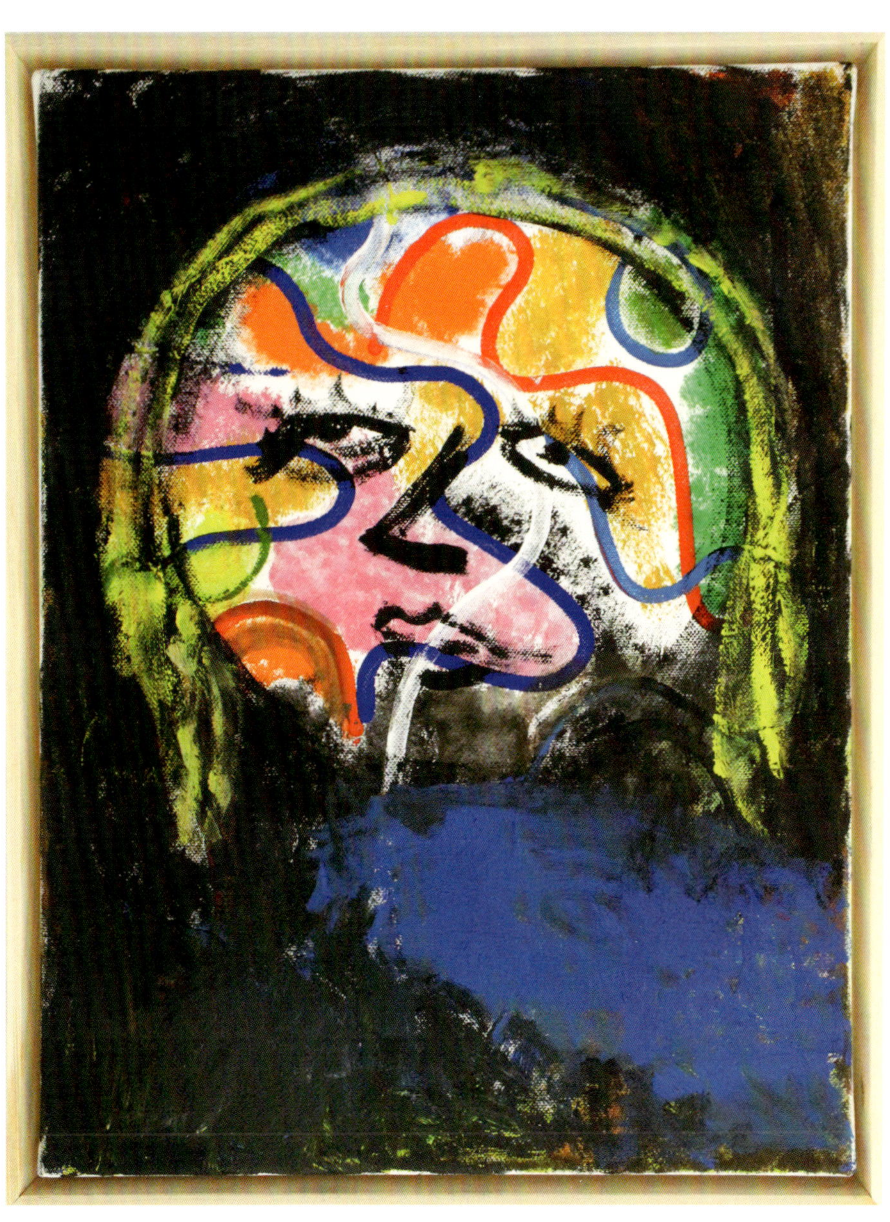

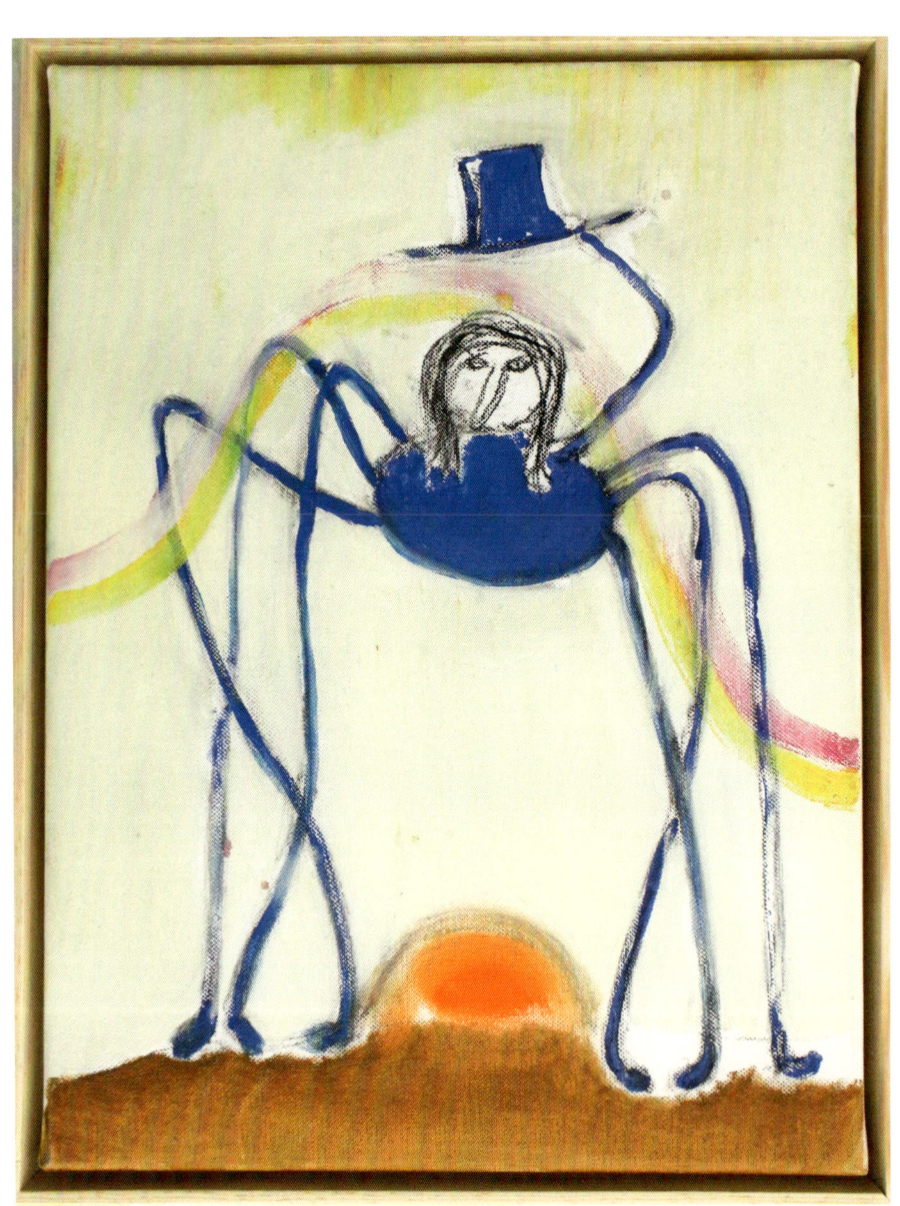

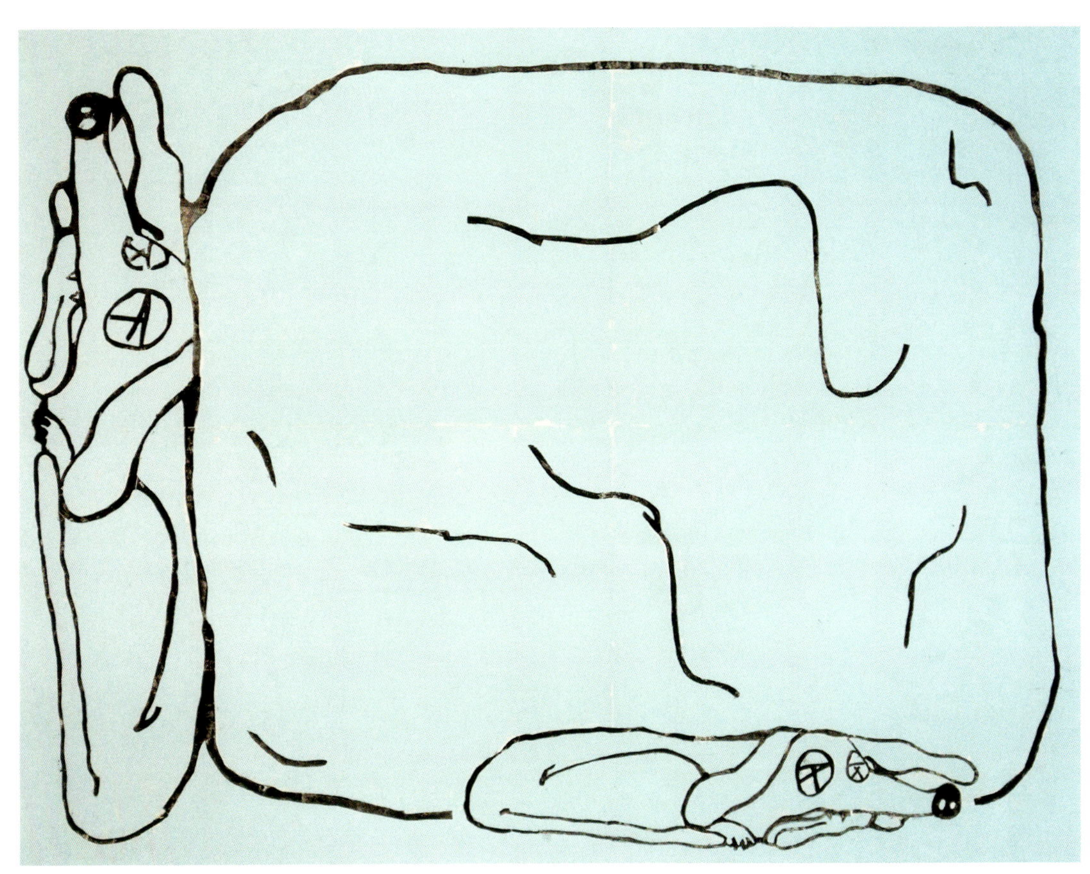

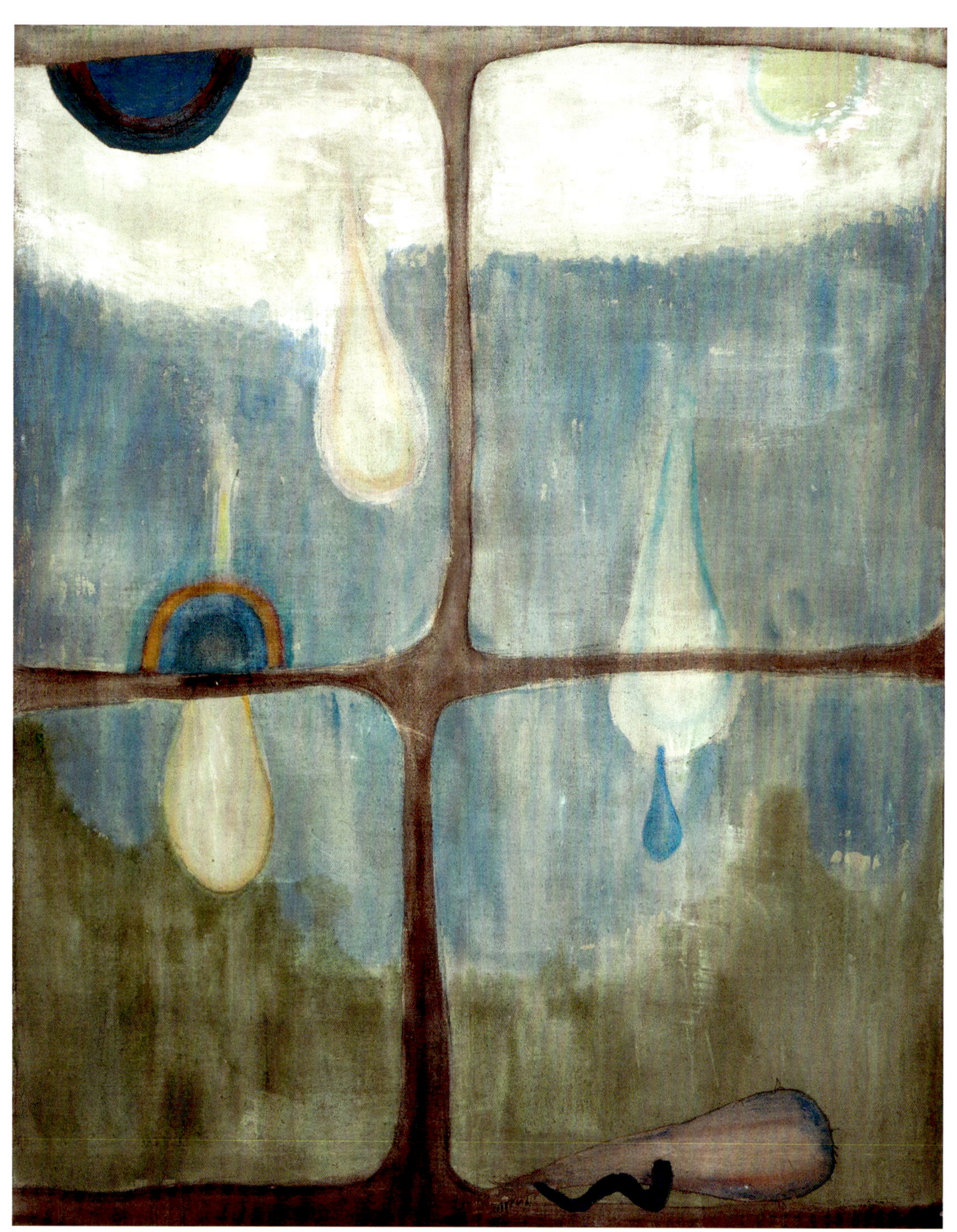

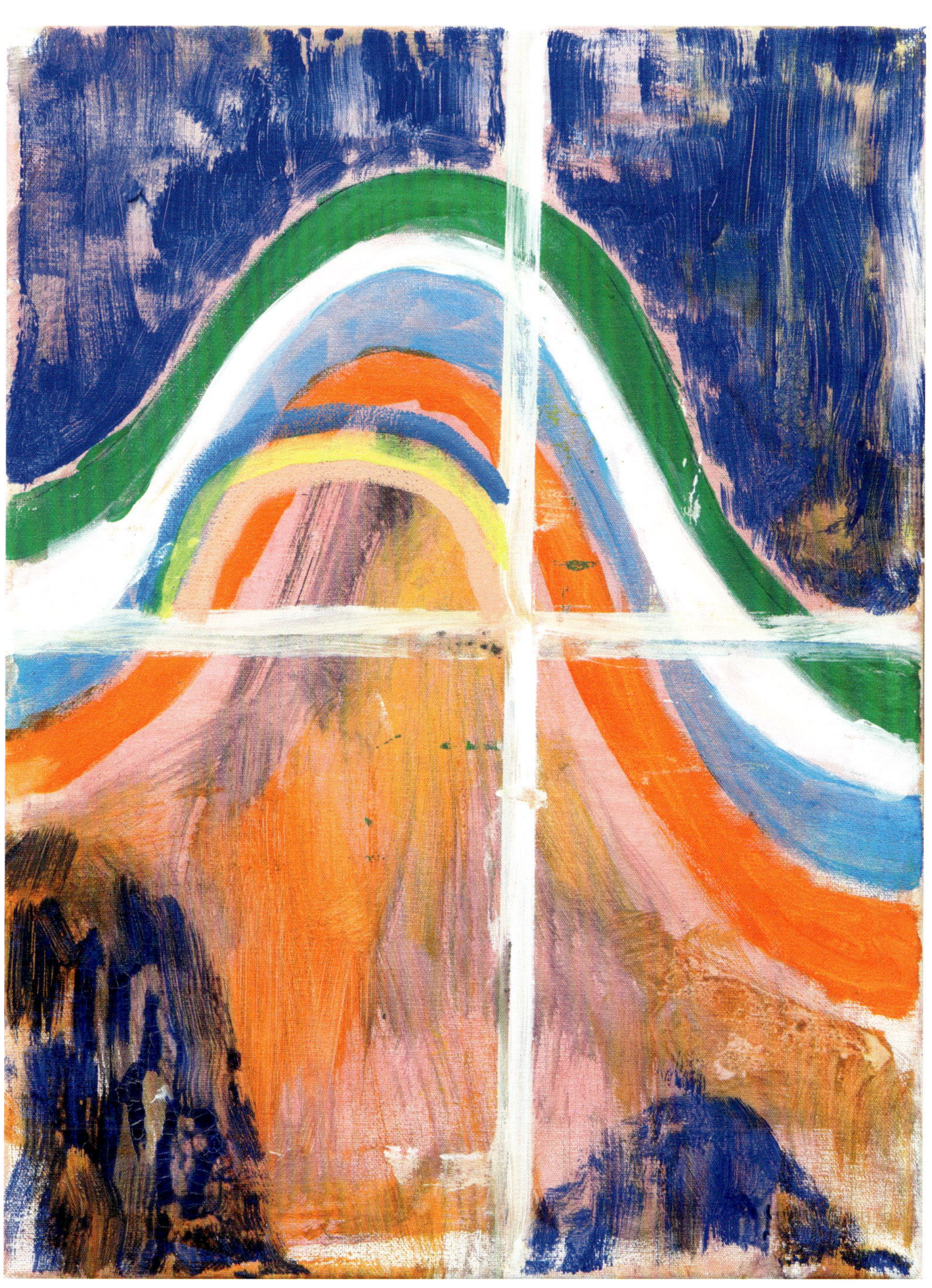

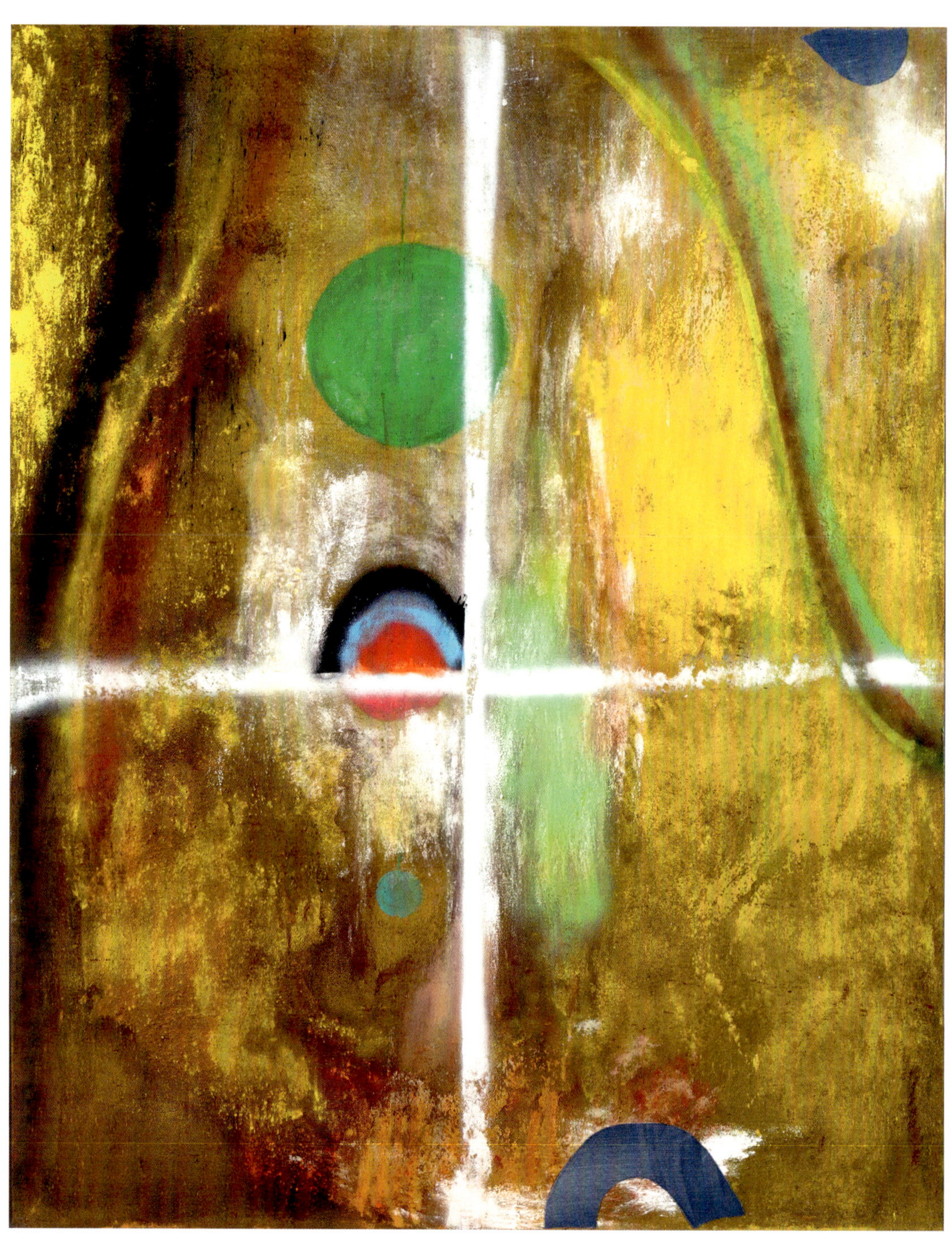

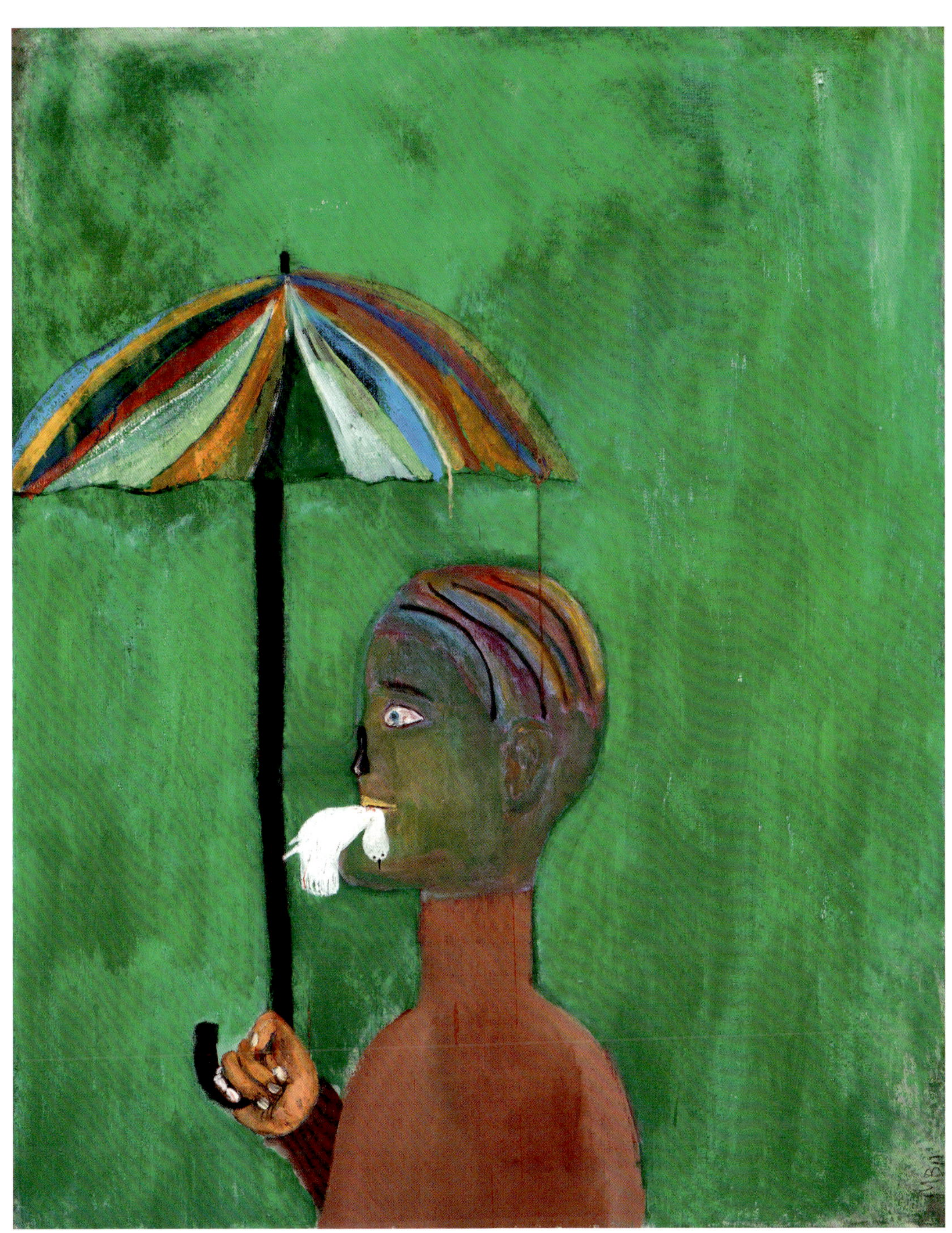

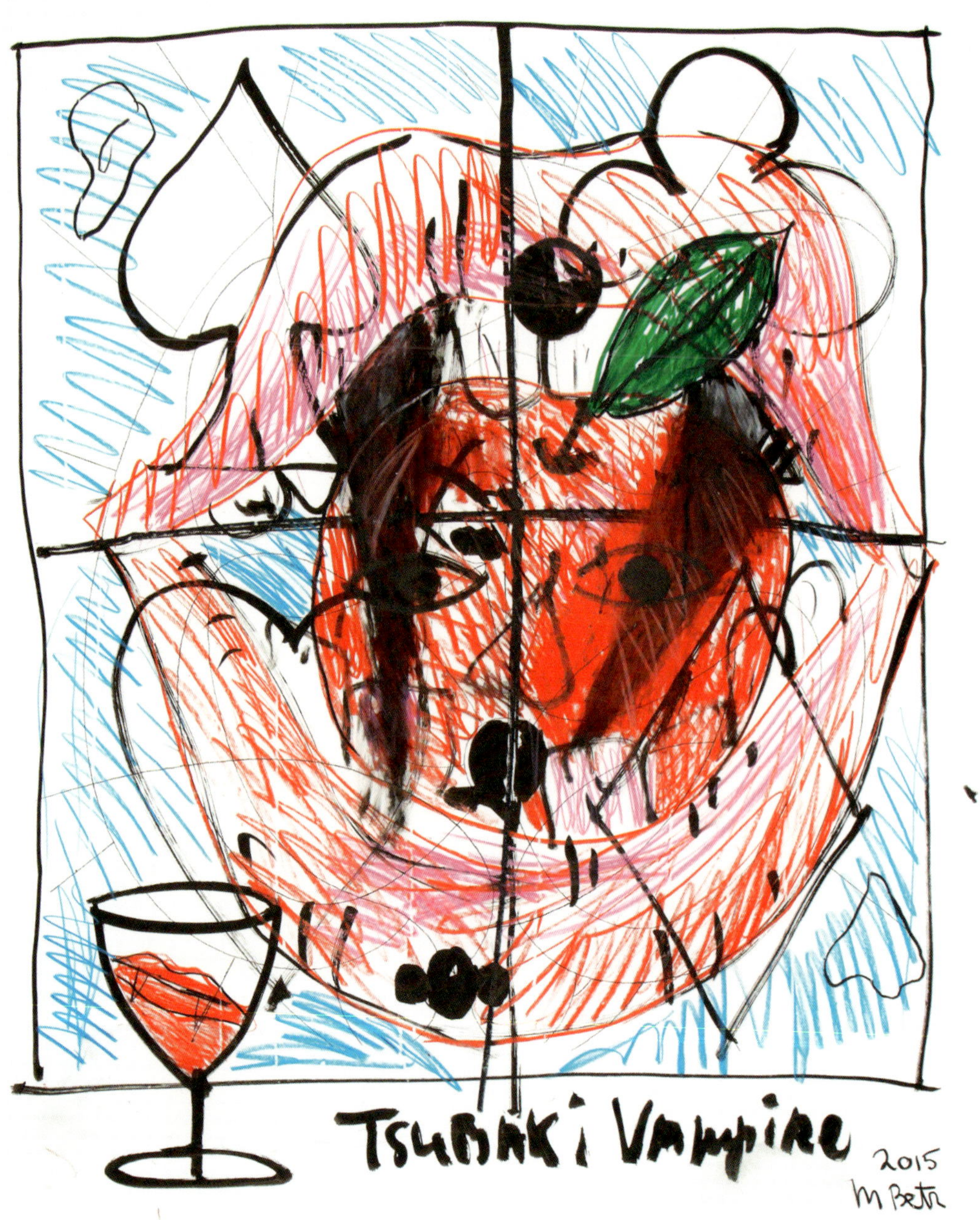
TSUBAKI VAMPIRE
2015

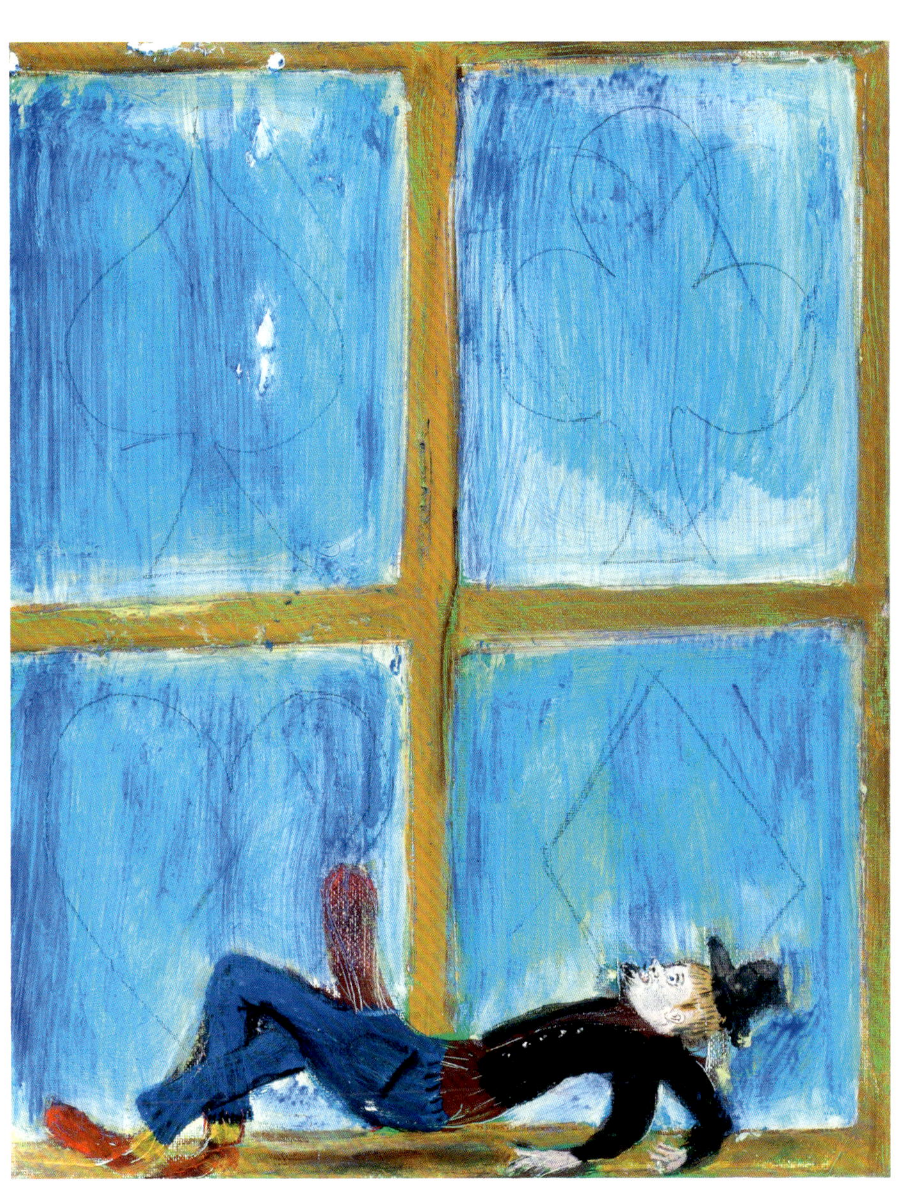

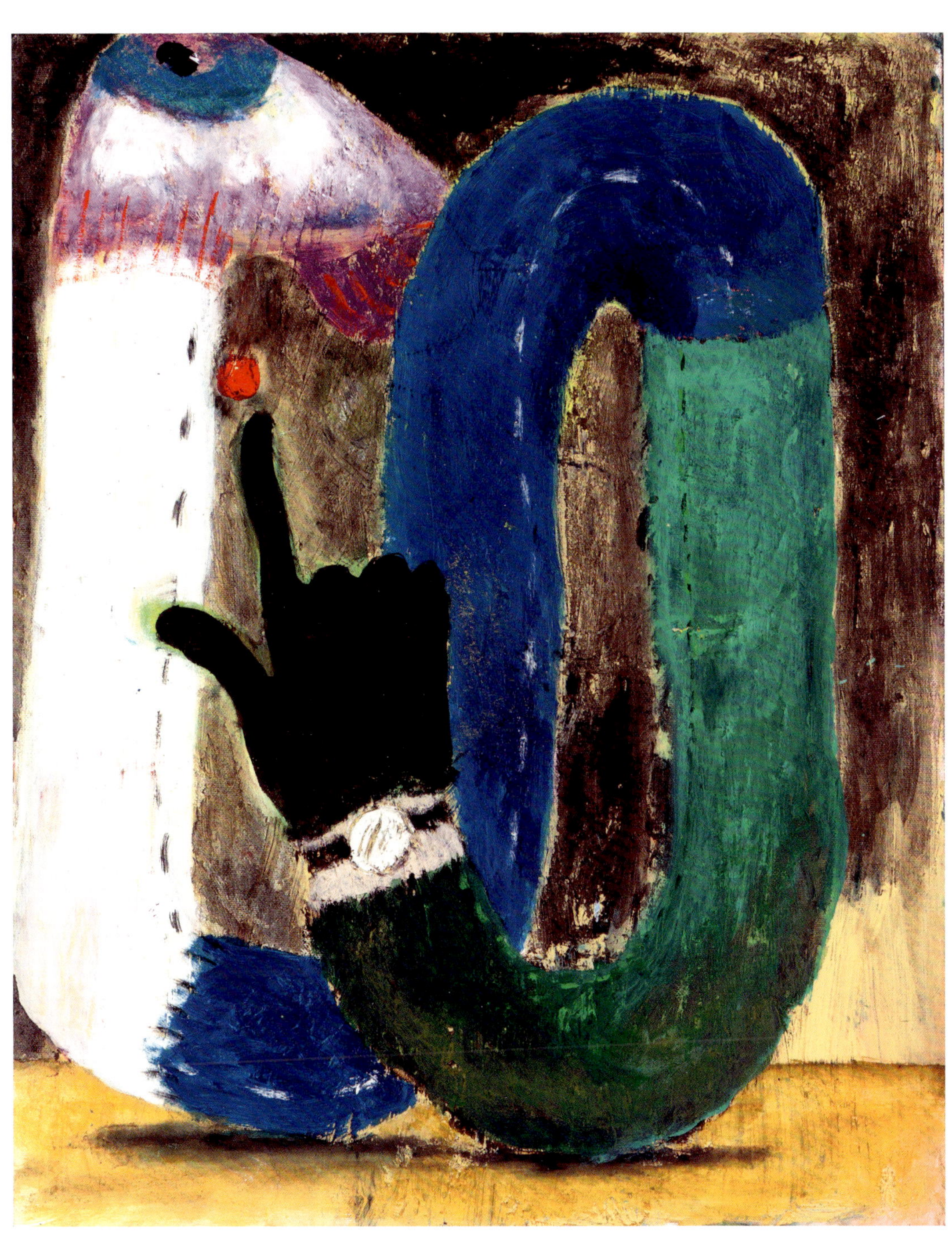

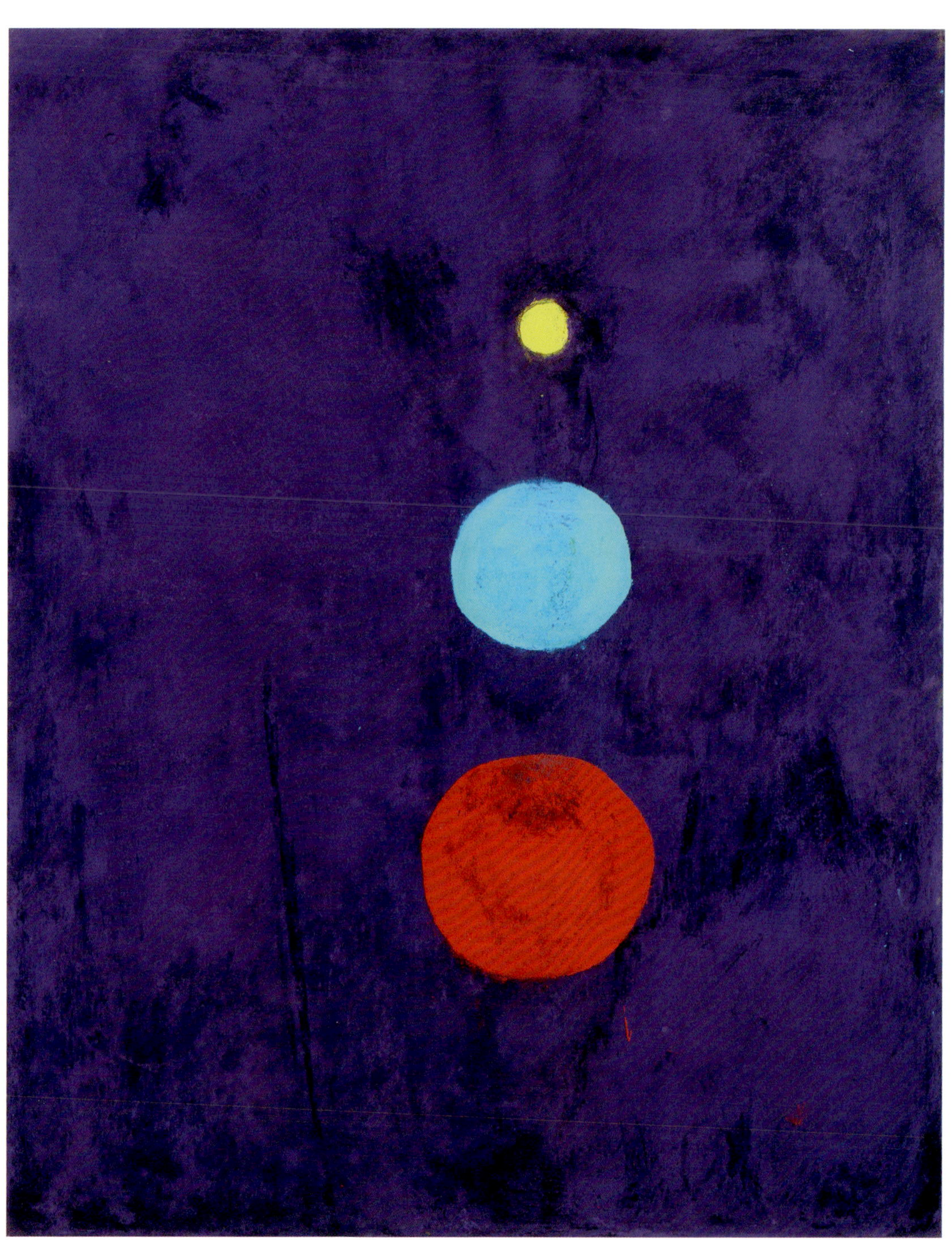

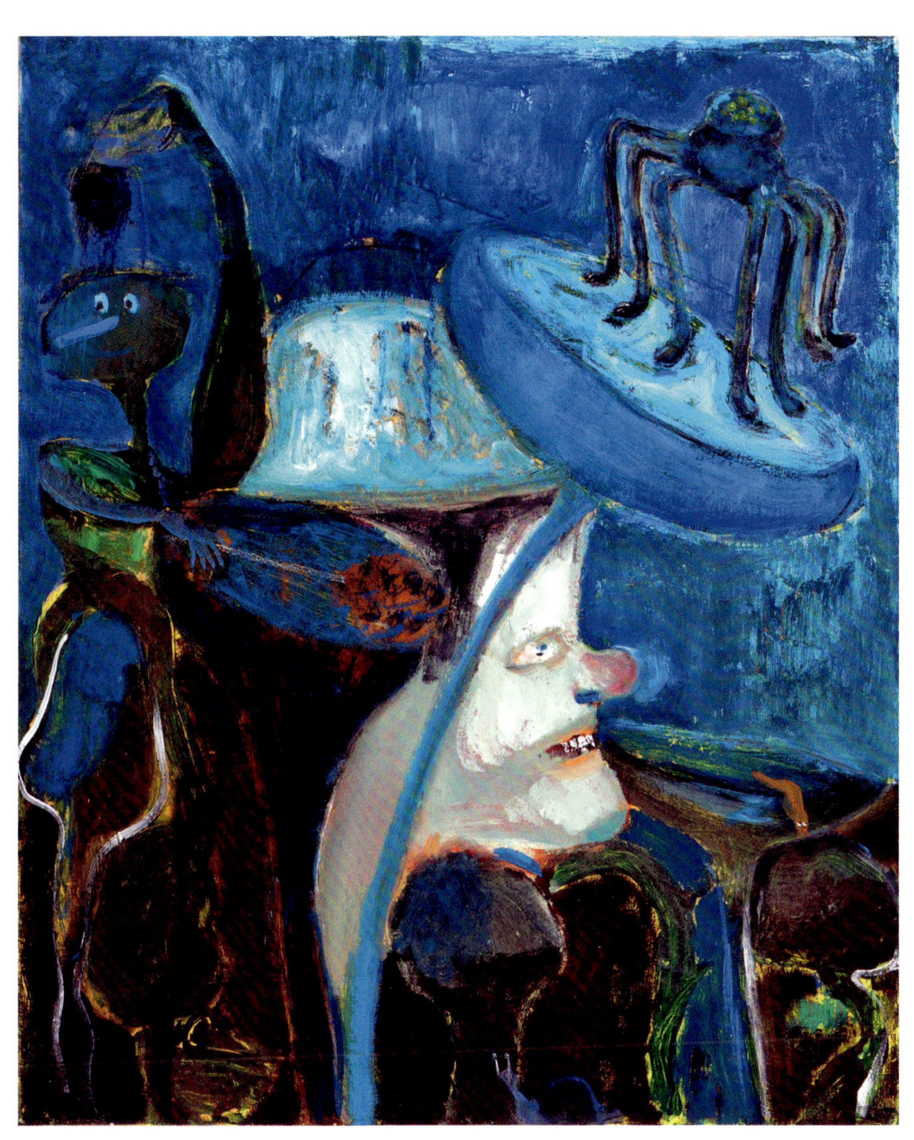

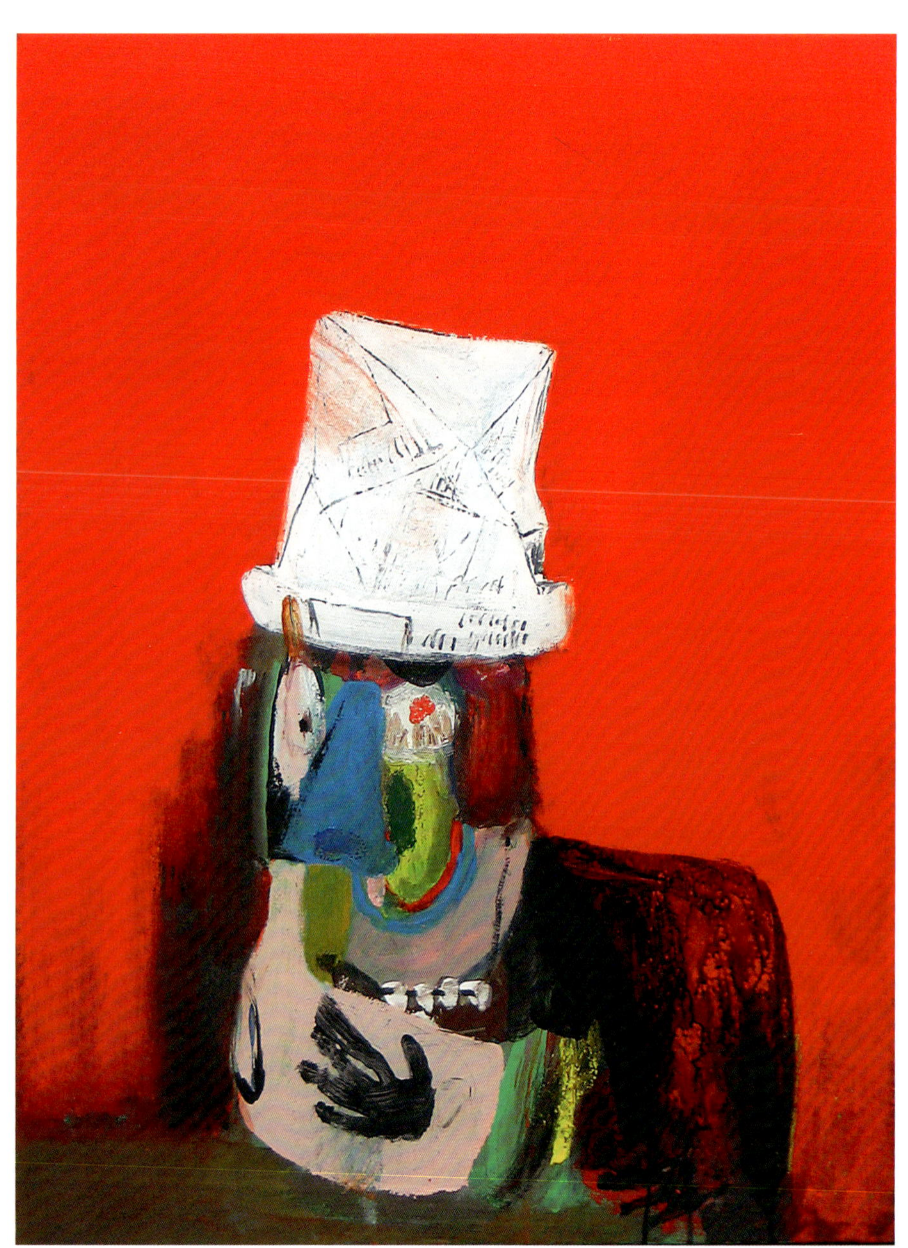

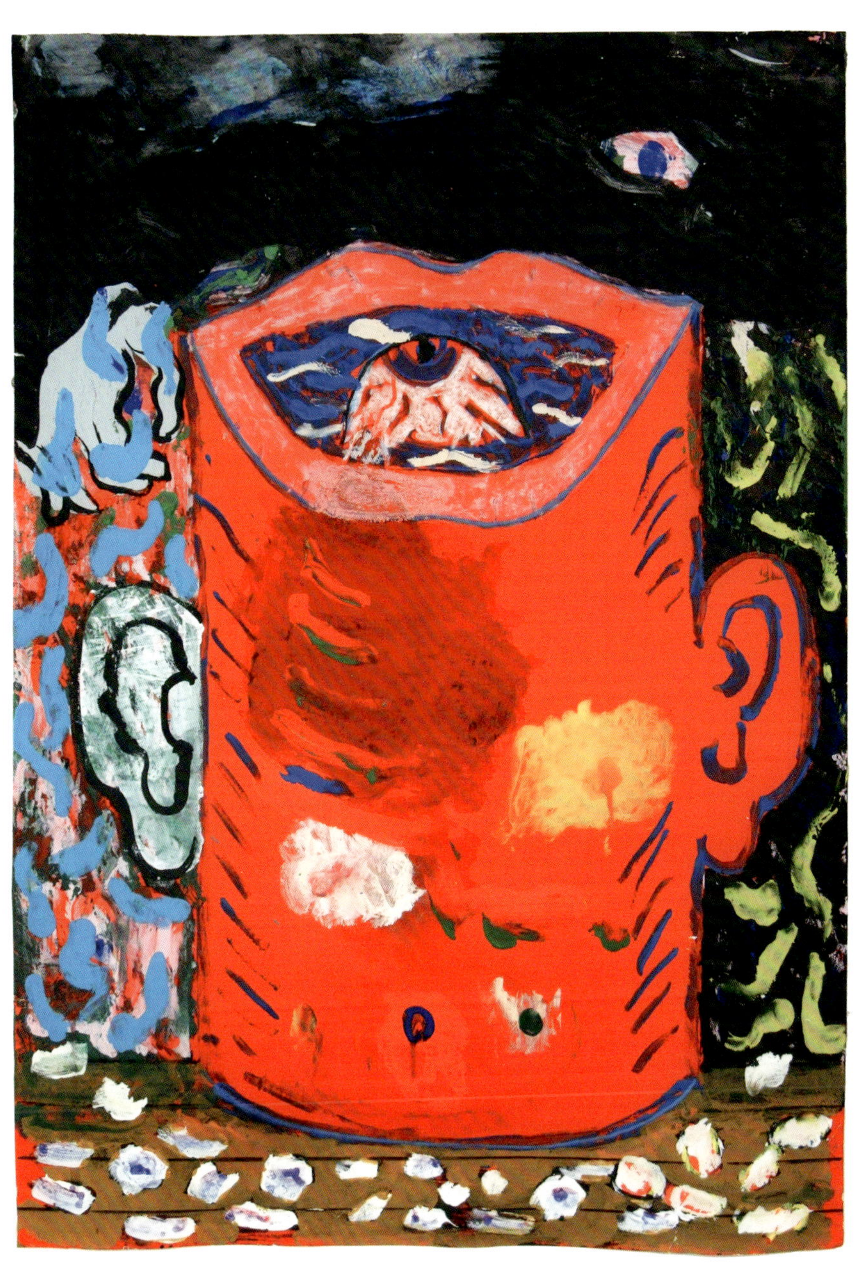

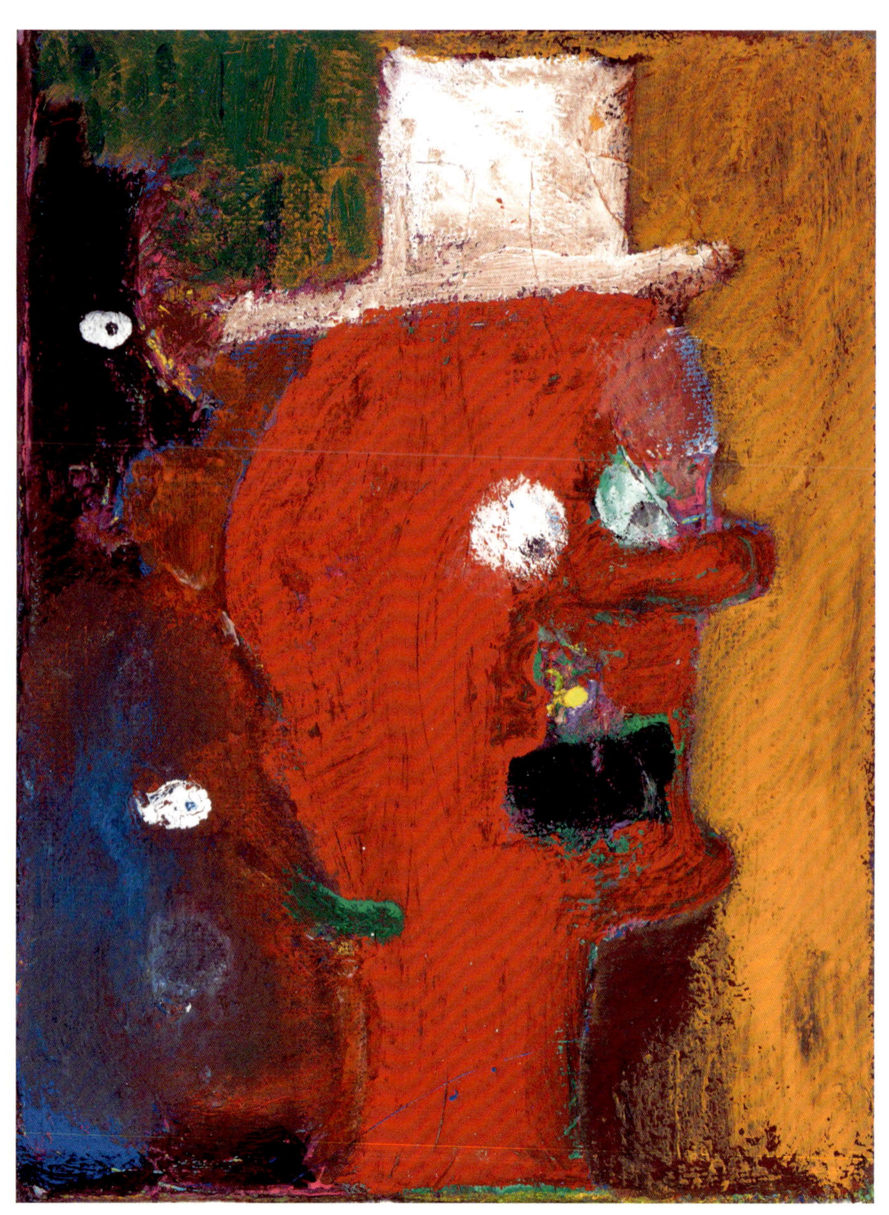

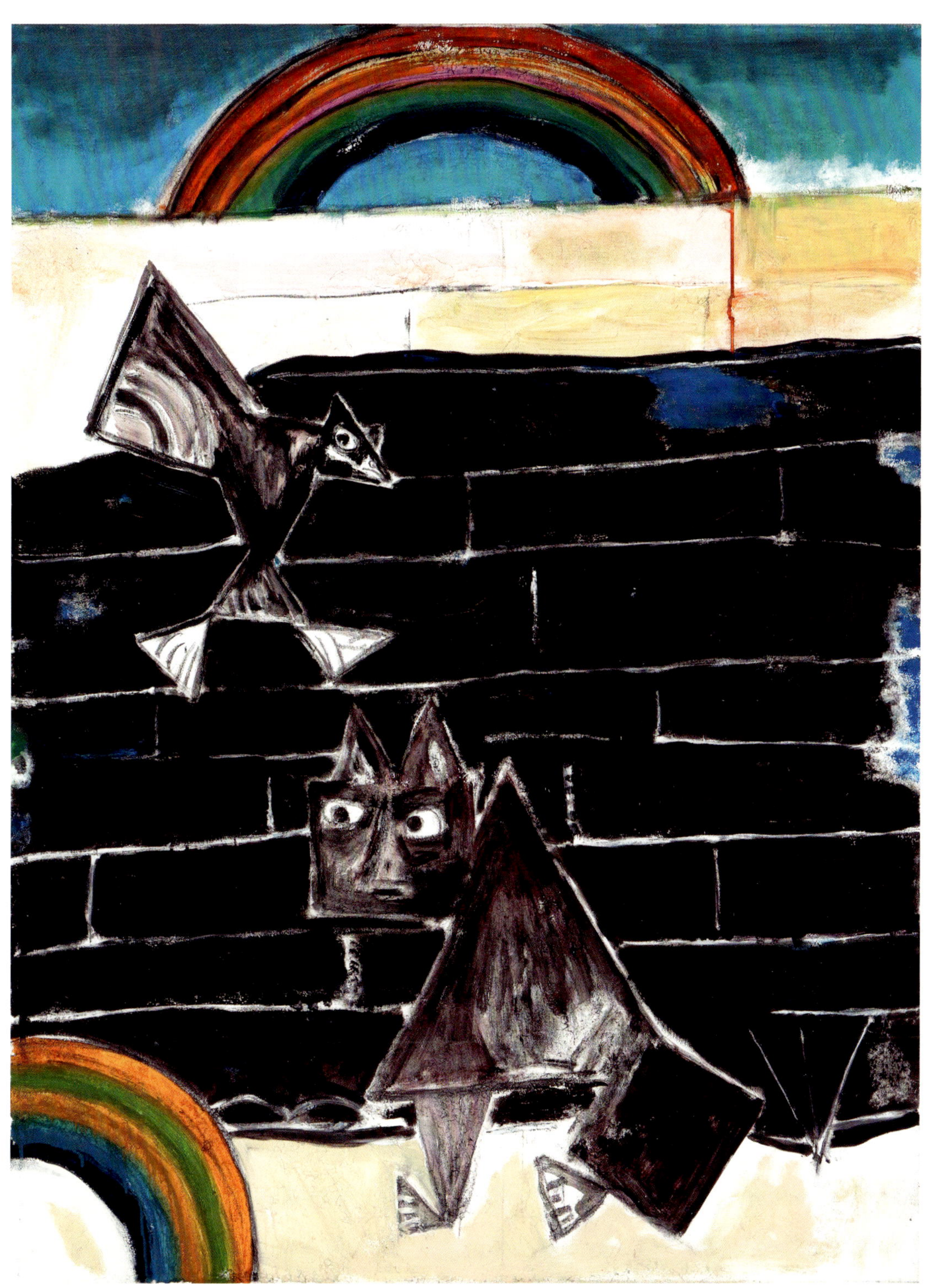

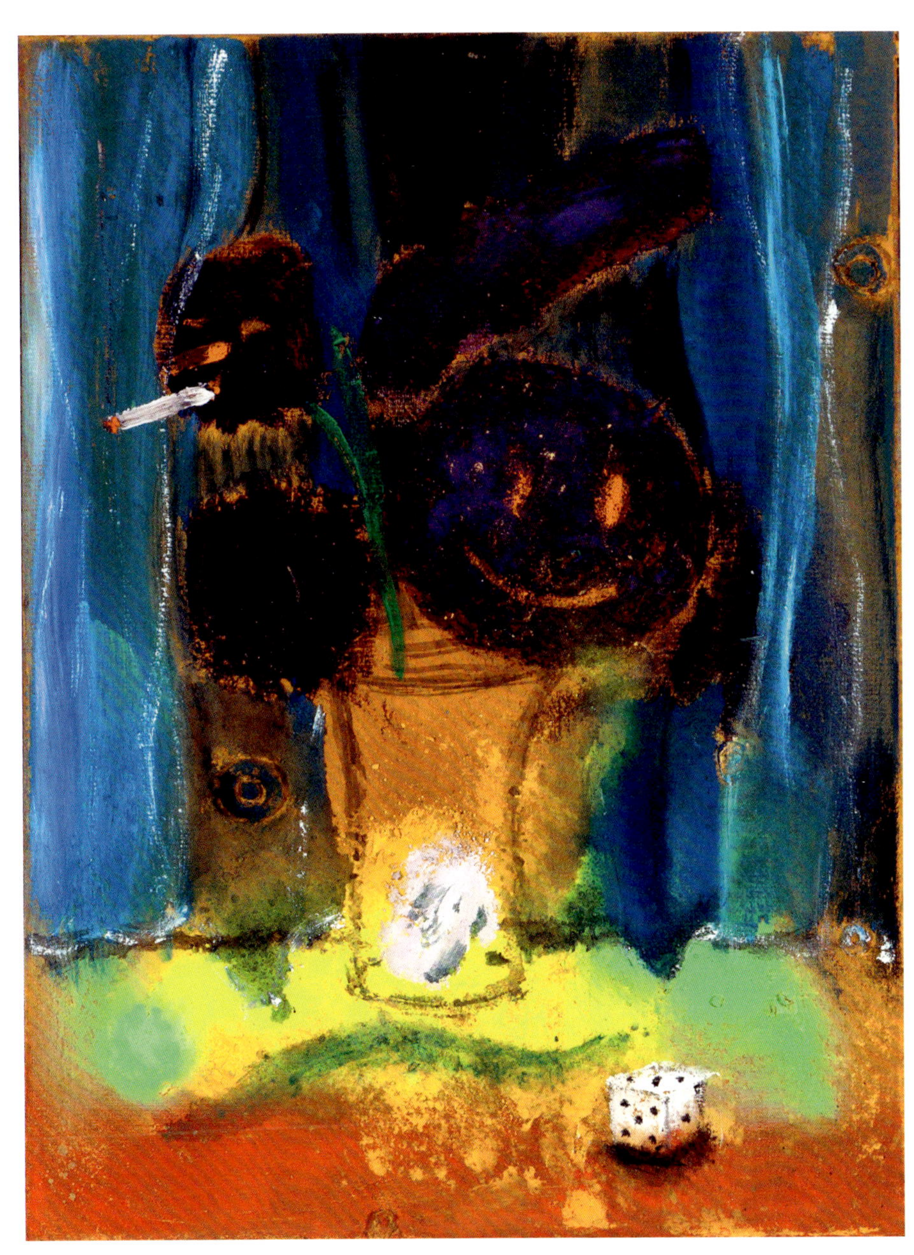

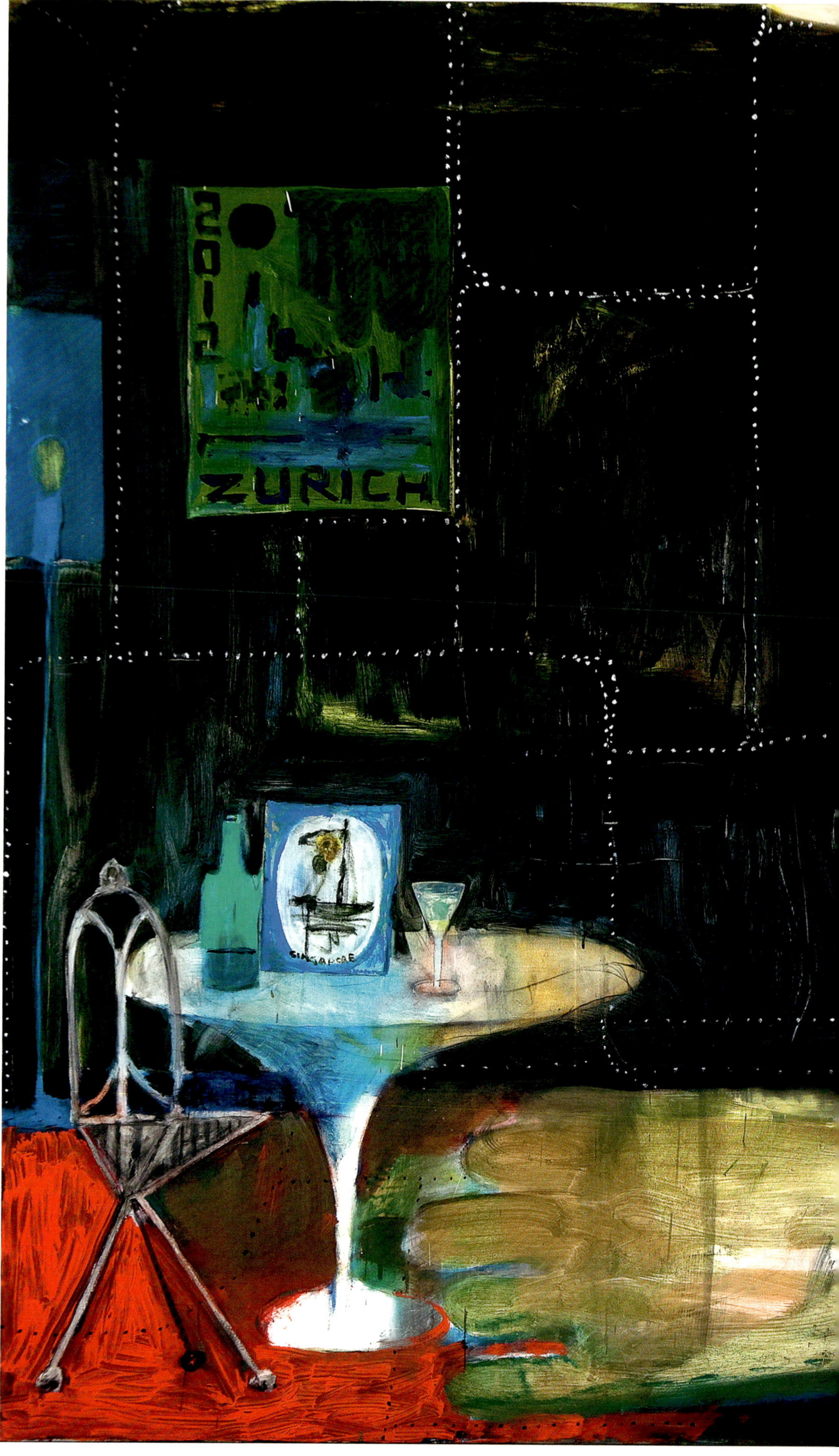
2012
ZURICH

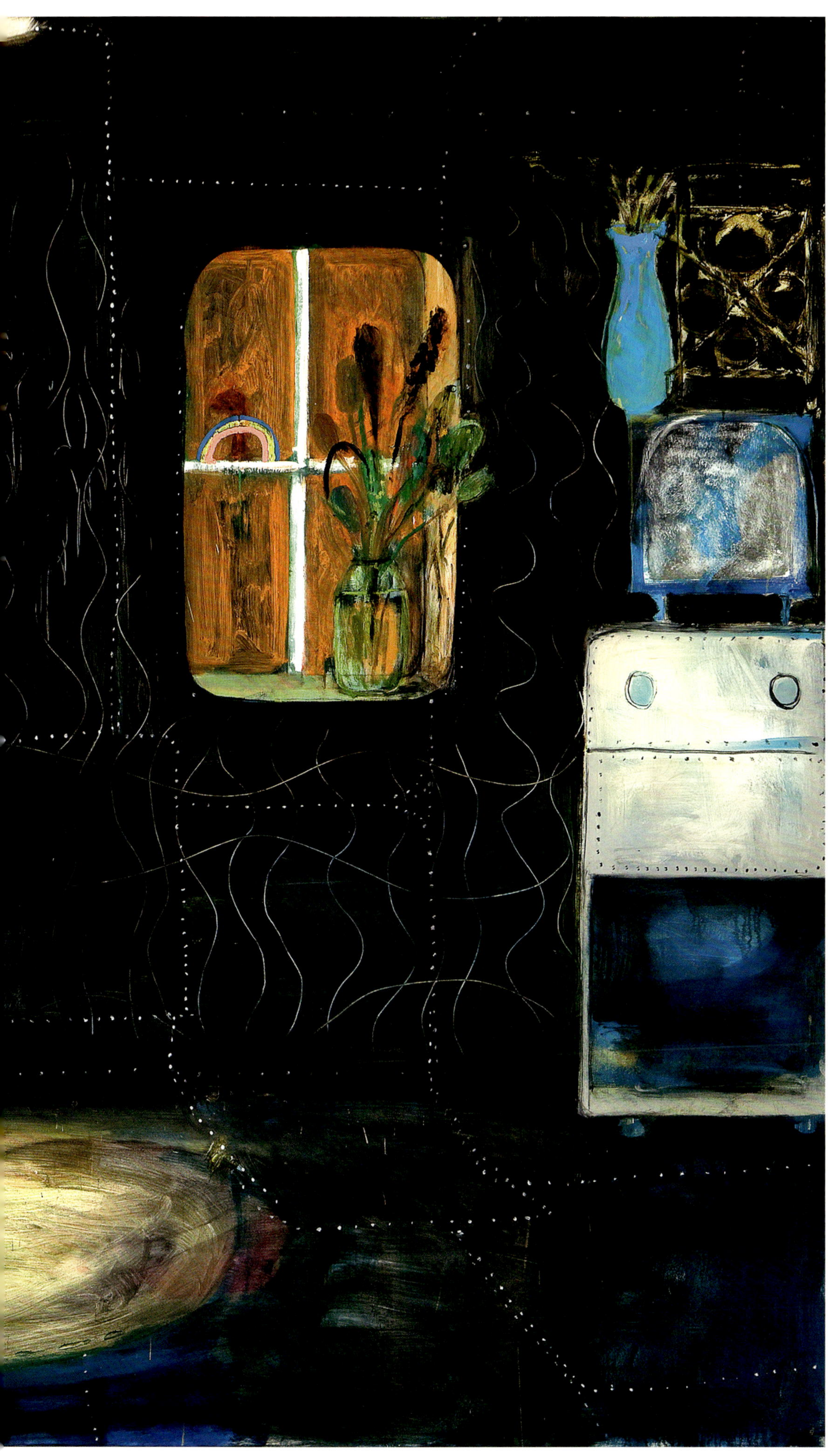

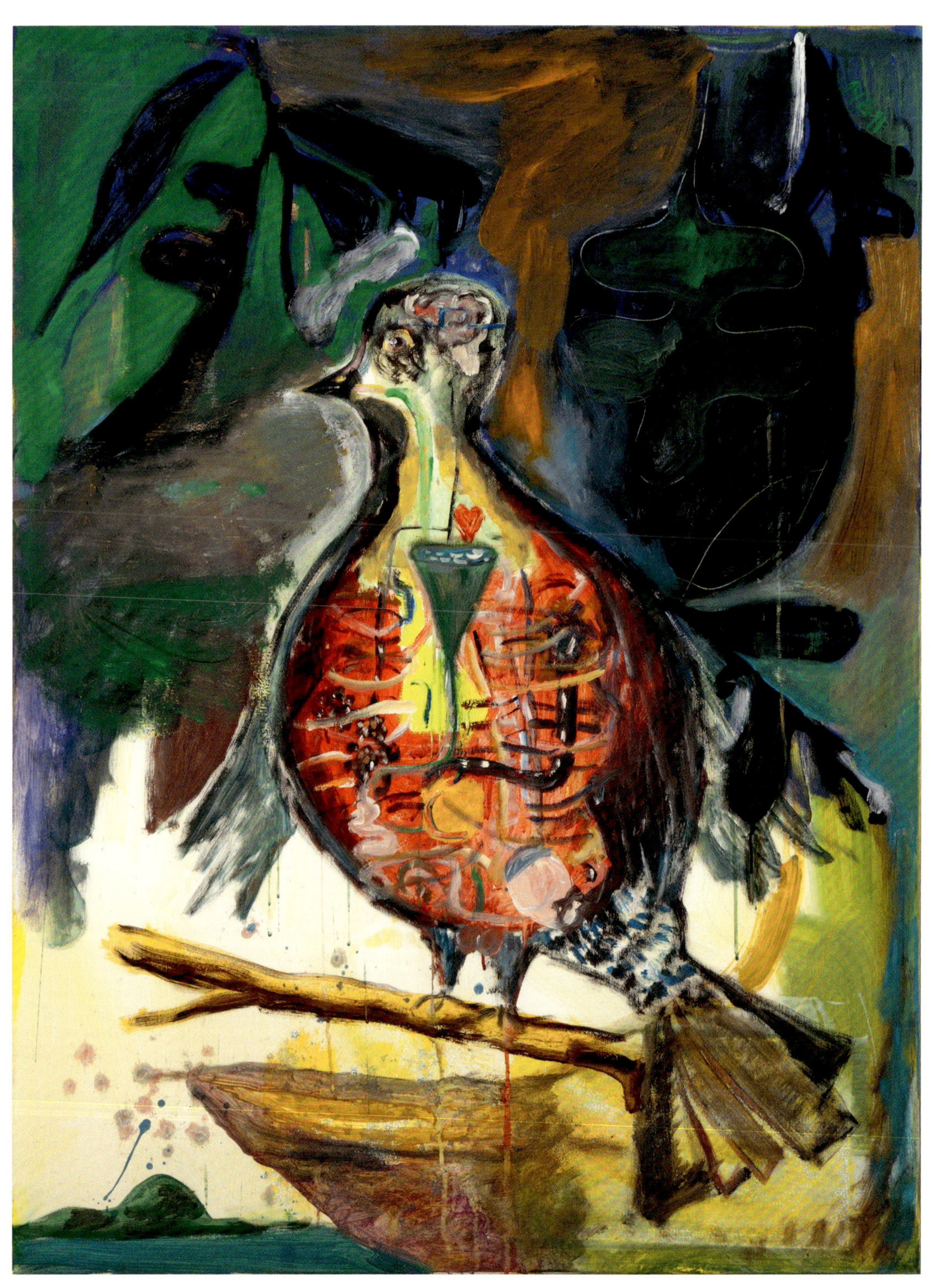

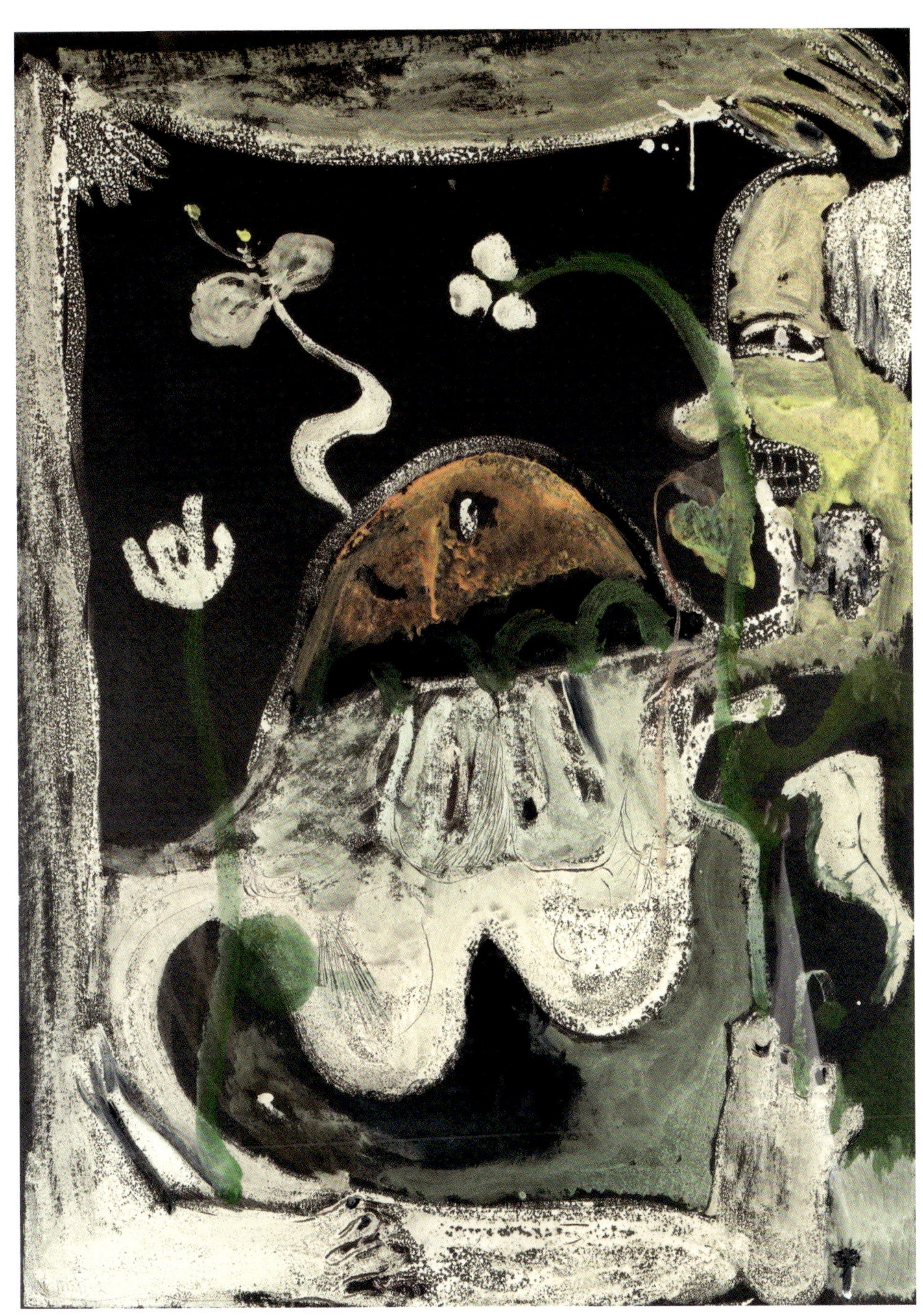

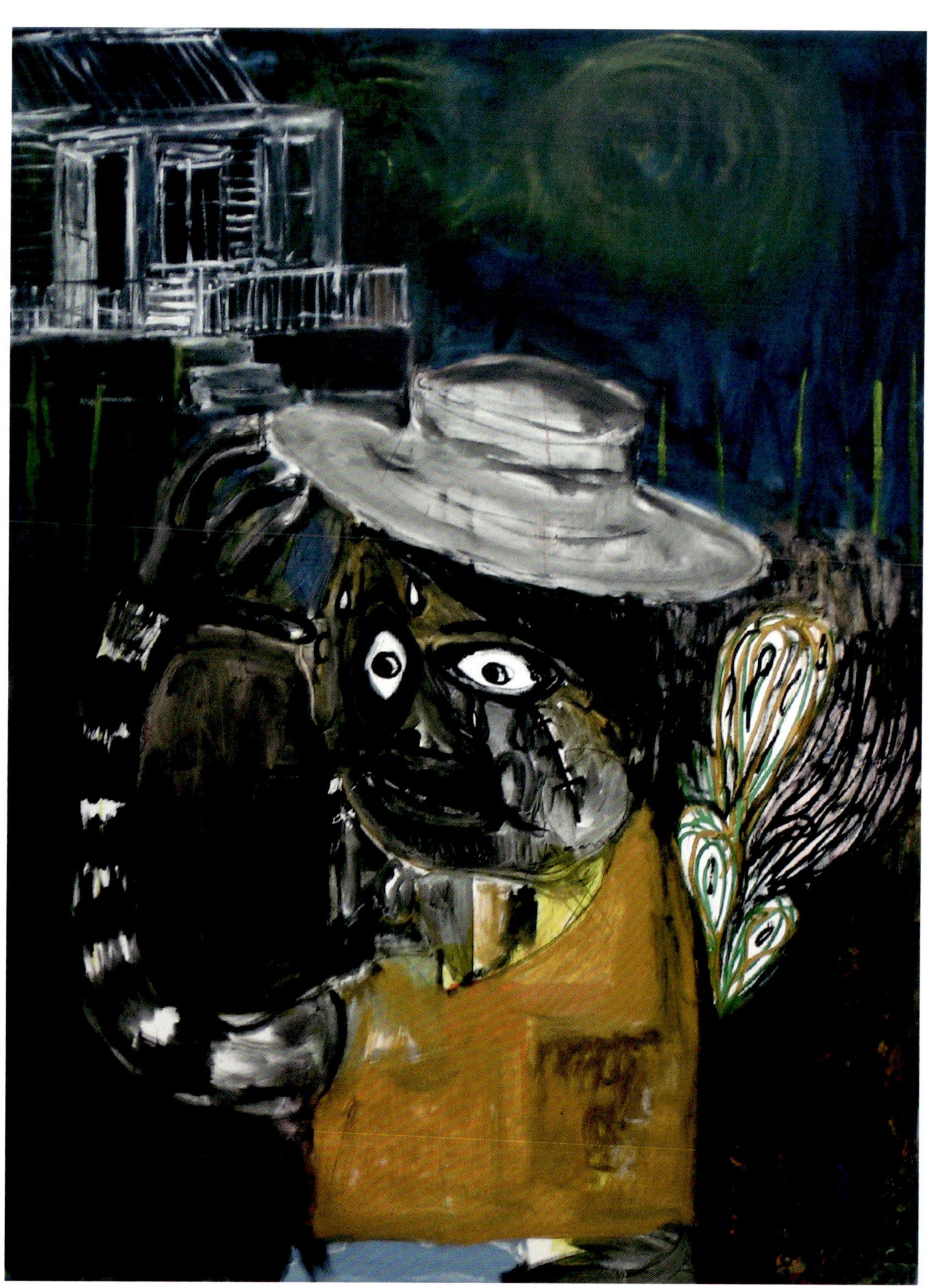

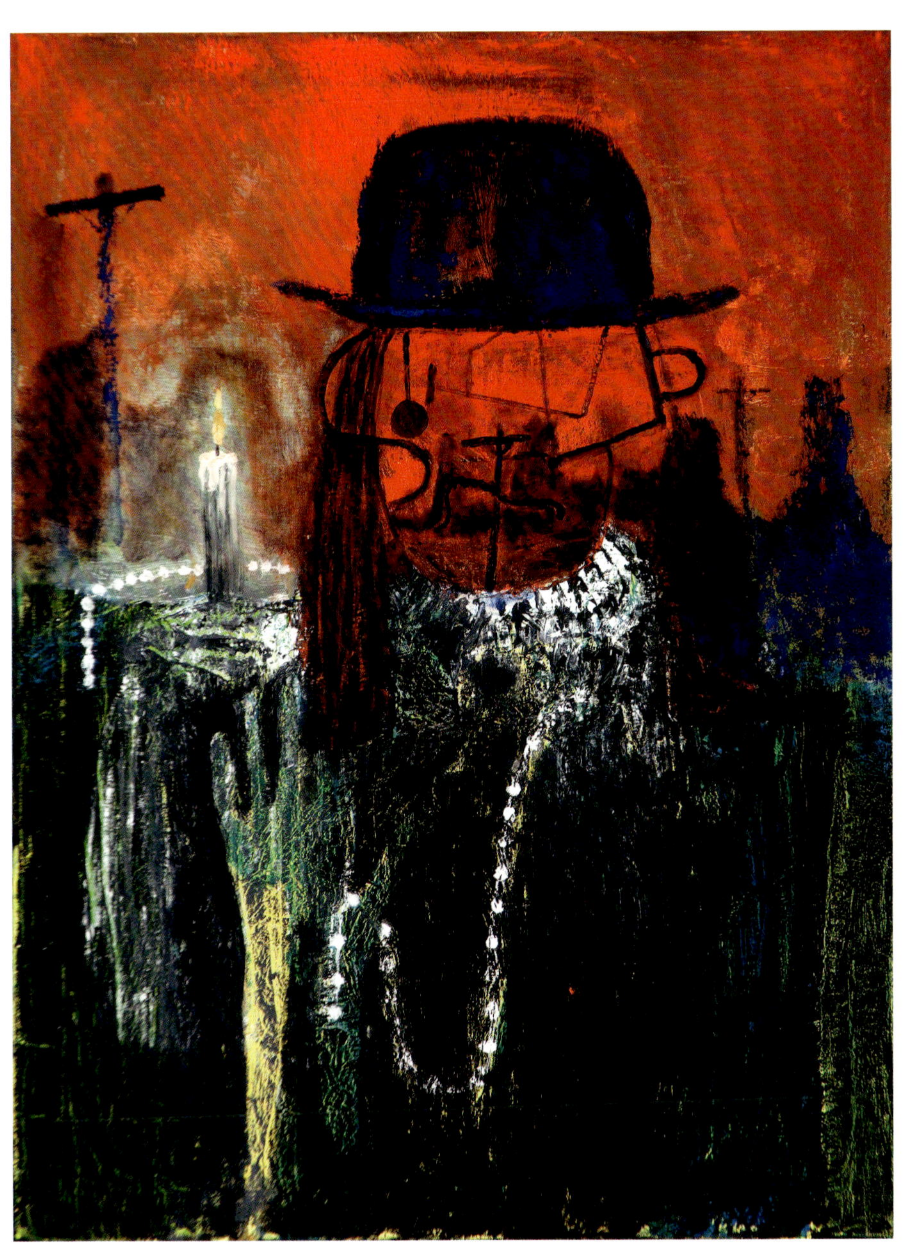

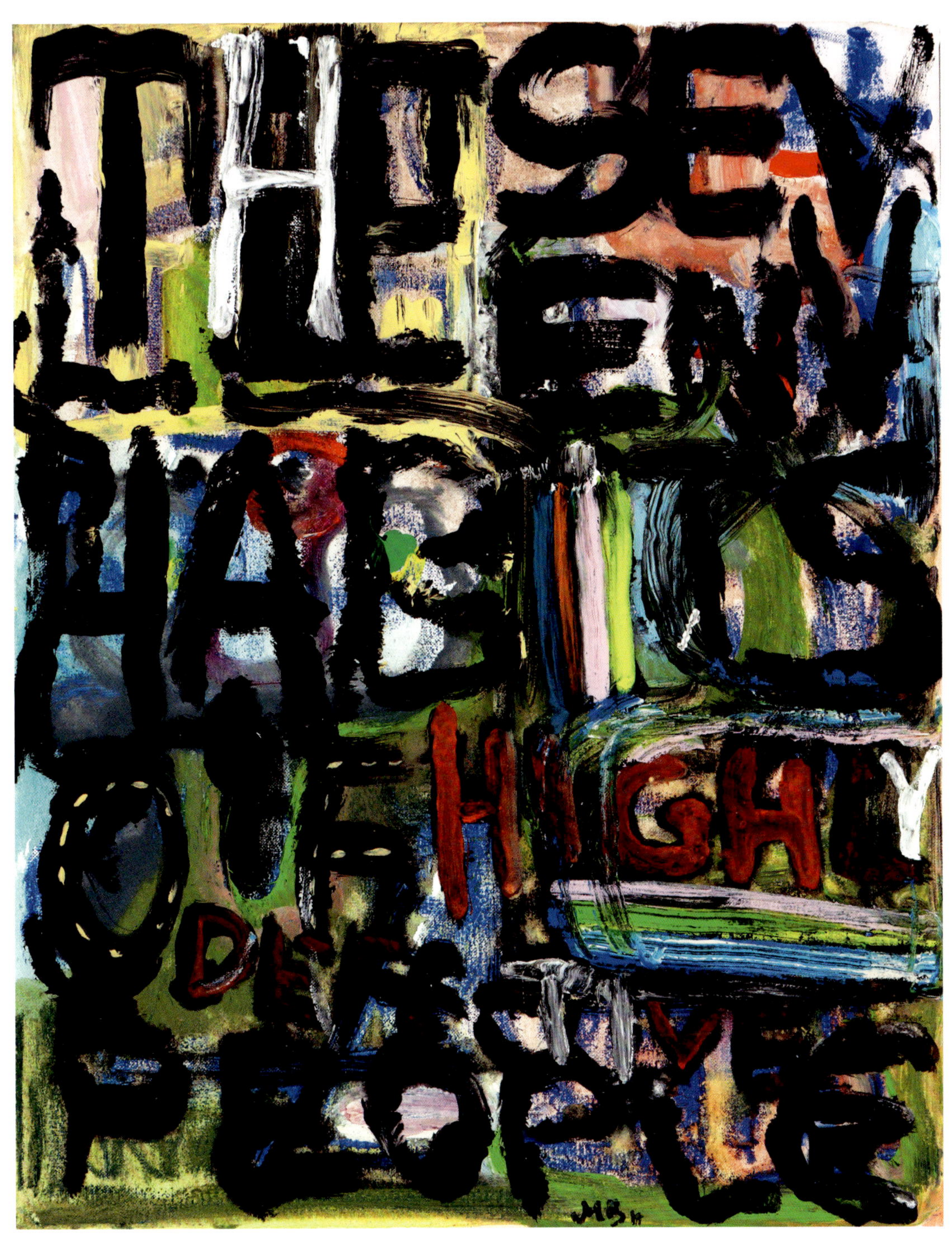
THE SEV
EN
HABITS
OF HIGHLY
PEOPLE

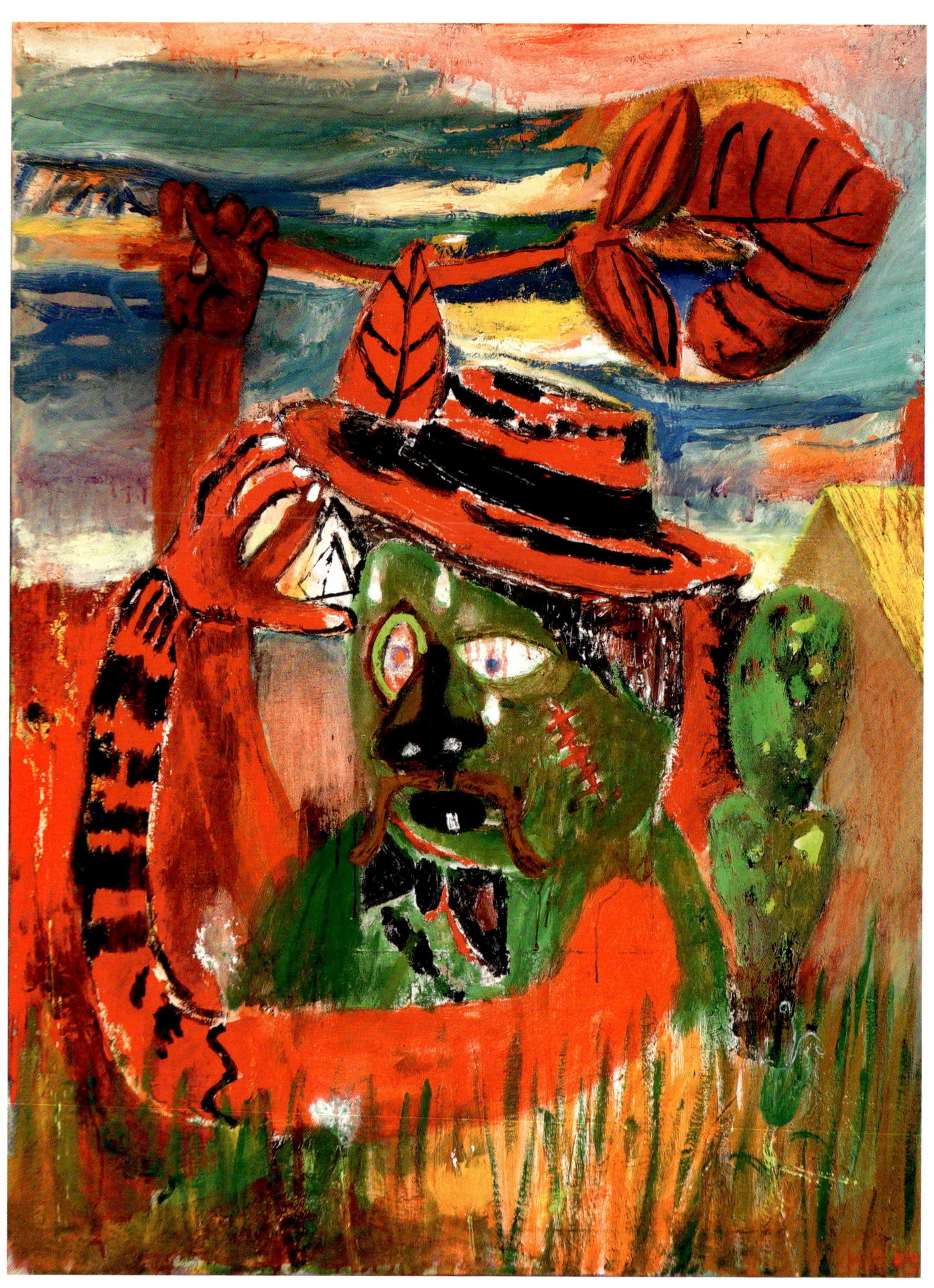

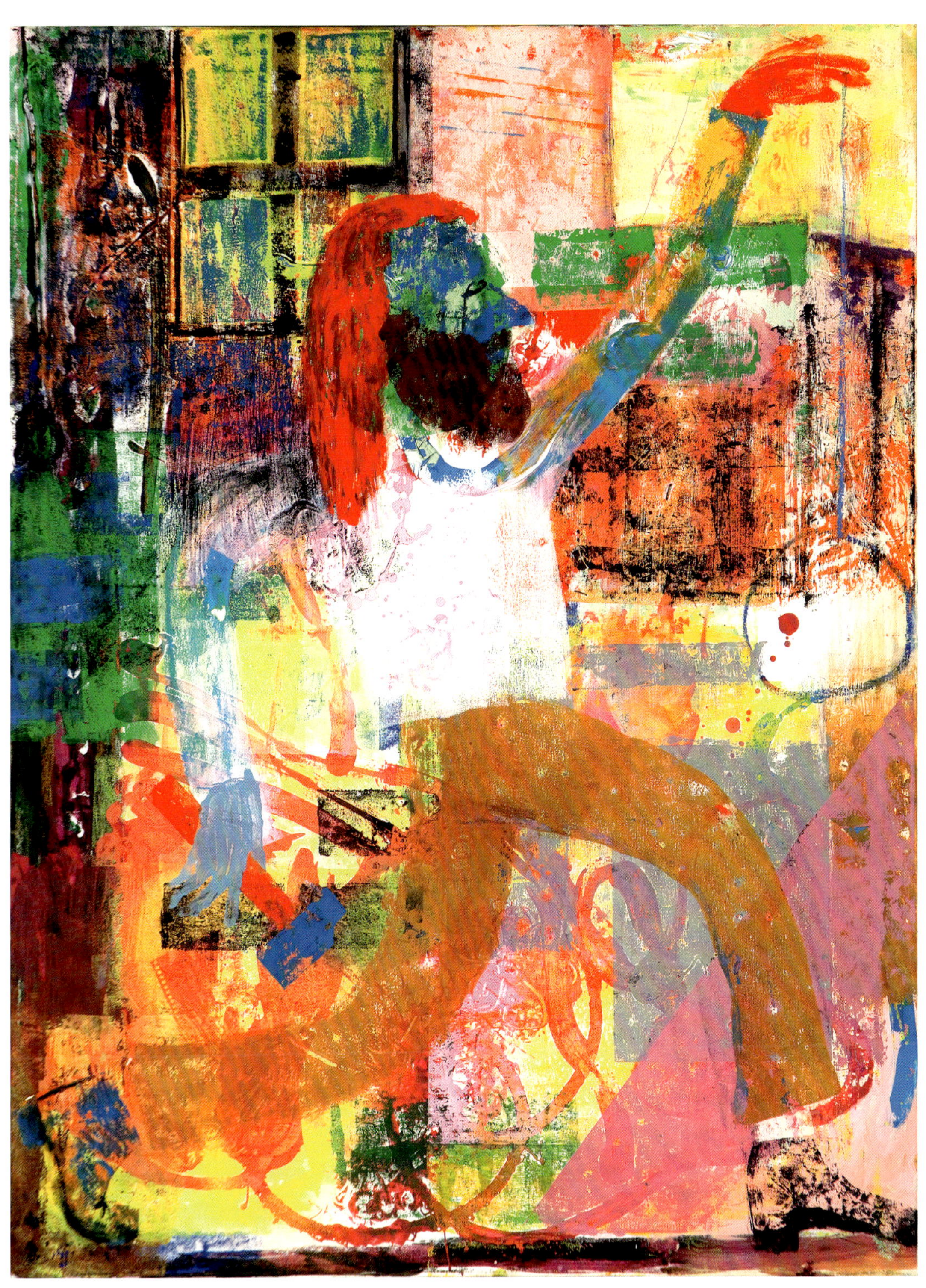

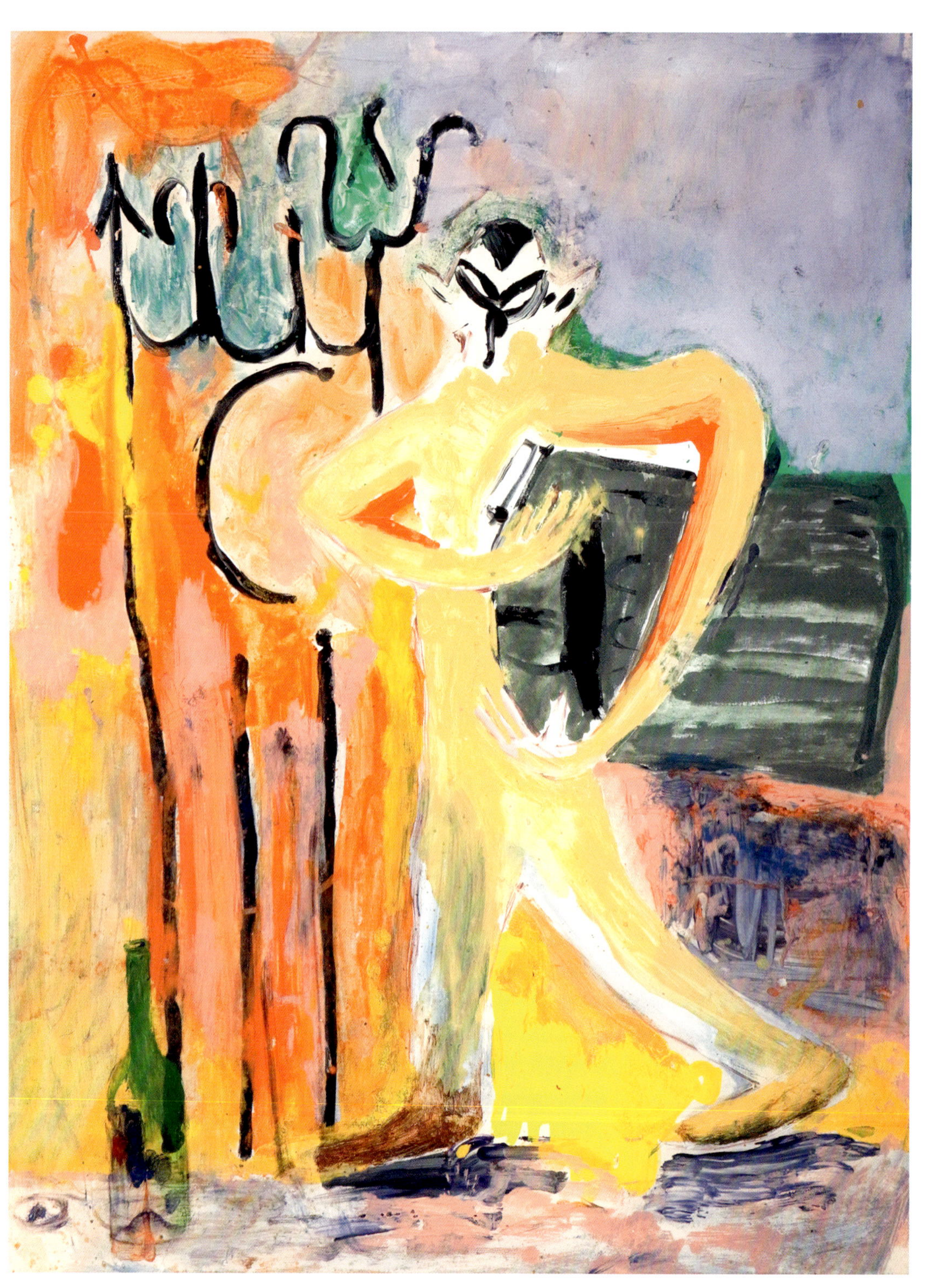

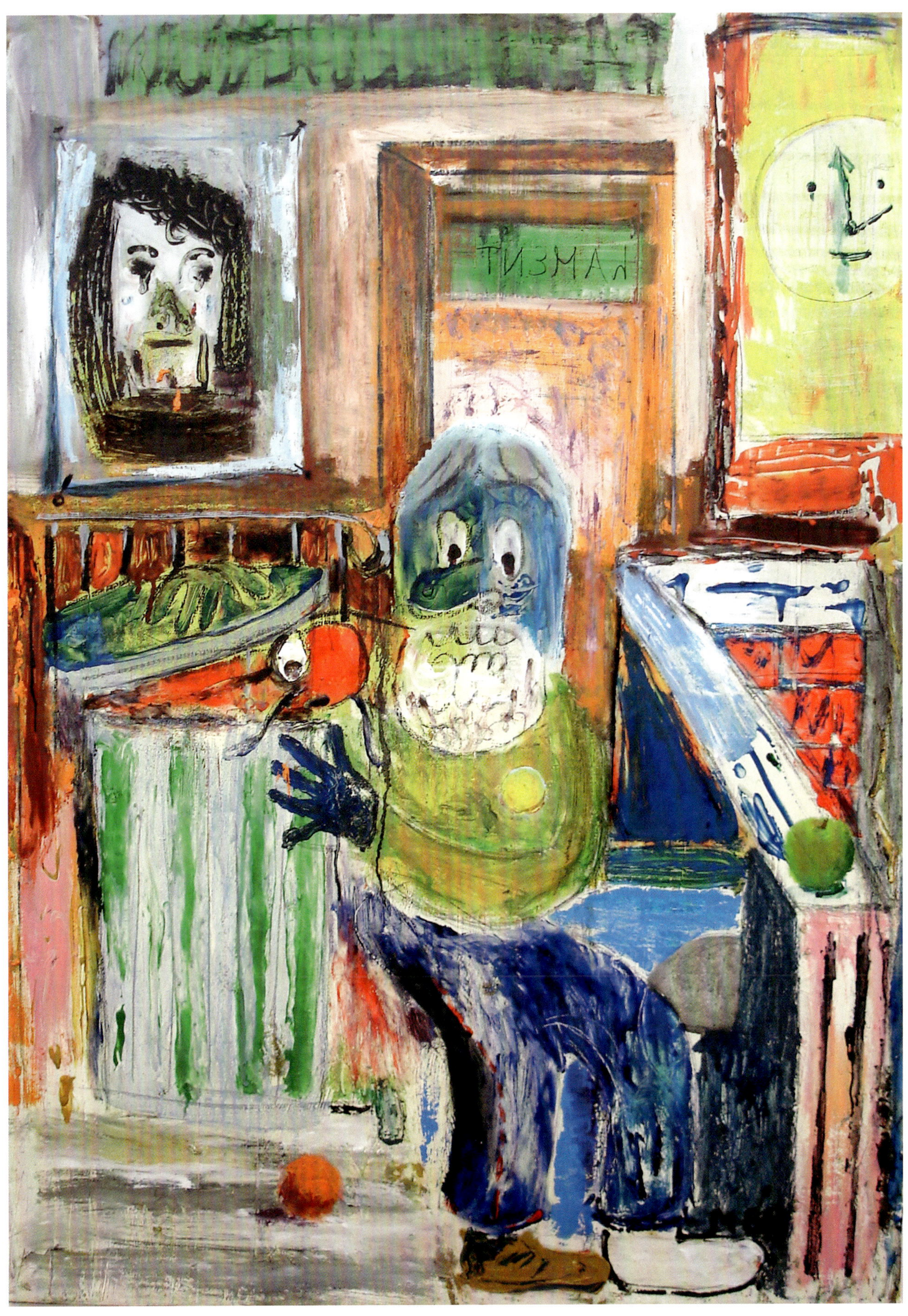
ТИЗМАЛ

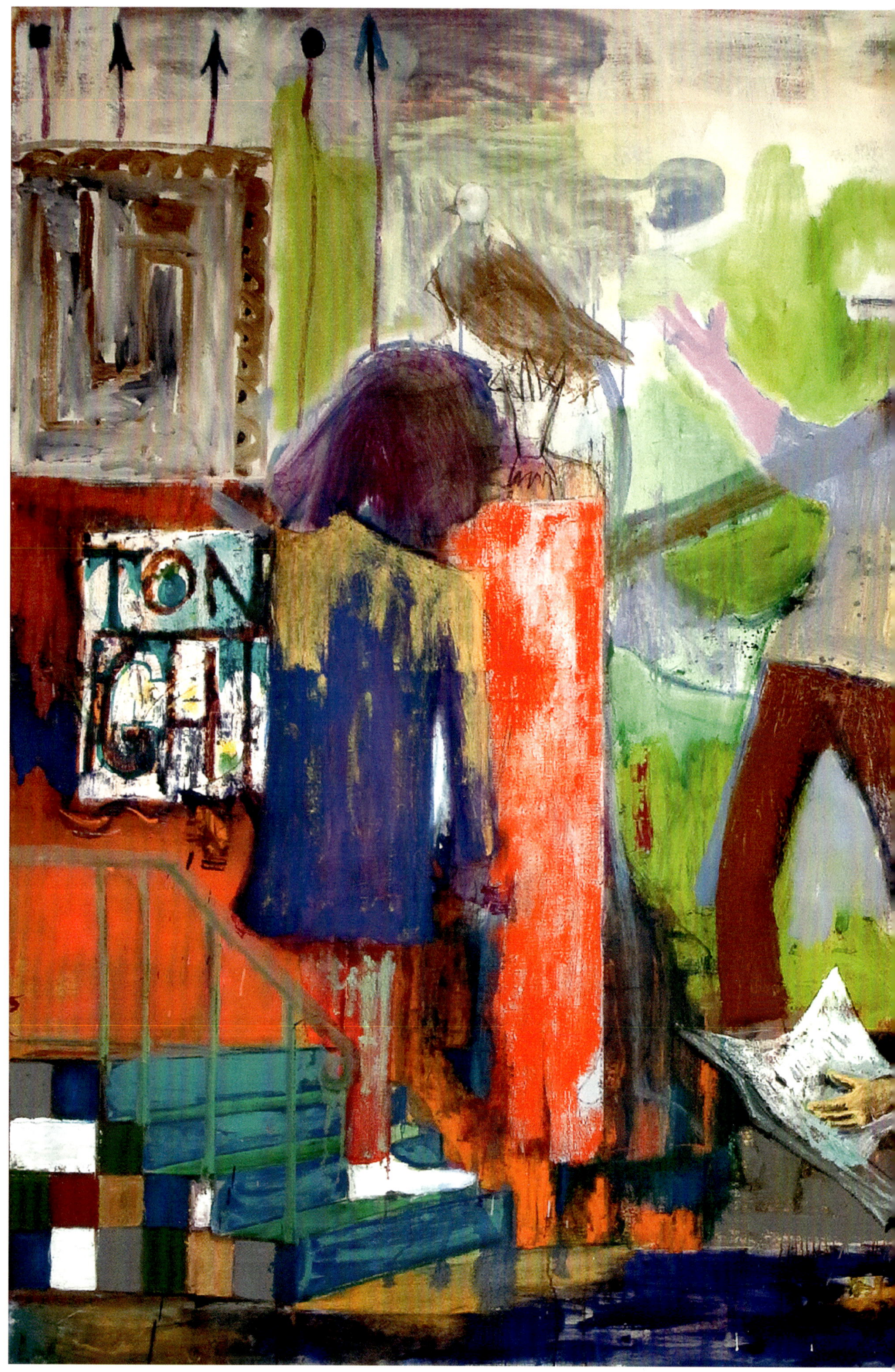
TON

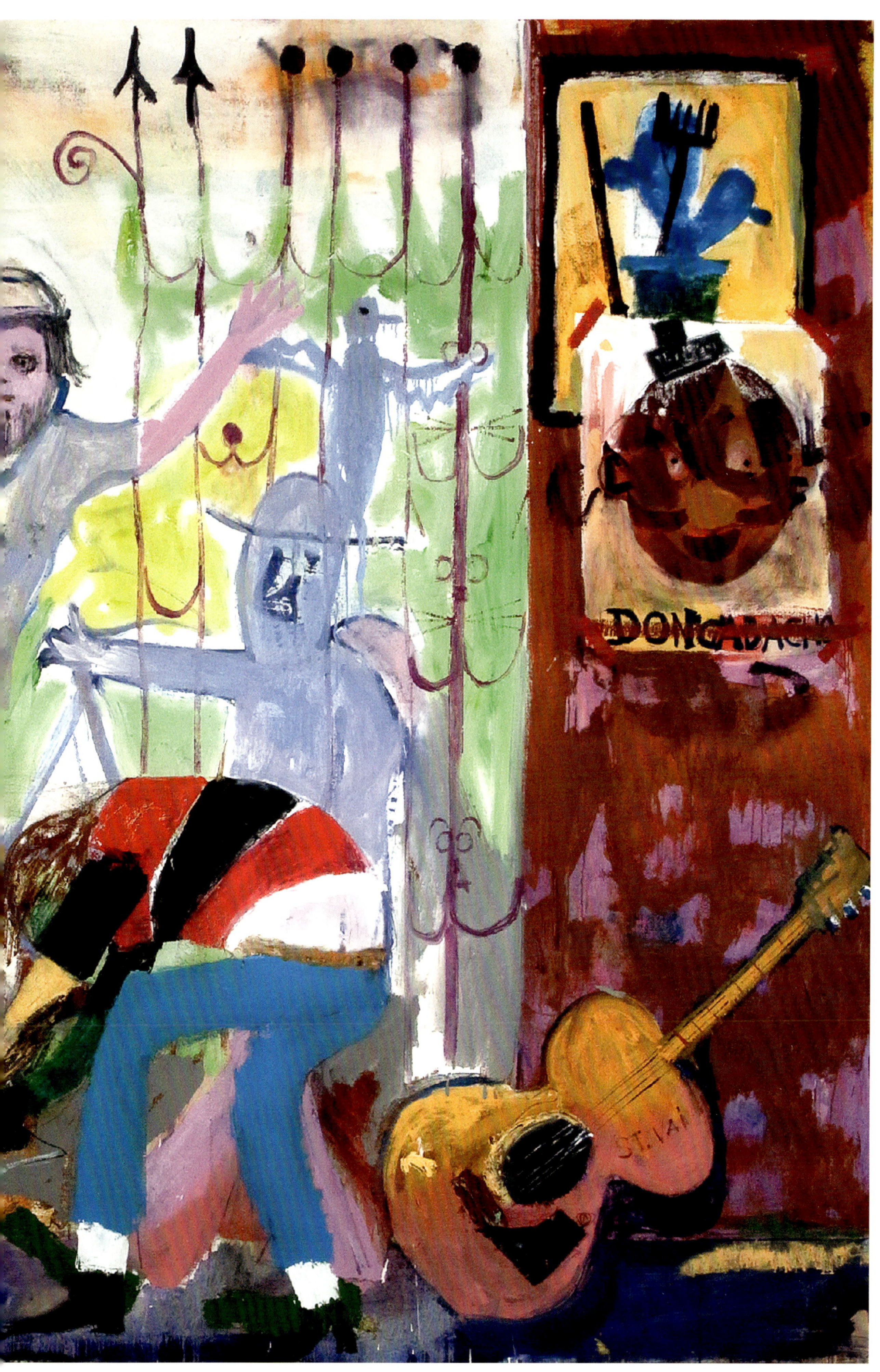

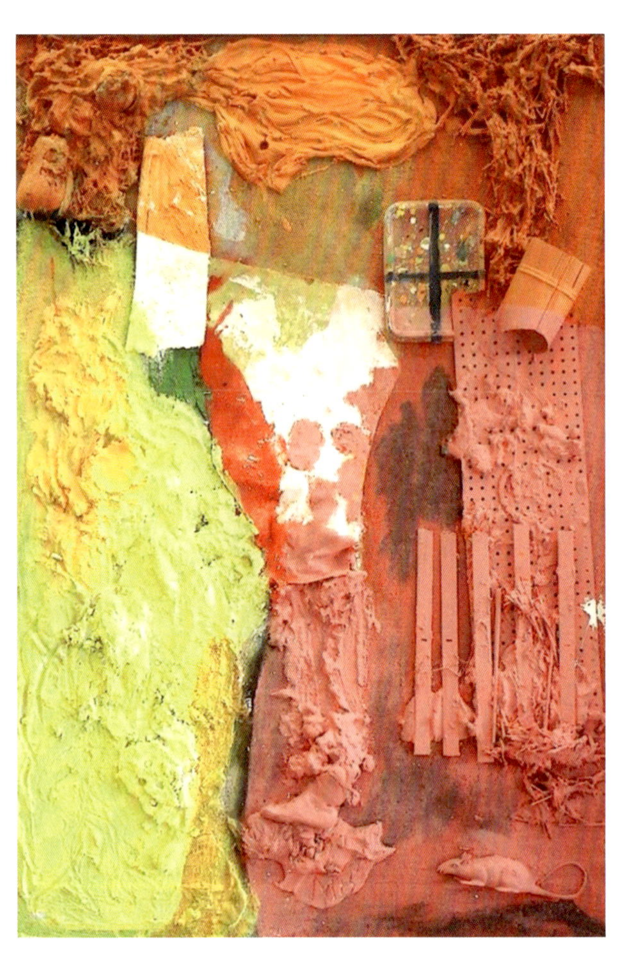

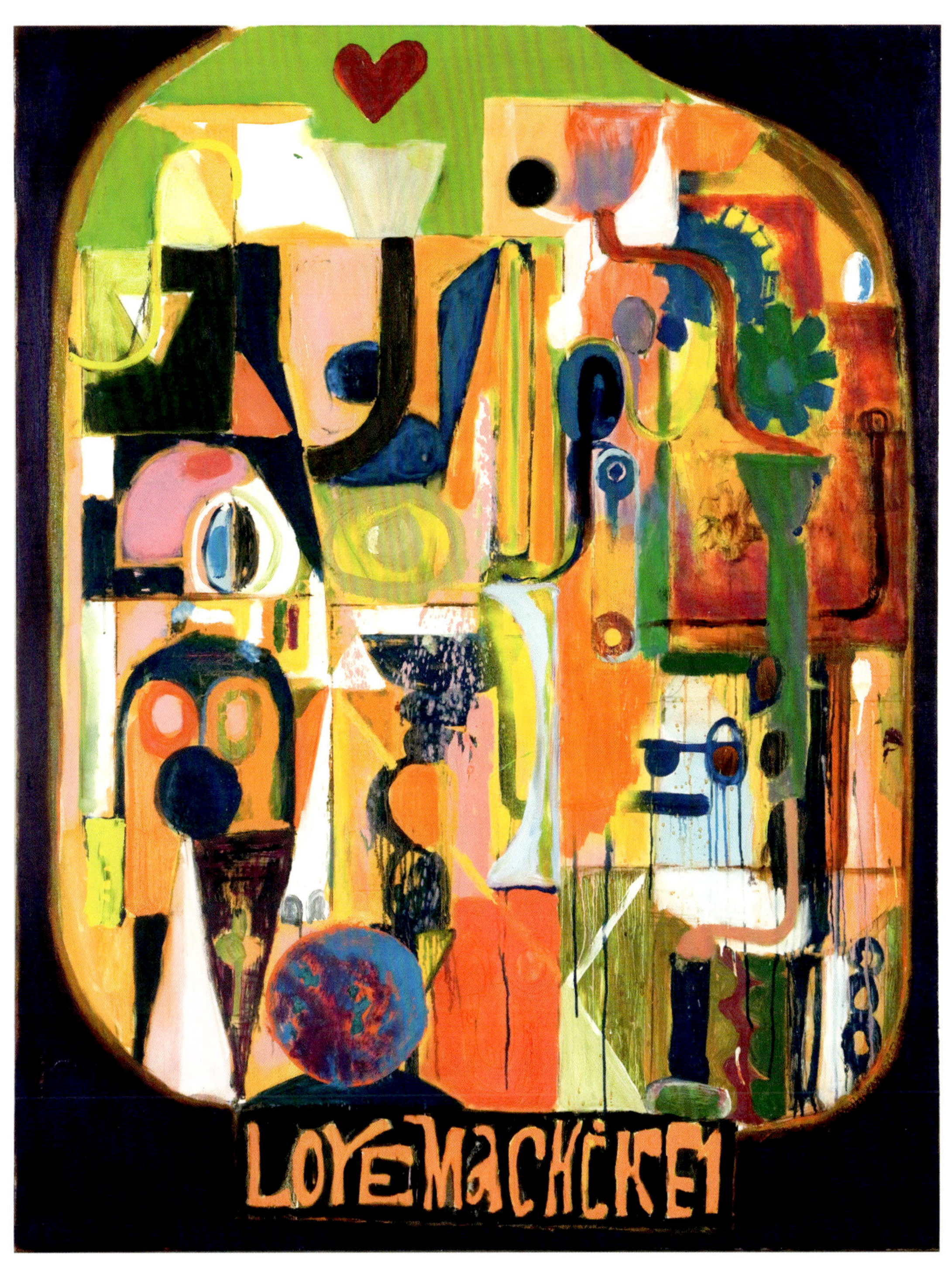

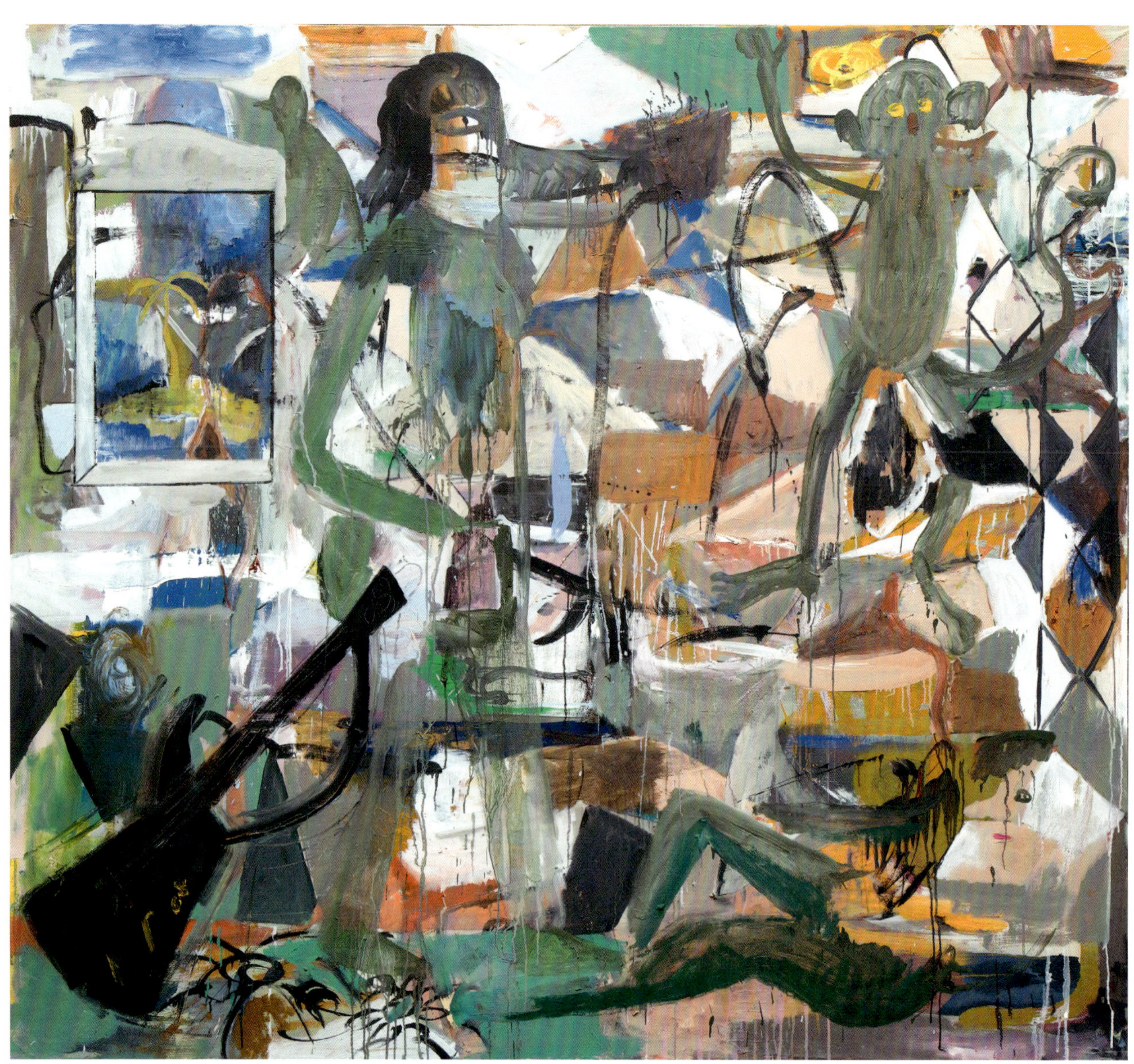

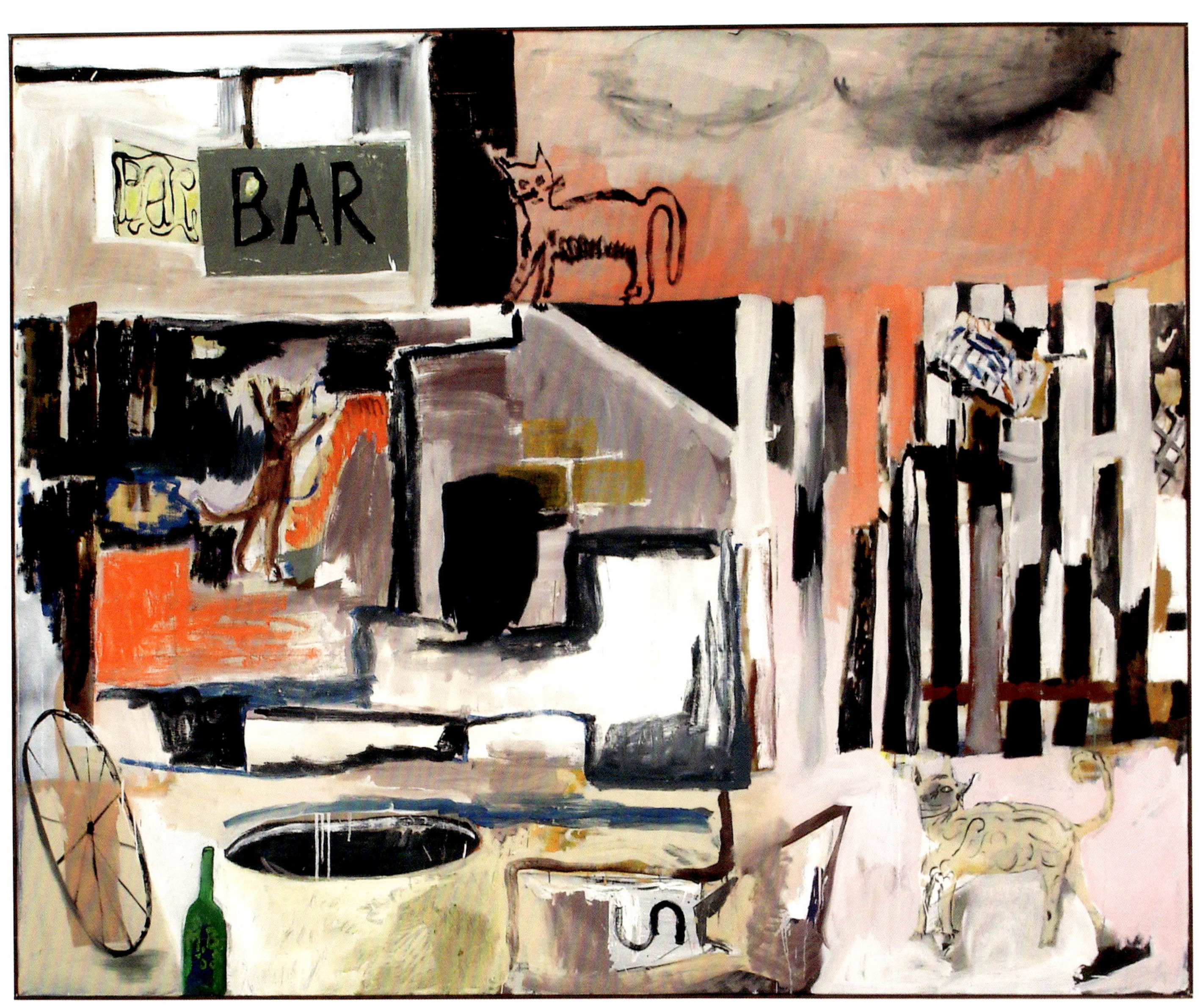
BAR

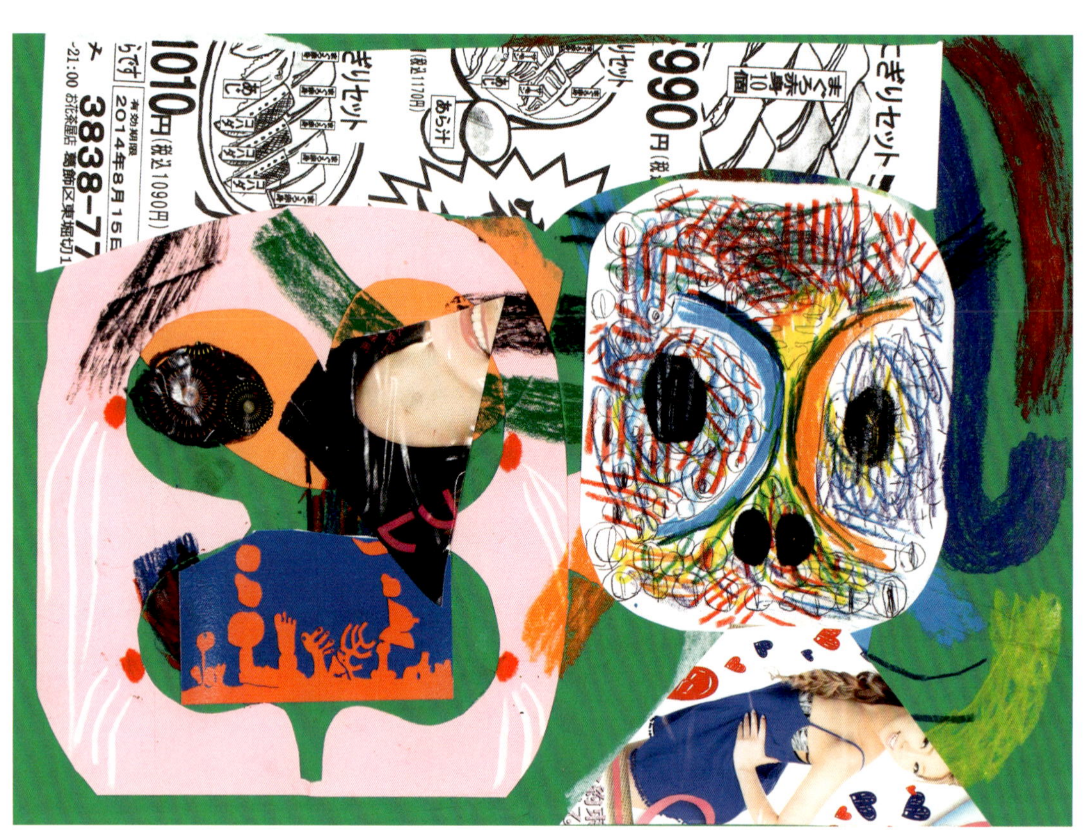

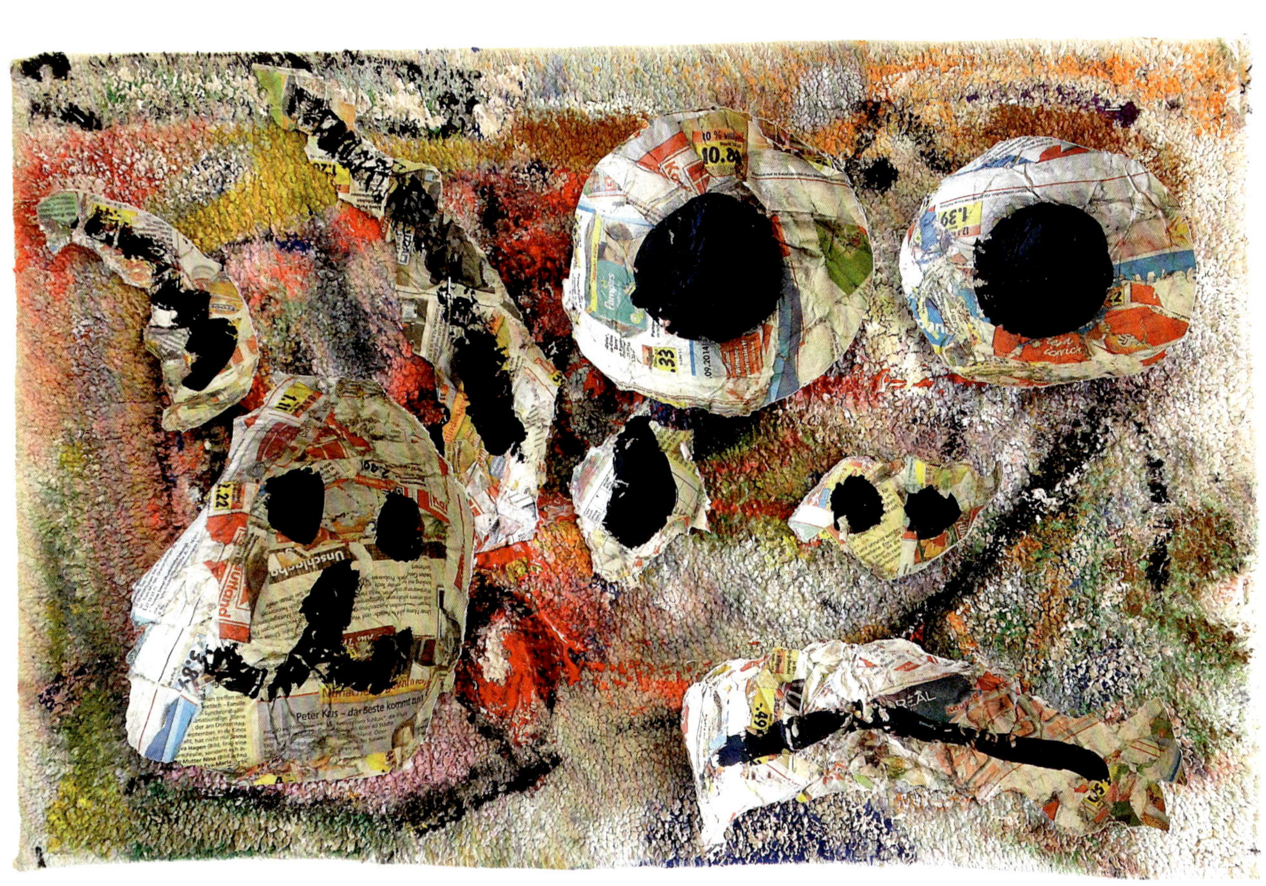

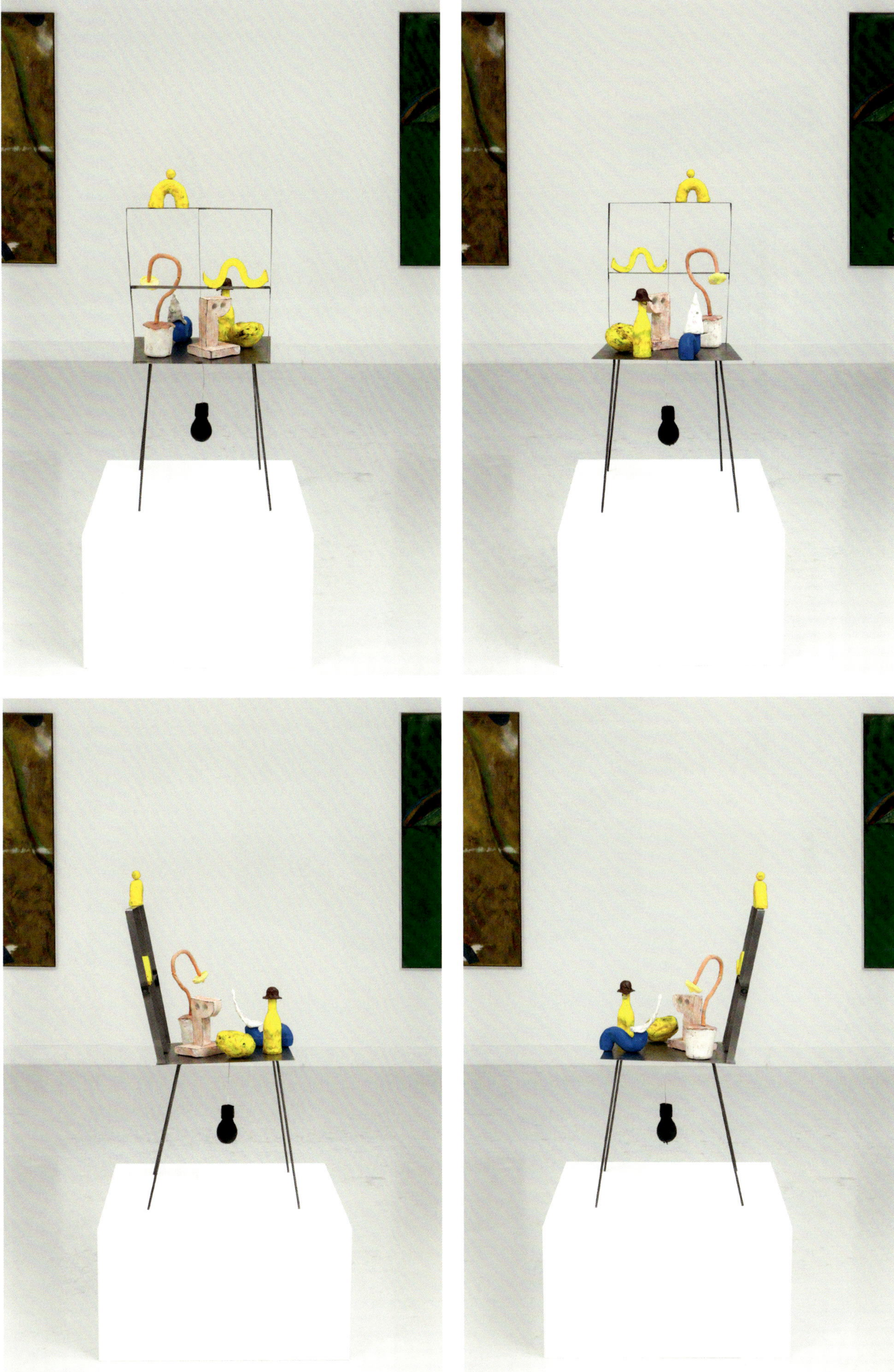

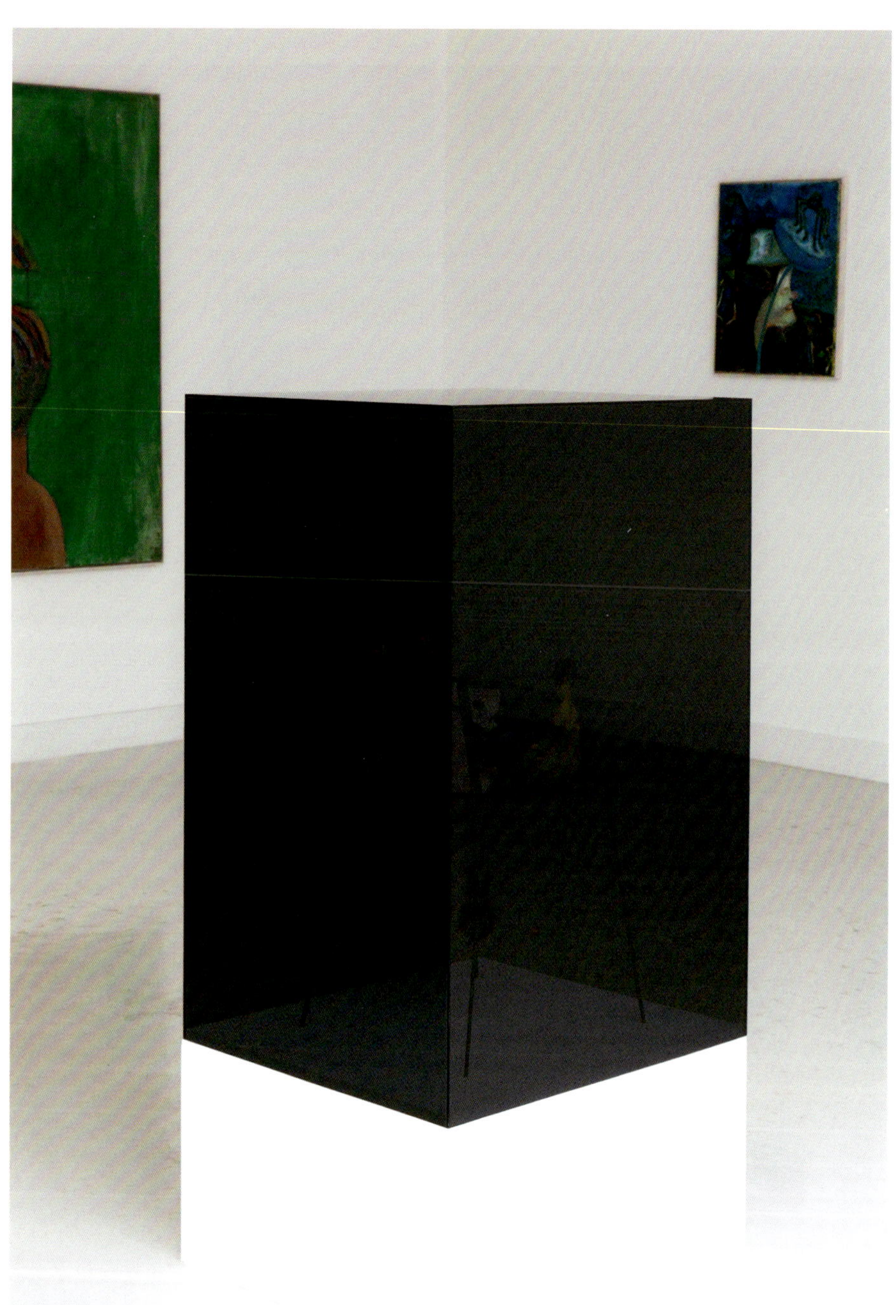

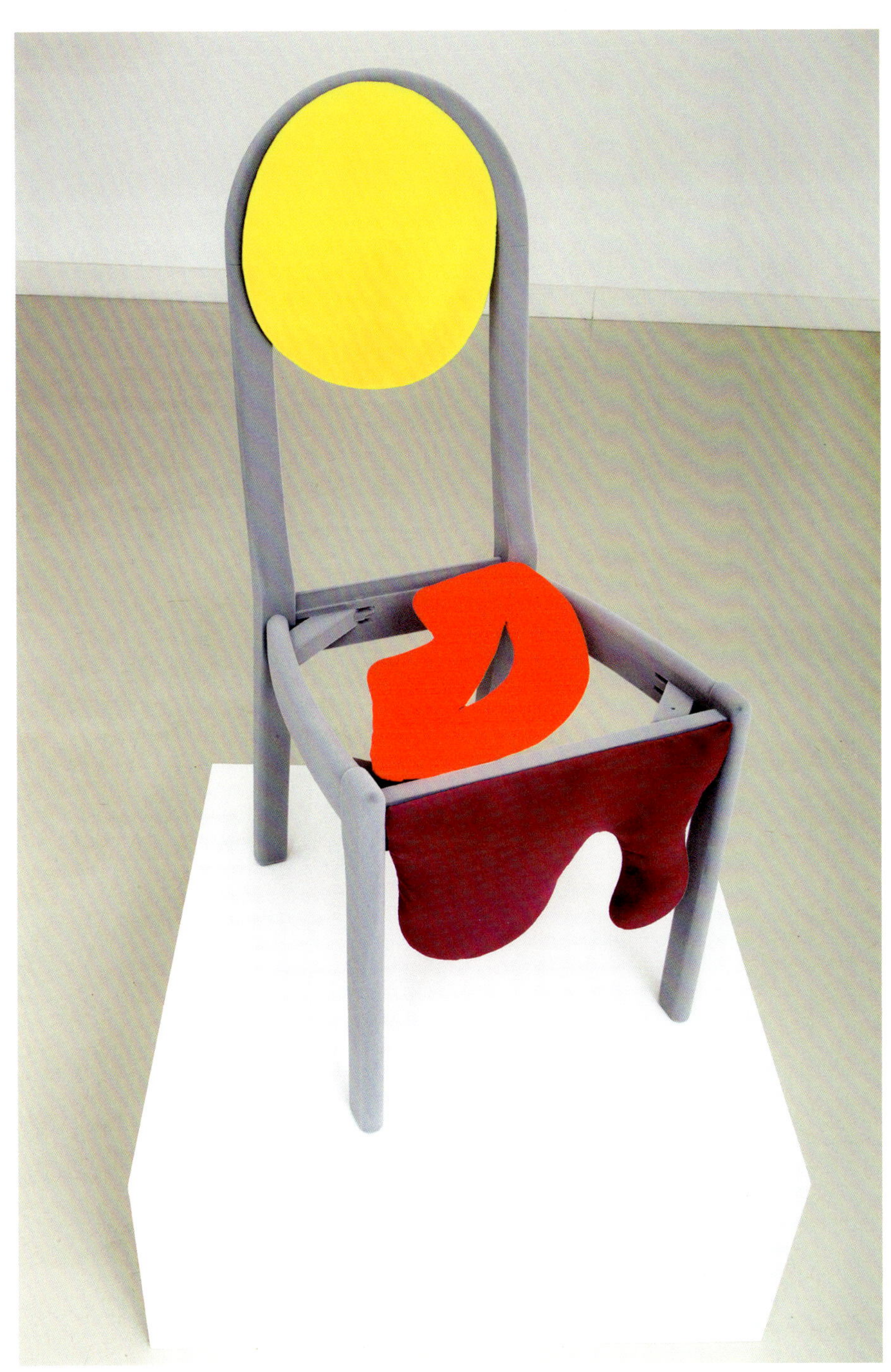

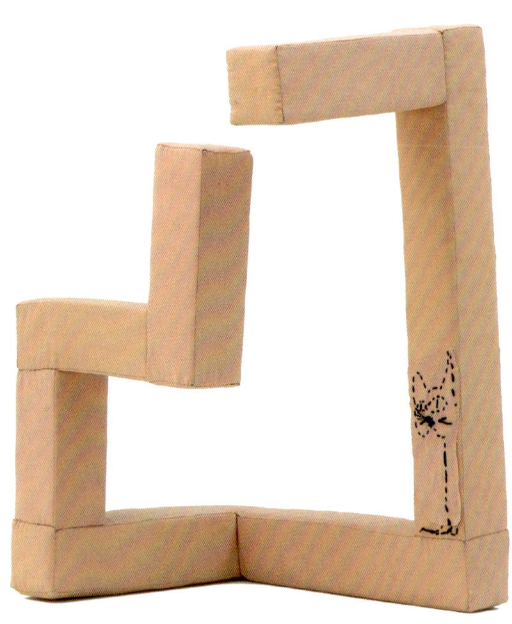

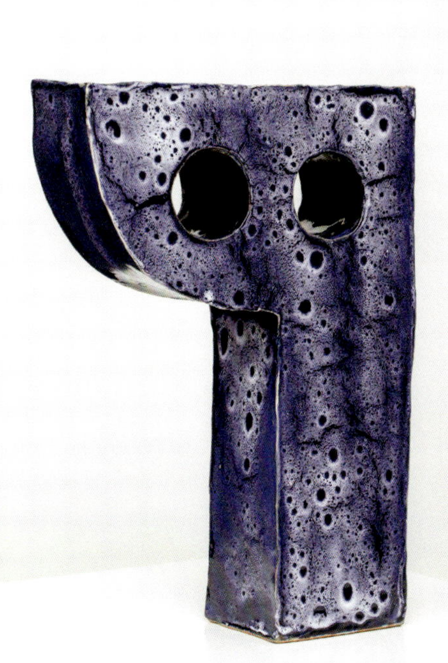

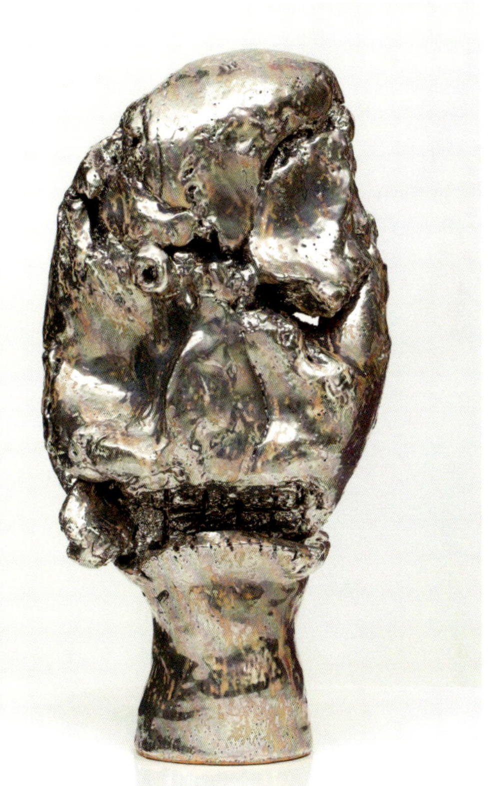

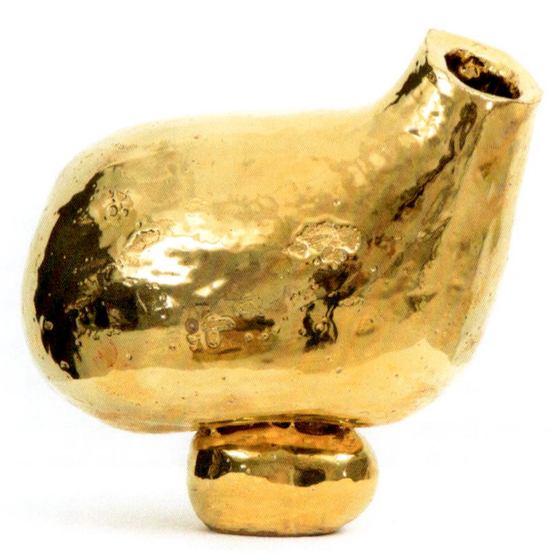

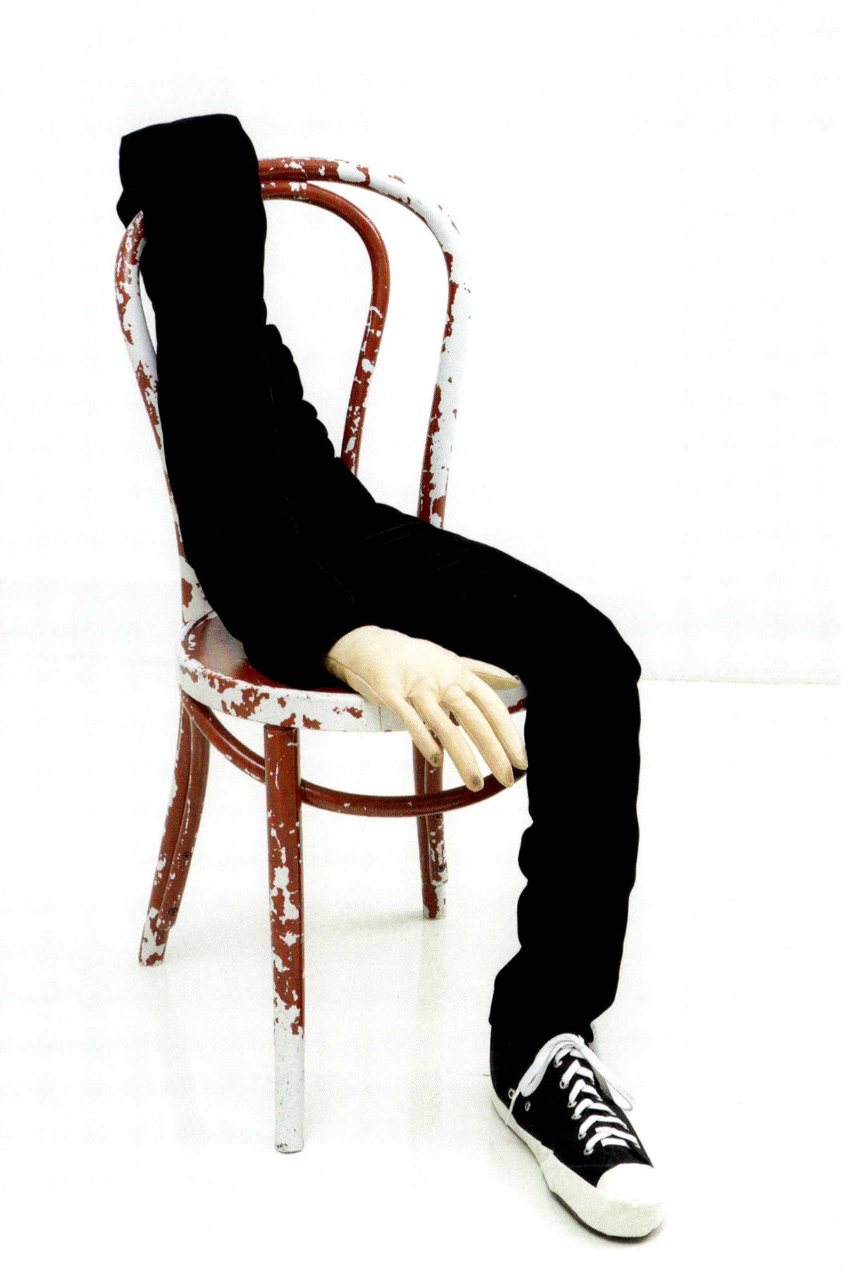

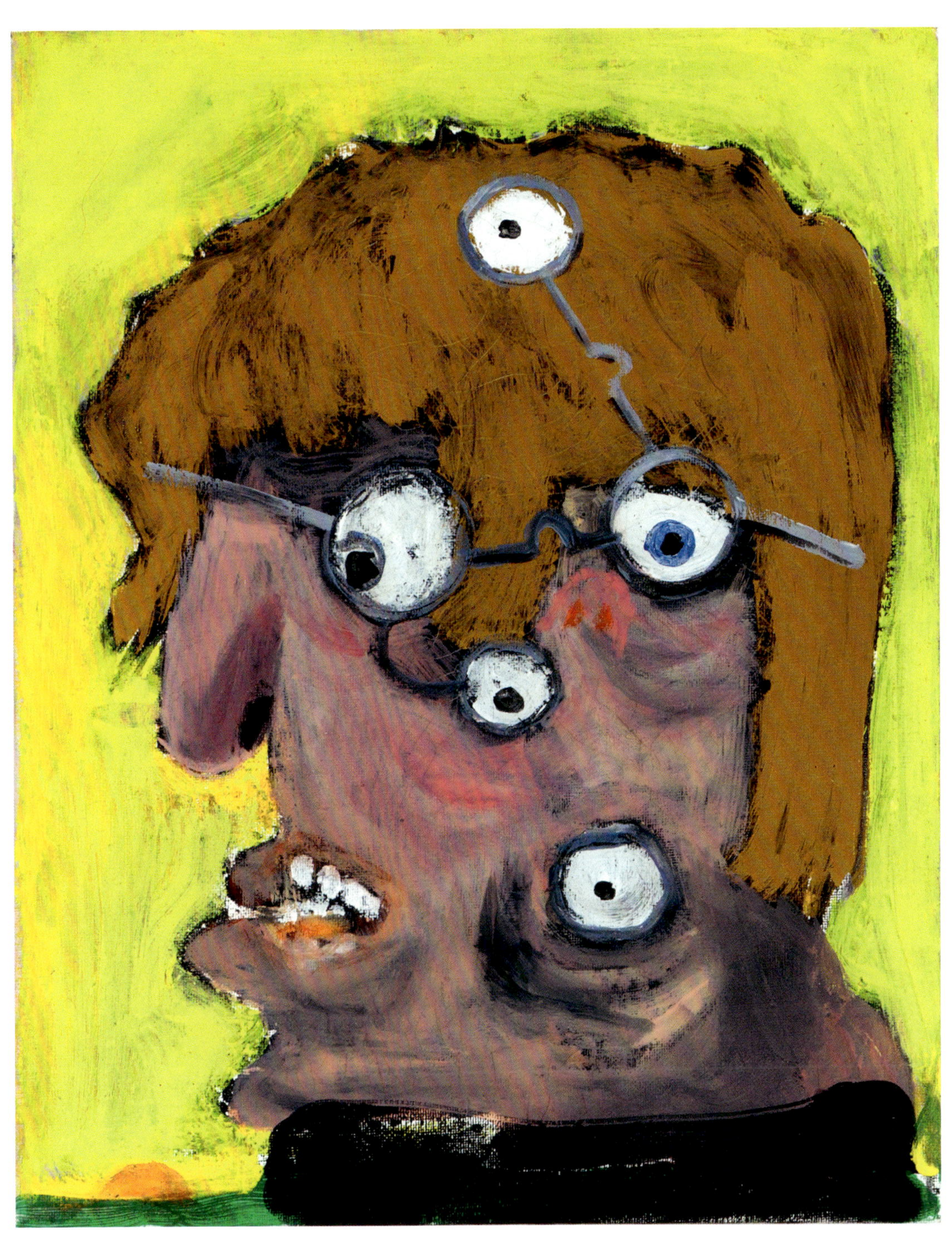

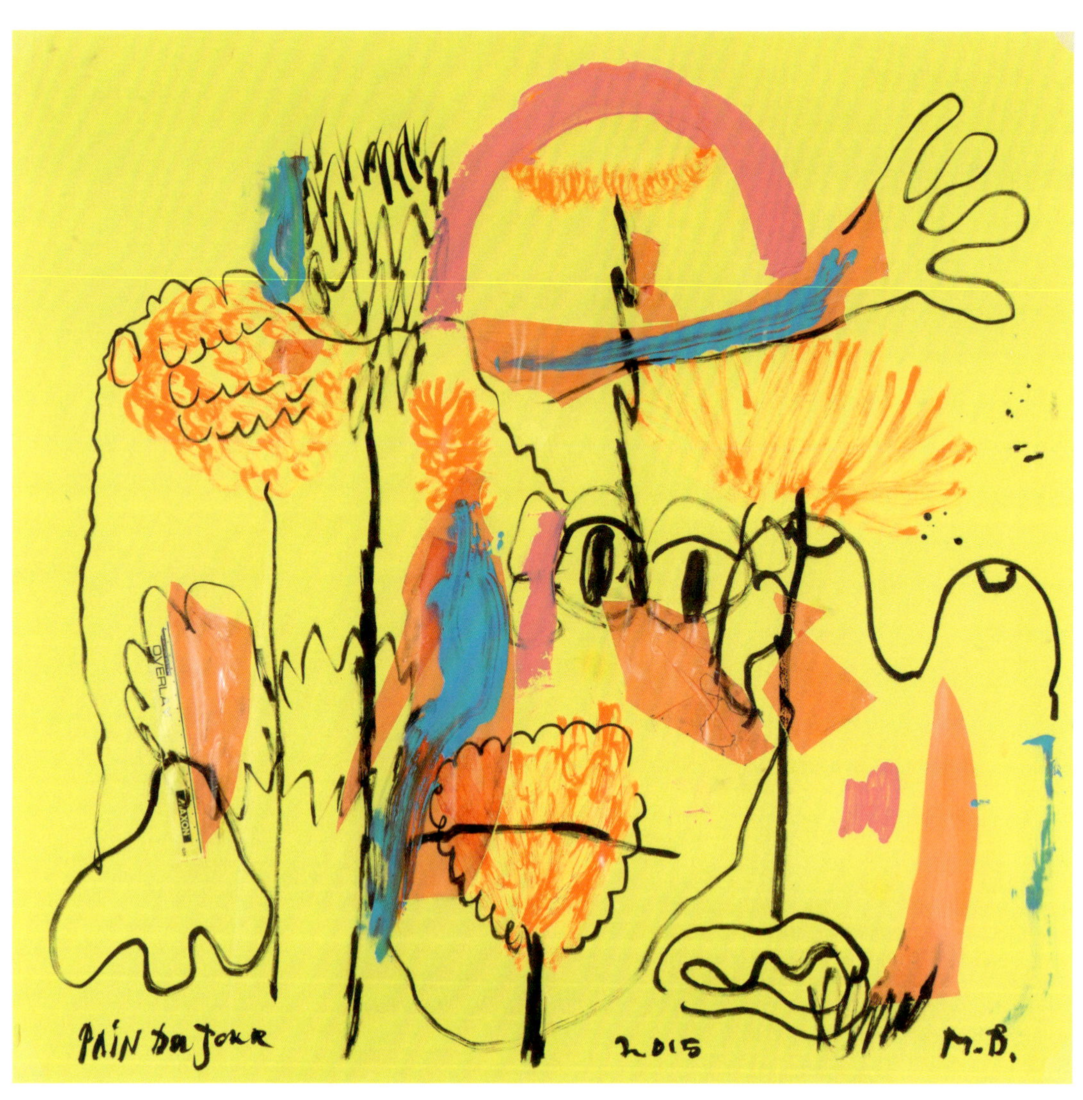
PAIN DU JOUR
2015
M.B.

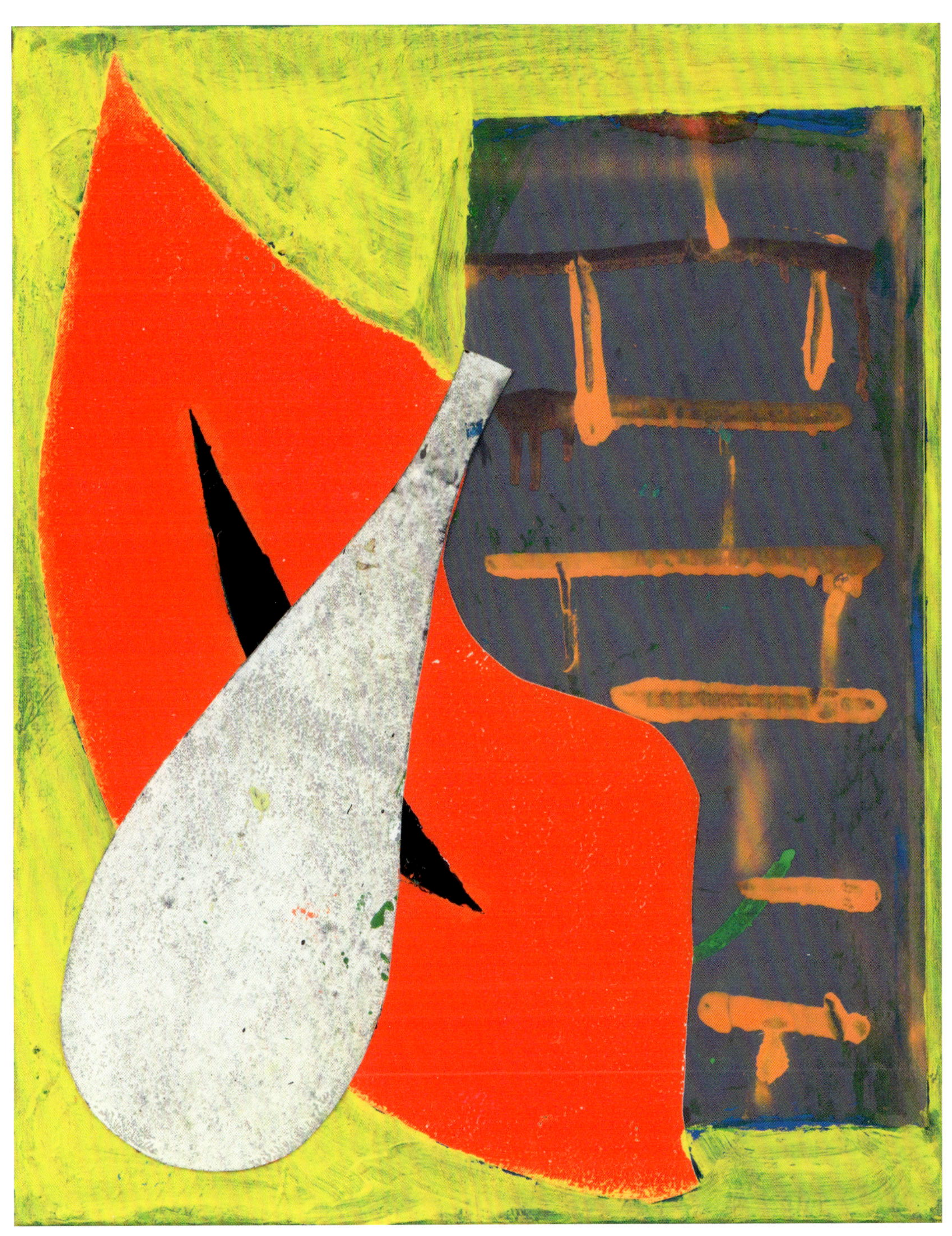

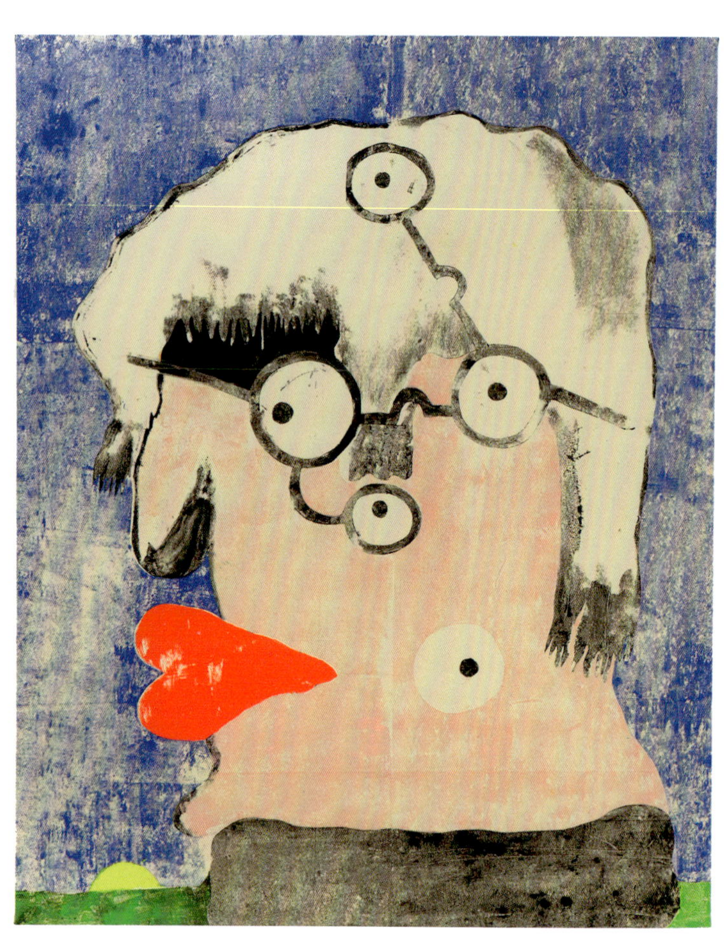

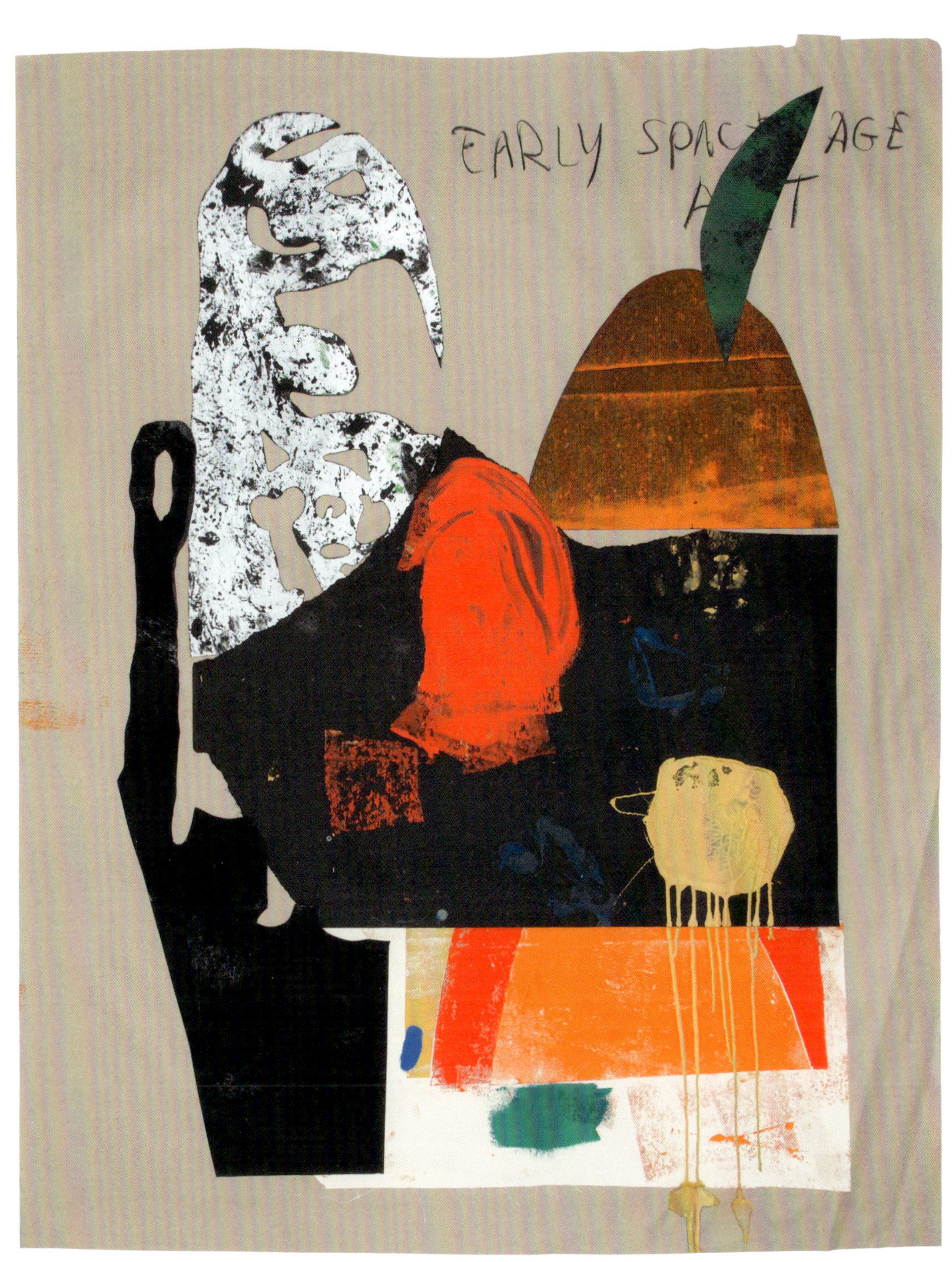
EARLY SPAC AGE

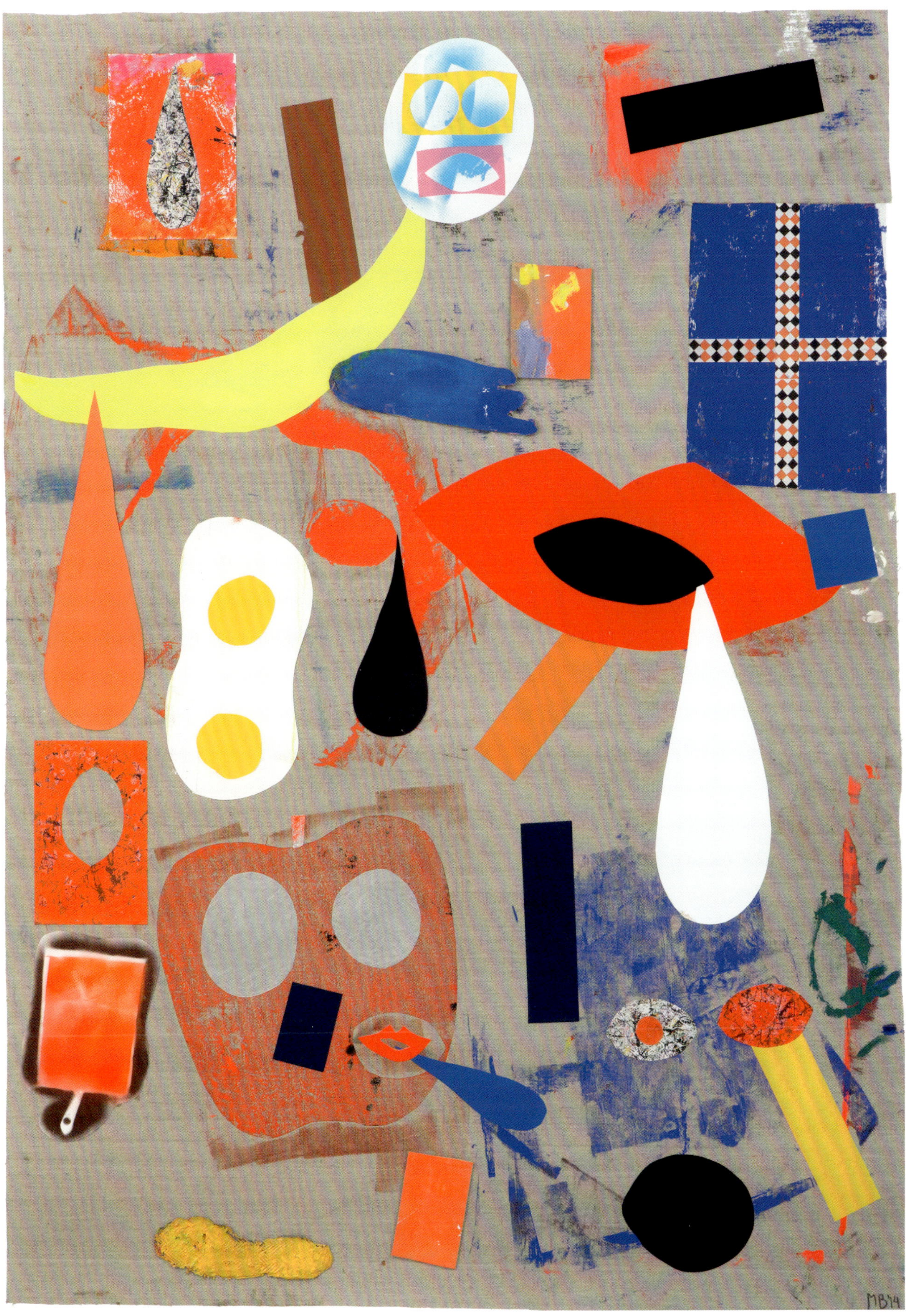

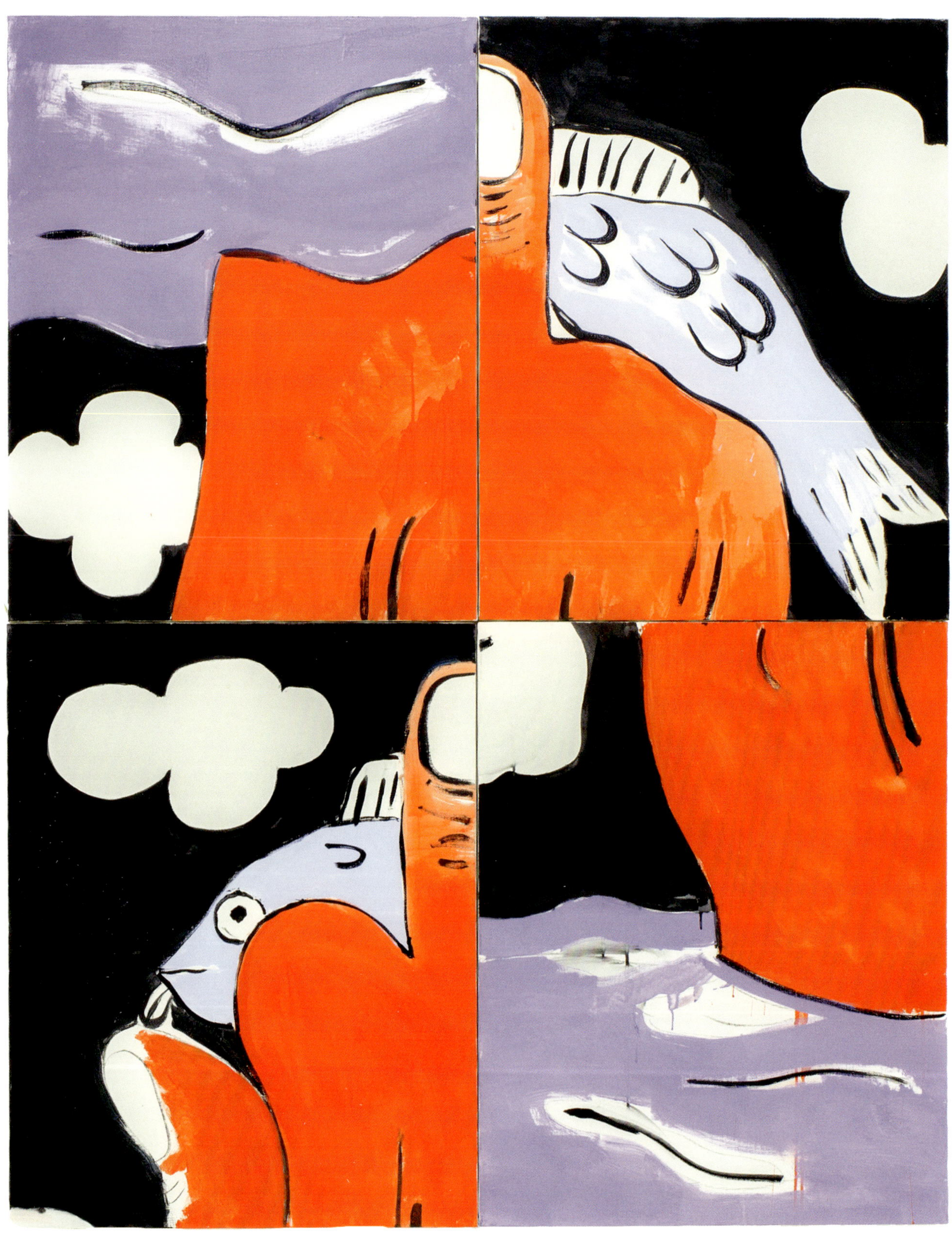

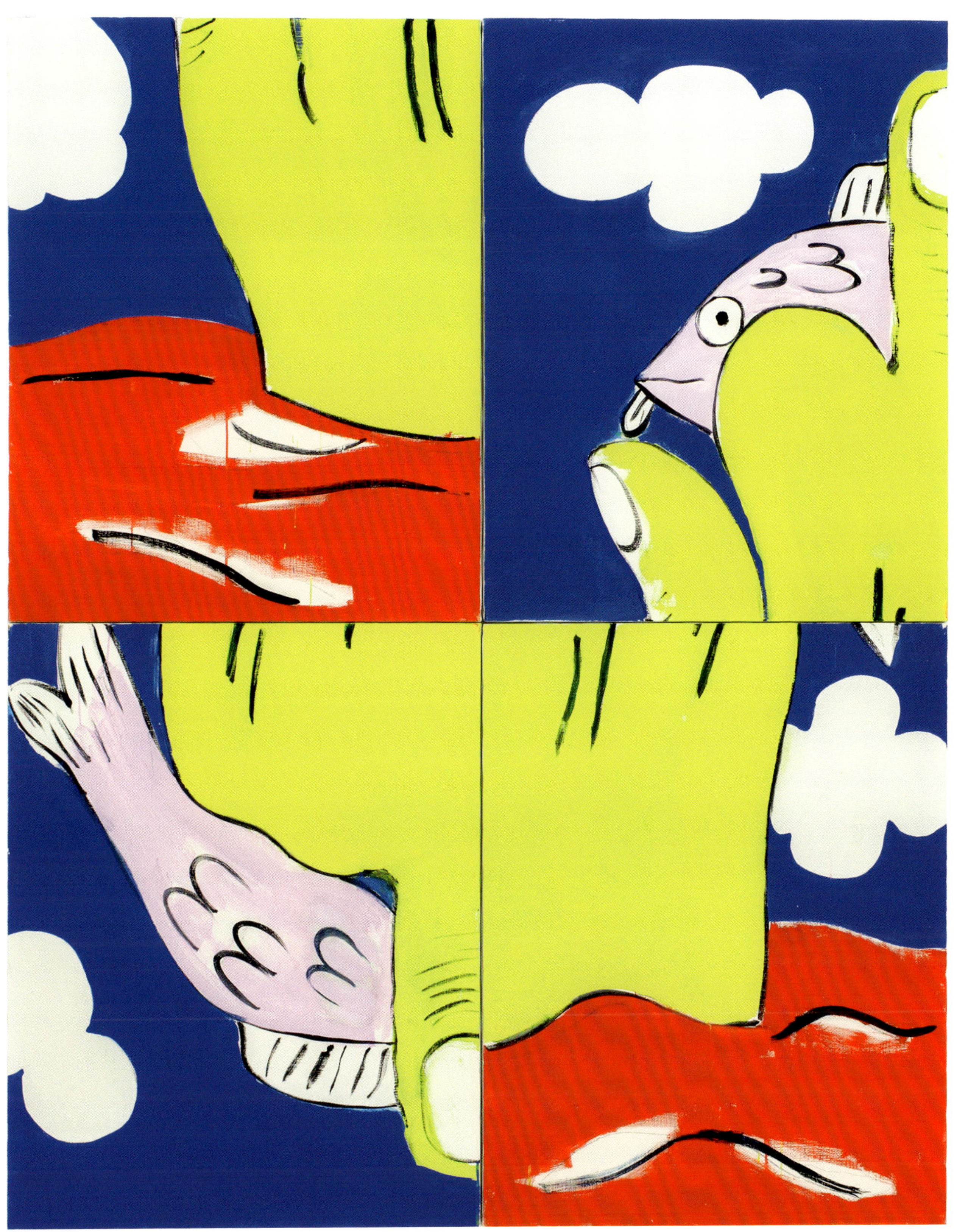

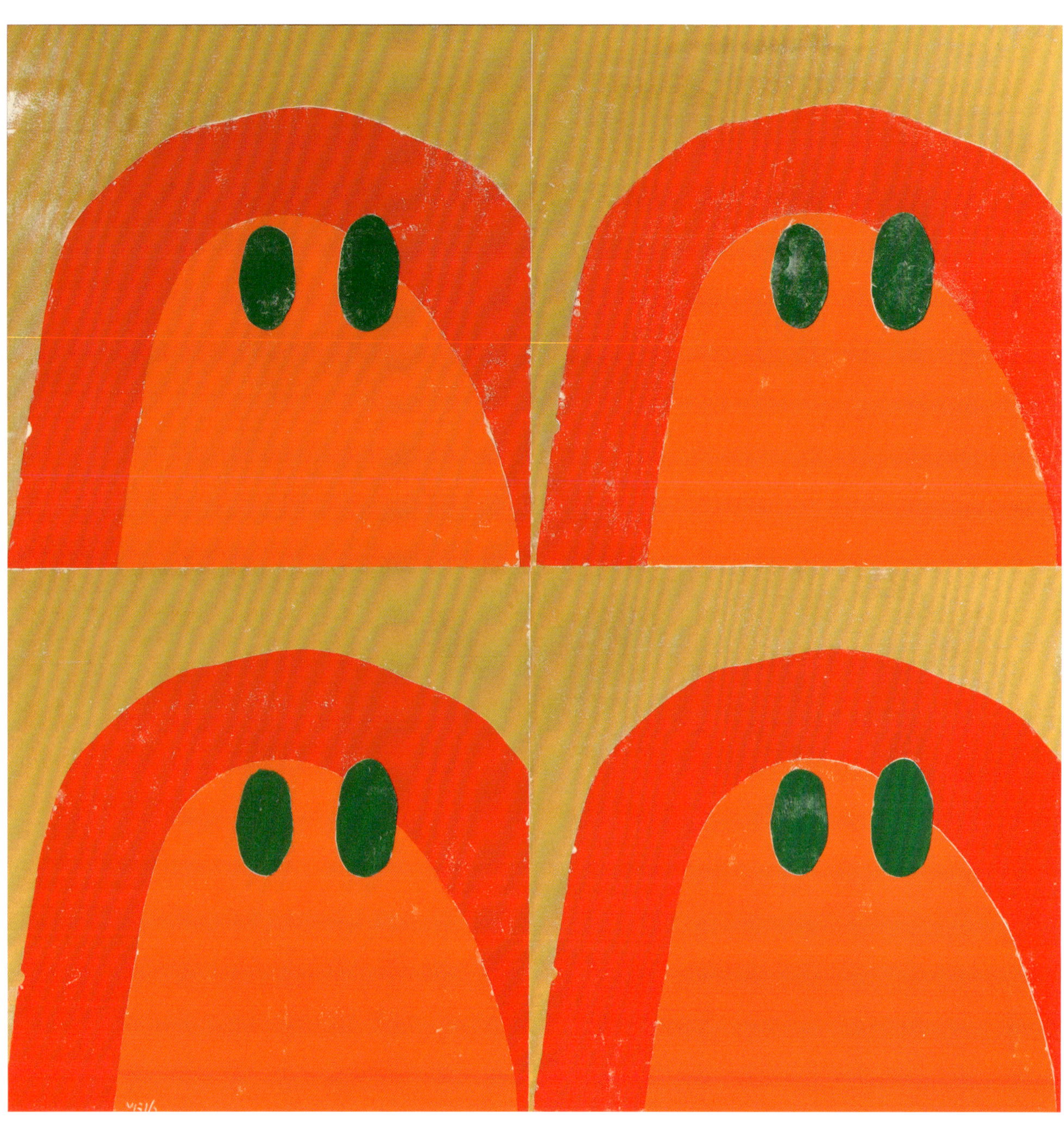

Morgan Betz

Flies on Milk, Green Eggs & Ham

Morgan Betz

Flies on Milk,
Green Eggs & Ham

Edited by
Hans Janssen & Willem Baars

Texts by
Benno Tempel, Dominic van den Boogerd,
Mischa Andriessen & Hans Janssen

Interview by
Johan Gustavsson

Gemeentemuseum Den Haag, The Hague
February 3 – June 3, 2018

Foreword
Benno Tempel, Director

More than ever, painting as a medium offers the artist a multitude of possibilities. Although today's image culture may be seen as a threat to the art of painting, it also provides unique opportunities. Morgan Betz (1974, Amsterdam) makes use of the many opportunities at his disposal, without lapsing into a bottomless pit. Drawing on a visual language that seems to blend Pop Art with Comics, he has succeeded in creating an idiom in its own right, in which the High Art of visual arts throughout history and the Low Art of comics and visual advertising intermingle.

Betz also explores the way in which the image takes shape on the canvas. The artist traditionally uses a paintbrush to do this, but Betz chooses to put a greater distance between artist and canvas. In his recent work, created especially for his exhibition in the project room at the Gemeentemuseum Den Haag, he uses a special technique to transfer the paint onto the canvas, by covering a piece of cardboard in paint and then pressing that medium onto the canvas. The resulting imperfections add tension to the work, ironically emphasising the artist's artisanal approach.

Betz partly developed his craft in Amsterdam's De Ateliers artists' institute before going on to explore the state of the art of painting in a unique manner—with boldness and irony.

Betz's first solo exhibition in a museum setting, proudly presented by the Gemeentemuseum, would not have been possible without the help of many people. First of all, I would like to thank Morgan Betz for the dedication with which he spent two years working on this exhibition. I would also like to thank Leendert Herkemij, Chris van Roon and Willem Baars for their generous support. Curator Hans Janssen coordinated the exhibition with the assistance of Michiel Simons and René Huijsman (who supervised the construction of the pond sculpture). The catalogue was published by the Gemeentemuseum and Zurich-based About Books and was beautifully designed by Bruno Margreth and Martina Brassel. The print was taken care of by Ron von Oven. It will keep the memory of this exhibition alive and will continue to delight lovers of art for many years to come.

Somewhere Over the Rainbow
Recent paintings by Morgan Betz
Dominic van den Boogerd

Morgan Betz's new paintings at the exhibition *Flies on Milk, Green Eggs and Ham* at the Gemeentemuseum Den Haag hang side by side in a row, like a frieze. They show large, recognizable figures: a garden fence, a rainbow behind a window pane, a clenched hand with a raised thumb. The visual idiom is as straightforward as that of emojis, the bold colors send the same powerful signal as a flag. Their simplicity, however, is deceptive. If you take a closer look, you will notice the refined color combinations and discover all kinds of false bottoms. With their exemplary conciseness the paintings of Morgan Betz clarify our view of the world without providing any explanations.

The technique stands out. In the past years Betz has developed his own method of painting: the paint is not applied on the canvas with brushes, but with stencils. The artist cuts the shapes that he wants to paint in thick, strengthened paper. The smooth side of the paper is then impregnated with a roller and transferred onto the canvas. Both the motif and the background are constructed in this way. The shapes are placed close to or against each other, thus enhancing the graphic, poster-like two-dimensionality of the work.

It would probably be quicker to use a brush, but the laborious stencil technique has its own charms. The composition of the image requires a methodical approach. Because the forms as they appear on the canvas are mirrored, the composition has to be fully worked out before the painting process begins. Betz wants the paint to penetrate the canvas and so doesn't apply any primer. In order to prevent the wet paint from causing the canvas to shrink so that the next cut-to-size stencils still fit, he first applies a layer of transparent gesso to the back of the canvas. The paint is a mixture of lino printing ink, acrylic colors and a medium. The color mixtures are tested on a number of proofs before determining the definitive color scheme. Each step in the work process is carefully prepared. Many of the representations are made up of large, even

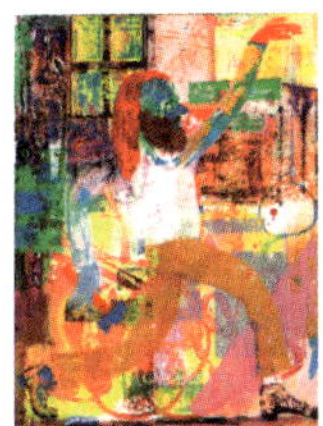

Say Yes to No NO, 2009
Linocut, oil and Flashe vinyl paint on canvas, 118 × 88 cm
Private collection

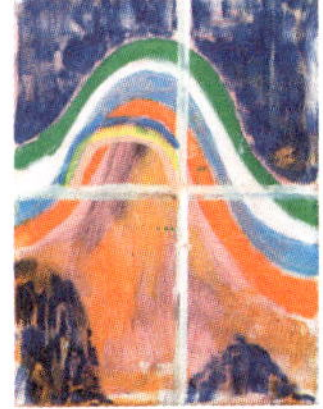

Five Easy Pieces, 2009
Oil on canvas, 189 × 233 cm
Private collection

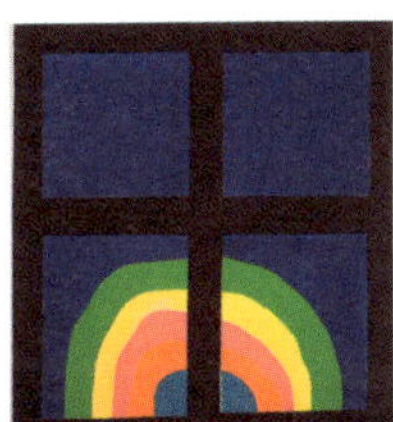

Untitled (Window), 2011
Gouache and water soluble oil paint on canvas, 40 × 30 cm
Private collection, Amsterdam

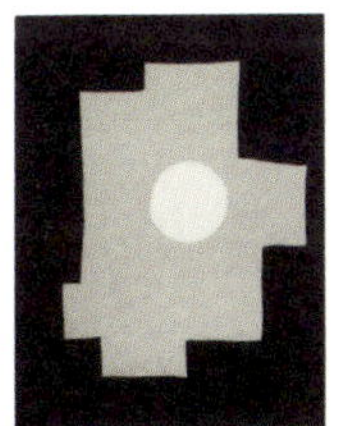

Flies on Milk (Neon), 2017
Block printing ink, block printing medium and acrylic on canvas, 200 × 189 cm
Willem Baars Projects, Amsterdam

Flies on Milk (Night), 2017
Block printing ink, block printing medium and acrylic on canvas, 200 × 152 cm
Willem Baars Projects, Amsterdam

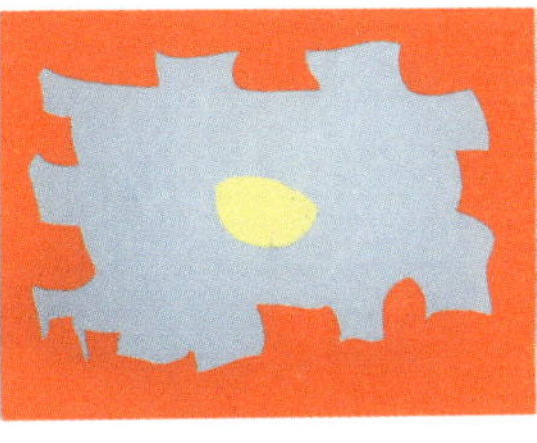

Flies on Milk (Day), 2017
Block printing ink, block printing medium and acrylic on canvas, 200 × 270 cm
Willem Baars Projects, Amsterdam

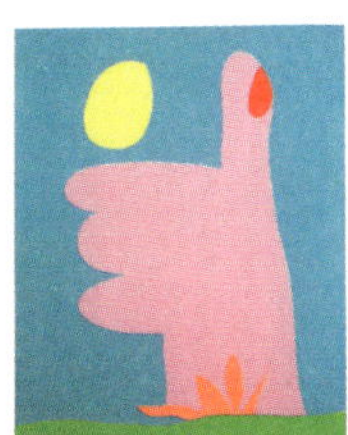

Flies on Milk (Yes), 2017
Block printing ink, block printing medium and acrylic on canvas, 200 × 164 cm
Willem Baars Projects, Amsterdam

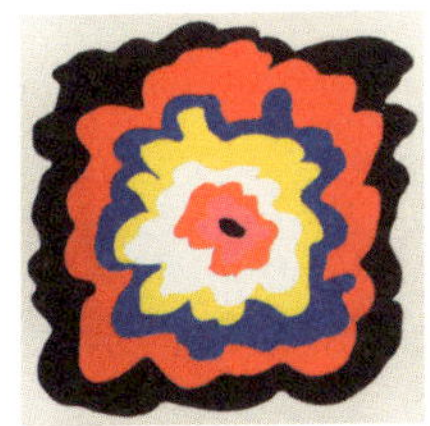

Flies on Milk (Blow up), 2017
Block printing ink, block printing medium and acrylic on canvas, 200 × 200 cm
Willem Baars Projects, Amsterdam

color fields. However, the paint is not transferred everywhere equally. Small imperfections result in a lively, varied texture. It is these imperfections that finish the painting. It is no coincidence that the contours of the shapes don't quite coincide with the edge of the painting, as it gives the composition a certain airiness and makes it appear less static.

Although the painter is in full control of his technique, he can never completely eliminate every risk and contingency in advance. On those rare occasions when he isn't fully satisfied with the printed form he retouches it by hand. Ironically, the decisive moment of this painting method, when the stencil is pressed against the canvas, is a 'blind' operation that escapes supervision. Besides, the larger shapes demand an extra pair of hands, implying that the artist literally and figuratively no longer has matters in his own hands. In the end, this painting method is no different from what happens in most painter's studios: a constant push and pull between control and letting go.

Betz first used the stencil technique in *Say Yes To No No* (2009). The main character in this work is a bearded carpenter holding a hammer in his hand who looks as if he has just emerged from a painting by Kazimir Malevich. There is a lot of 'white noise' in the painting, a large amount of visual information that doesn't exactly clarify things. By contrast the figures in recent paintings have a certain monumental simplicity—as if they have been reduced to their true essence.

'Green eggs & Ham', the last part of the exhibition's title, is derived from a children's book by Dr. Seuss which Betz vividly remembers from his childhood. The paintings also look as if they are based on illustrations from children's books, but that is not the case. Many of these figures originated in the darkest recesses of the artist's subconscious and have already featured in his earlier work. The rainbow behind the window, for example, first appeared in *Five Easy Pieces* (2009) as an unobtrusive detail in the background. Three years later, it has increased in size, becoming a familiar motif in *Untitled (Window)* (2011). In *Flies on Milk (Neon)* (2017), finally, the window with the rainbow fills the entire surface of the image and has the self-evident presence of a gas station logo. The view of a patch of sky surrounded by the contours of high-rise buildings in *Flies on Milk (Night)* and *Flies on Milk (Day)* (2017) is also an earlier subject: it first appeared in two paintings from 2013. Betz calls the figures in the recent series his guilty pleasures, motifs that he used to tuck away in a corner of the painting, but which he now has decided to bring into the spotlight.

Again and again, almost obsessively, the artist returns to his subjects, and with each repeat the figures become larger, simpler and, paradoxically, more mysterious. The huge pink hand with its thumb in the air, which appeared earlier in *Untitled (green)* (2015), could be seen as an expression of positive feelings—a 'like', to say it in Facebook speak—but the red fingernail could also pass for a drop of blood. Although we might have no difficulty in recognizing the image, in a sense it remains ambiguous. Sometimes it is a question of scale and it remains unclear whether what we see is enormous or microscopically small. For example, is that yellow circle a ball or a sun? Does the figure in *Flies on Milk (Blow up)* (2017) represent an enormous explosion or a flower? Betz paints his meticulously stylized signs without telling us what they mean, something which we as viewers initially fail to notice. We simply assume that those parallel swerves of green, yellow, pink, orange and light blue represent a rainbow, overlooking the fact that the order of colors doesn't correspond with that of the natural spectrum. And doesn't it strike us as unusual that this rainbow has appeared in the sky in the dead of night?

In his daydreams, the motifs that the artist regularly uses have merged with personal memories, associations and feelings. Fences, windows and doors often act as metaphors for an entrance to another world, a gateway to the realm of the imagination. The wooden garden fence that first appears in *Pinot Noir* (2008) is derived from Malevich's *Carpenter* (1908–1910/1929). In the latter, the fence separates the path in the foreground from the village in the background and at the same time, the boundary is permeable, allowing you a partial view of what is behind it. In *Flies on Milk (Fence)* (2017) the garden fence seems to be looking back at us, staring straight into our eyes like some impudent messenger from an imaginary world. This constant back-and-forth between two worlds, between here and there, interior and exterior, large and small, is the driving force behind much of Betz's work.

What the series as a whole expresses is difficult to determine. The more paintings the artist adds to the series, the more you get the impression that the collected images could simply be a mirror image of himself. Know thyself, was the advice of the Oracle of Delphi. However, this is easier said than done. Betz quotes from a poem by François Villon, a fourteenth-century French poet and leader of a band of robbers, a rogue who was accused of murder and probably died on the gallows. His 'Ballade' (here in an English translation) tells of the way he learned to understand everything

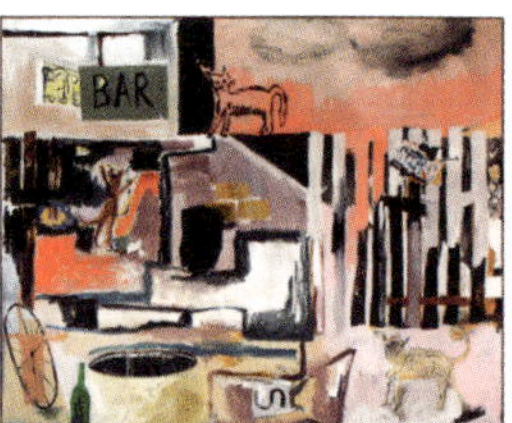

Pinot Noir, 2008
Oil on canvas, 200 × 240 cm
Private collection, Austria

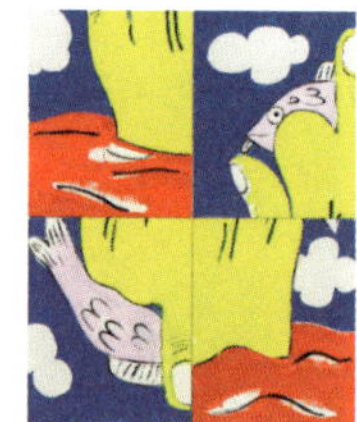

Untitled (Fish Fingers Day), 2015
Gouache and acrylic on canvas, 182 × 146 cm
Private collection

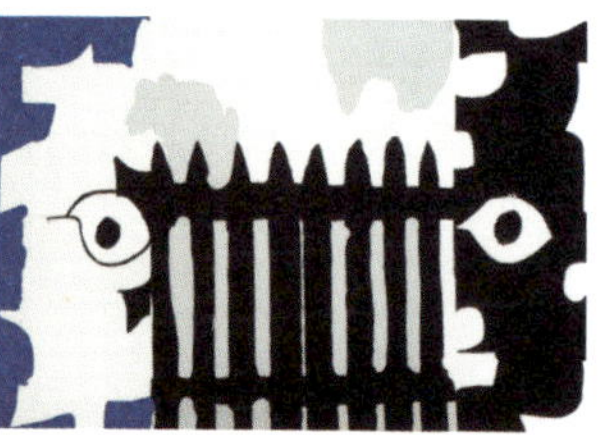

Flies on Milk (Fence), 2017
Block printing ink, block printing medium and acrylic on canvas, 200 × 300 cm
Willem Baars Projects, Amsterdam

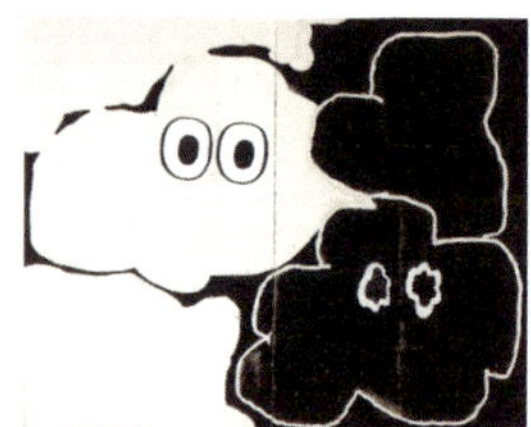

Popcorn and Sakura, 2015
Block printing ink on canvas, 225.5 × 280 cm
Collection Ph Deceuninck

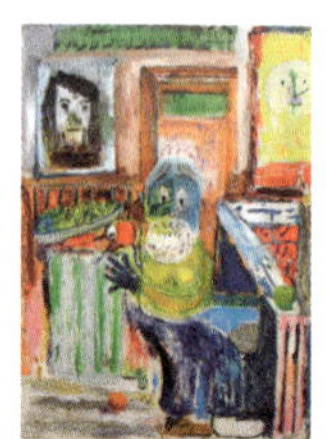

One House Ago, 2009
Oil on canvas, 125 × 90 cm
Collection Auke van der Werff

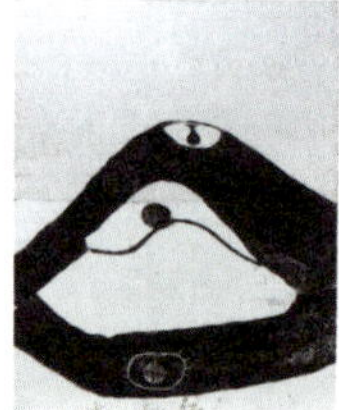

LL, 2013
Block printing ink on linen, 150 × 120 cm
Private collection

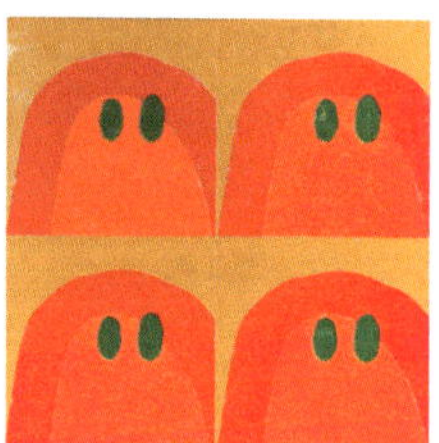

Hmptydmtymf, 2016
Block printing ink on canvas, 195 × 195 cm
Private collection

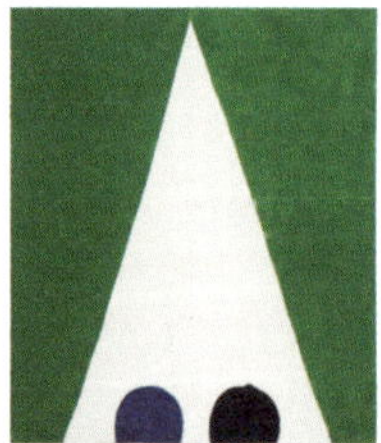

Flies on Milk (Road), 2017
Block printing ink, block printing medium and acrylic on canvas, 200 × 174 cm
Willem Baars Projects, Amsterdam

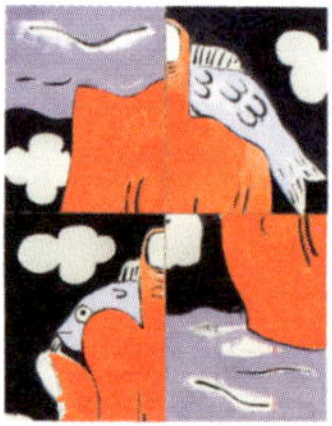

Untitled (Fish Fingers Night), 2015
Gouache and acrylic on canvas, 182 × 146 cm
De VandenBroek Foundation

in the world, save himself: *I know flies in milk / I know the man by his clothes / I know fair weather from foul / I know the apple by the tree / I know the tree when I see the sap / I know when all is one / I know who labours and who loafs / I know everything but myself*. Betz's paintings are similar to the lines of the poem: you can infer all kinds of things from them, but what do they tell you about the artist? Do these images of his dreams, feelings and desires actually reflect his views on the world of today? Could we reasonably expect a bunch of symbols and metaphors to encapsulate a life in the same way as a deck of tarot cards?

Although he was born and raised in the Netherlands, Morgan Betz is not a typical Dutch painter. The artist has lived in Amsterdam, New York and Tokyo and has a studio apartment in Berlin since 2008. Traces of his travels around the world can be found in his work. There are affinities with Dutch painters like Toon Verhoef (the repetition and transformation of greatly reduced motifs), but also certain links with American pop art. Like Roy Lichtenstein, Jasper Johns and other pop artists from the '50s and '60s, Betz borrows his motifs from the entertainment industry and consumer culture (for example, Oscar the Grouch from Sesame Street features in *One House Ago*, 2009). Japan's refined visual culture also had a considerable impact on Betz's work, from the woodcuts prints of Katsushika Hokusai to the anime produced by Studio Ghibli.

Warholian repetition is manifest in *Hmptydmtymf* (2016), a painting based on a child's drawing of a face that the artist found by chance. For reasons unknown, the single transposition of the image wasn't enough, so Betz decided to reproduce it four times. The multiplication of the image takes the focus off its uniqueness and creates something new: the beginning of a grid, a pattern. Although the stamping technique could easily lead to this conclusion, repetition here is not aimed at serialization and standardization. On the contrary, for Betz it apparently has to do with the minimal differences that occur when the image is repeated, like with Humpty Dumpty in the English nursery rhyme. The figure is painted in gold ochre, vermillion red and orange, with two grass green ovals as eyes. The soft, exquisite color palette and the repetition of the motif bring to mind the dreamlike, sensual paintings of John Wesley.

Besides this multiplication of the motif, there is also the segmentation of the motif. In *Untitled (Fishfingers) Day* and *Untitled (Fishfingers) Night*, both from 2015, the image is cut into four parts which then have been shifted in relation to each other. Looking at this quartered representation, you feel the urge to recombine the fragments, like the pieces of a puzzle, into a coherent whole, a complete image which, however, has been lost forever and only still exists as fiction. The disturbed relationship between part and whole, between individual and group was actually the subject of the original representation, in which the fish stand for the Japanese people and the raised middle finger is directed against the *gaijin*, the 'foreigners' or, rather, the 'non-Japanese'.

References to American pop art intermingle with references to Japanese culture in the succinct and monumental painting *Popcorn and Sakura* (2015). A piece of popcorn appears side by side with a clump of cherry blossom (*sakura* in Japanese)—its cloud-like form looks a bit like the quintessential American snack. *Sakura* symbolizes life, which is just as short and beautiful as the blooming period of the cherry tree. It also has a dark side: during World War II the Japanese Empire propagated the belief that the souls of dead kamikaze pilots would reincarnate as cherry blossoms. Both sides—life and death, joy and fear—are reflected in the sharp contrast between black and white, positive and negative. At first sight, Betz's paintings might look funny and innocent, yet the subtext sometimes can be grim or dejected. Humor, Octavio Paz wrote, renders ambiguous everything it touches. Betz's humor is a kind of slapstick that is meant to soften the pain of failure and the absurdity of our inadequacy.

Betz's subtle play with asymmetrical compositions and leaps in scale echo Hokusai's most famous print, *The Great Wave off Kanagawa* (1831). It shows huge waves threatening to engulf a number of small boats. The largest wave towers over everything like a fearsome monster with white crests as its claws. The smaller wave in the foreground reflects the silhouette of Mount Fuji which is visible in the distant background (the woodcut is part of the series *Thirty-six Views of Mount Fuji*, which actually comprises 46 prints). A wave that is also a mountain—for Betz this is perfectly plausible. In his painting *LL* (2015) we see a snowy mountain that could just as well be a woman's breast seen through the legs of a cowboy. The ambiguous motif has been further stylized in *Flies on Milk (Road)* (2017), which, unlike other works in the series, is executed in light pastels such as lilac, salmon pink and cream.

The dreamlike quality of Betz's seemingly childlike imagery, in which something can simply change into something else and reality sometimes seamlessly slips into fantasy, reflects something of Japanese anime: animated films that aren't aimed at children, but also address adult issues such as self-conscience and loss of identity. One example is *Paprika* (2006) by Satoshi Kon, about a psychiatrist who helps patients to access their own dreams. The film is a gripping, whirling, breathtaking mind trip of the kind that you only find in digital animations by the British artist Ed Atkins and the Chinese artist Lu Yang. In *Delusional Mandala* (2015) Yang recreates herself as a genderless avatar who explores her own consciousness through deep brain stimulation and finds a neurological cause for the belief in God. Betz feels at home on the slippery slopes of psychofiction. His paintings reflect the ambivalent relation between reality and the virtual, which has become increasingly muddled in the digital age.

The boundary between reality and fiction, between real and fake is explicitly addressed in the most recent works at the exhibition. In *White Window* (2017), Betz returns to the motif of the rainbow behind the window, but gives it a three-dimensional twist. The painting is a cast in white plastic material of a cardboard cut-out window frame that has been embedded in the wall and bears an uncanny resemblance with a real window. This architectural folly is intended for a permanent installation in a canal house in Amsterdam, in which the four walls of the piano room have been painted blue, green, yellow and orange (with complementary colors on opposite walls) and the color of each wall encroaches on the next. The view from the window into the derelict garden is represented by a crude mesh of sisal that is suspended upside down from the ceiling like a hanging garden, while the floor has been covered with the kind of long narrow slats that are found in old New York lofts. The anthropomorphous piano stool consists of a long arm that twists and turns, a motif that first appeared in an untitled surrealist painting from 2011. This installation could be seen as a three-dimensional painting; the artist compares it to a life-size child's diorama. In addition to the blind window, the installation features a pink false door that is also encased in the wall (*Pink Door*, 2017). All of Betz's well-known themes converge in this installation, which can be summarized as the great confusion between the world as we perceive it and the world as we imagine it.

All works of art are like a window open on creation, Émile Zola wrote. In *Flies on Milk (Neon)* (2017), a key work from the series, painting and window become one: the four window panes form a cross that coincides

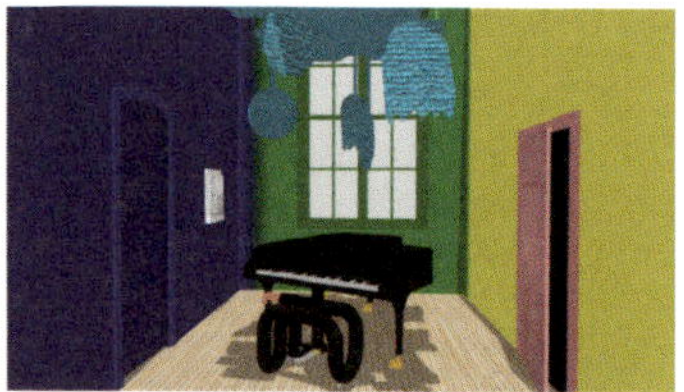

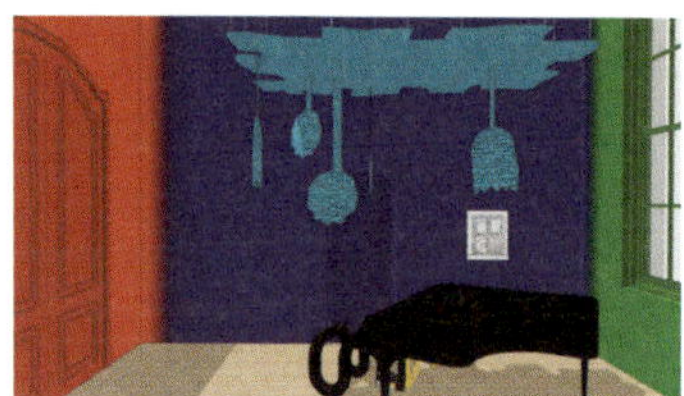

Green Room, 2018
Paint, plastic, polyester, fabric
Private collection

with the cross bars of the stretcher that is hidden behind the canvas. The window or painting opens on a dark blue nocturnal sky. Everything that goes on behind a dark windowpane, Charles Baudelaire wrote, is more interesting than what happens in the sunlight, it is more profound, more mysterious, a black expanse where 'life lives, life dreams, life suffers' (*Paris Spleen*, 1869). Behind the dark window, in the strange, intangible world of the imaginary, there is a shimmering rainbow. An age-old symbol of the bond between God and man. The shortest line between earthly reality and the incomprehensibility of existence. This symbol, this majestic symbol of hope, has taken on the appearance of a plastic sticker in garish colors that looks like it has been stuck on the back of the glass. The stuff of which Judy Garland's dreams are made of turns out to be ordinary adhesive vinyl. It would be funny if it wasn't so disconcerting.

Double-Edged Simultaneity
Eleven approaches to Morgan Betz
Mischa Andriessen

1

An Indian tribe believes that the universe consists of three worlds. They are laid on one another like the layers of a wedding cake. The two upper worlds rest on tall trees that line the outer edge of the lower world. They can all be reached via these trees. The Indians, who live in the middle world, can climb up or down. The lower world is where the animals, the illnesses, the enemies are. Only a madman would want to go there. The upper world is home to deceased relatives, and although it would be nice to see them again, you can't get married there: there are no wedding ceremonies in the upper world. Life there may be blissful, but it is also dull. That is why the Indians settle for the belief that those two other worlds exist and are accessible, but choose to stay where they are, in the middle.

2

Can something that is depicted on a painting be filled in and left empty at the same time? The question is raised by a painting by Morgan Betz which is essentially composed of two color fields. One is a fallow pinkish orange that tends towards the color of the bricks that were used to build many residential buildings in Berlin. The other is light blue. The light blue field is reminiscent of a piece in a jigsaw puzzle. Has it been removed, has it been flipped over and is what we see its white back side? It could be a trompe l'oeil, a painting of a puzzle with a puzzle piece that seems to have been removed, flipped over etc. The reference to a puzzle immediately creates a certain tension. The two color fields could be seen as residual forms of each other, but they remain complementary. The idea that they can't exist without each other corresponds with the idea of a puzzle. A puzzle can be solved—it may take a short or a long time, and sometimes there is more than one way to reach a solution—but a jigsaw puzzle has only one 'correct' outcome, since we always can see at once that a piece is missing. On this deceptively simple canvas Betz has painted an order in which something is missing. The thing that represents unity simultaneously represents its opposite: a fragmented whole.

There is also a little circle, somewhat right of center. It could be a sun, or a thumbprint, as can be seen on another canvas by Betz, with a similar circle next to it.

There is something else that is strange about this painting. The contrast between the two colors creates a sense of depth. The white field becomes an opening, a space that arises from a flat surface.

At one point during my visit to Betz in his Berlin studio he draws my attention to something outside. Standing in the courtyard and looking straight up, you recognize the shape of the puzzle piece: a segment of sky, framed by pinkish orange façades.

What looks like depth is apparently derived from an upwards view. This does not mean that Betz precludes the first way of seeing, better still, his paintings discreetly urge the viewer to *look through* the different points of view that the painting has to offer—in the same way you would *think through* a philosophical problem.

Depth can be height and vice versa, so whether you describe the inner surface or the circumference, the form or the residual form, it often turns out that the roles can be reversed or at least aren't clearly defined. In Betz's work there is always an image and a counter-image, and both are equally important. A filled-in shape, therefore, can also be a cut-out, although this obviously doesn't solve anything, because it is just a possibility, a way of seeing that presents itself and that is not necessarily dominant because the opposite is also true.

3

In March 1960, the Philadelphia Museum School of Art hosted a panel discussion between the artists Philip Guston, Ad Reinhardt, Robert Motherwell and Jack Tworkov. That day, the art critic Harold Rosenberg acts as moderator. The discussion has been going on for quite a while when Reinhardt begins to enumerate a long list of don'ts, of things that he feels artists should avoid doing. When Reinhardt is finally done, Rosenberg asks the others to comment. Guston is the first to speak. He declares that he has nothing to say except that 'Ad wants to be right'. Rosenberg then asks: 'Would you make that an additional "Thou shalt not"?' to which Guston replies: 'The artist should not want to be right.'

Being right or asserting your authority is an important issue in contemporary art. Regardless of the question whether the artists themselves want to be right: how many interpretations does a work by Jeff Koons allow the viewer? How much freedom does the work of Damien Hirst give the public to discover something in it that is different from what he has invested in it? These are just two examples of artists who discipline the viewer. Of course there are also instances of the opposite, of artists who are completely surprised by their own work. The unexpected in what you make is also important for Betz. This is reflected in a statement by Woody Allen, one of Betz's favorite quotes:

'What people who don't write don't understand is that they think you make up the line consciously—but you don't. It proceeds from your unconscious. So it's the same surprise to you when it emerges as it is to the audience when the comic says it. I don't think of the joke and then say it. I say it and then realize what I've said. And I laugh at it, because I'm hearing it for the first time myself.'

There is an unmistakable tension in Betz's work between spontaneity and control. His paintings, drawings and sculptures are clearly the product of a lot of thought, a sharp eye and a critical attitude: nothing is taken for granted, but his work also shows a great immediacy which is associated with surrealist art as well as reminding us of cartoons. Betz directs the viewer only to then give him complete freedom. Or vice versa: his best paintings reproduce what he has seen in such a manner that the moment of surprise has been preserved.

Artists like Hirst and Koons apparently can manage without viewers. The work is finished. Other art, the kind of art that is called 'fundamentally open', exists almost purely by virtue of a viewer who finishes the work by seeing something in it. The Italian art historian Dario Gamboni has studied so-called 'potential images', images that are ambiguous and open to multiple interpretations: a cloud can also be an angel, a landscape can also be a woman. The key word here is 'also'. It is both, at the same time. Artists who make such 'potential images' often come up with somewhat amorphous representations that aren't clearly outlined, whose contours are fuzzy and blurred, giving the viewer more room for interpretation. Betz's lines, however, are notably sharp and clear. Ambiguity may not necessarily be something he strives for, but he does accept it.

4

A green hand with a raised middle finger, its nail shining brightly. The hand stands out against a red background. On the bottom left of the canvas there is a small yellow field with next to it three deep blue elliptical forms. They could be folds in a puff sleeve, but this is where the image becomes unclear. This confusion is exacerbated by the strange angle of the fingers and the unnatural color of the hand.

I read the title of the work, 'Boat', and only then I see it: the raised middle finger is a steam pipe, the curvature in the blue surface is the wake of the boat, and the yellow crescent could just be the farthest reaches of the mainland.

The strange thing is that the context provided by reading the title brings only momentary clarity. Even though I now know that the painting is called 'Boat', the first thing I see is still the hand with its raised middle finger, and only then a boat. Furthermore, the colors that were used also evoke associations with a plant. The sleeves or waves form the pot, the hand or ship is the plant itself, and I notice that I even connect the red background with the plant—the representation sparks the imagination in such a way that I see things on the canvas that are inconsistent with what the image logically allows, and I find once again that my mind is distracted by what the painting is unintentionally saying.

5

'You came up with that retrospectively.' During our conversation Betz repeatedly expresses doubts—both sincere and fundamental doubts that spare nothing and no-one, especially Betz himself. Yes, he is looking for images that have the potential of an icon or a symbol, but at the same time turn out to be layered or even highly charged—images that might appear immediately intelligible, but are in fact ambiguous and anything but clear-cut.

I doubt whether this has anything to do with the way we look. Betz's work can be fully seen at a glance. There are no details that only reveal themselves after long scrutiny, on the contrary, everything is there from the outset. However, what you see represents more than one thing at the same time. If you take a longer look, you will not discover anything that you haven't already seen, but on closer examination the lines, shapes and colors take on a totally different appearance, causing a second image to appear next to the first one. It is as if the brain rather than the eyes reveals those deeper layers, because you immediately see everything there is to see.

There is something odd about the balance between the forms, the position of the lines, the colors and the shapes. They obviously aren't subjected to the constraints of symmetry and the golden section, otherwise the work would be dull and lack tension, but these images aren't noticeably off balance either. It apparently takes a while before you see it, but once your brain registers the shift in balance, undermining your first impression, you are no longer sure about what you saw. It is as if although no information has been added, still everything you saw earlier has been cast into doubt. However stable the forms on the canvas may look, what they signify and represent gradually becomes fluid.

This is partly Betz's intention, but also partly the result of chance. Which part of this chance occurrence can an artist claim as his own achievement? When a work is not one hundred percent preconceived, why would you retrospectively say that you are responsible for the whole thing and that something which essentially ended up there by accident is an added value that has been bestowed upon you? Yves Klein once said that his works were only the ashes of his art—in other words, what remains after the fire. Betz isn't convinced. There is no point in cheating and slipping into the romantic role of the artist as visionary, but the pragmatic approach doesn't tell the whole story either: the same lines, colors and shapes allow for totally different interpretations that don't cancel each other out.

6

The American writer Raymond Carver published a short but brilliant essay on writing. It is simply called like that: 'On Writing'. In it Carver gives a few pointers which he stuck on the wall of his writing room like post-its. One of those is 'No cheap tricks'. He later amended the advice he gave himself—and other writers—to 'No tricks'.

Betz is well aware of the fact that the public can see through each cover-up, each game that isn't played to its conclusion, regardless of the consequences, each hackneyed allusion. 'People can smell a rat,' he says, 'they immediately recognize it.'

The recognizable allusions in Betz's work to illustrious predecessors like Philip Guston and Henri Matisse are not just quotations from the work of others. They are not meant as an enrichment of his own work, but rather as a brave attempt to understand the essence of their oeuvres. Betz does not stand on the shoulders of giants to make himself look taller, on the contrary, it may allow him to reach higher but also to fall deeper. Betz accepts all the consequences of his artistic practice and is prepared to go to extremes, but not on a whim or because it might be charming or mediagenic. It doesn't work that way. Betz is only willing to fully accept those consequences when there is a beginning of understanding.

7

The day after my visit to Betz's studio I was wandering through Berlin. It turned out to be the day of German unification and all the places of interest were closed. So I walked for hours to kill time. I noticed how inventive the people were in finding solutions were to deal with the lack of space in this *Grossstadt*. Every last free plot seems to have been used. A remaining green strip next to a parking lot had been converted into a playground, a small wedge of land between a fence and a motorway was apparently just large enough to accommodate a sportsground. Four men were jogging and working up a sweat in this small arena. Some doors have dozens of doorbells, occasionally one of those doors would open, revealing a courtyard with entrances leading to multiple apartments. These attempts to make the most of available space are especially notable because that same space was once so lavishly squandered. The ridiculously wide Kurfürstendamm, which chancellor Otto von Bismarck had planned to extend all the way to Paris, is the most striking example of this.

I knew from earlier visits that the immensity of Berlin with its towering apartment buildings, its ostentatious architecture and closed façades, can be very confrontational. Its high-rise buildings and broad avenues leave you feeling literally overshadowed and overly exposed.

Betz's work always seems aware of its surroundings and of the fact that however humble the artist may be, making art is basically an arrogant act because it always wants to add something and isn't satisfied with what is already there. Betz certainly does not suffer from false modesty, but his work seems suffused with the idea that an artist must manifest himself and speak out.

Clearly Betz is aware of artistic tradition and also sees through the sometimes insane contradictions that are inherent to it—for example, that the tradition that has weened him is also one that is constantly breaking with traditions.

There is a certain unease in this. Betz says he likes to use elementary but highly charged forms, like a heart. The question is how to use such a clichéd image in a sincere and non-banal way. The question isn't new. Betz knows that, but being innovative isn't his first concern.

Over a century ago there was a group of poets in Russia who worked closely with avant-garde painters like Malevich and Pavel Filonov. A first version of the *Black Square* already featured as a piece of stage decoration in the 1913 opera *Victory over the Sun* by the poets Velimir Khlebnikov and Alexei Kruchenykh. Those same poets developed a self-made, transrational language they called 'Zaum', which means 'beyond reason'. Their motivation is very similar to Betz's. For example, Kruchenykh said that he could no longer use the word rose because it had been tainted by the bourgeoisie. Betz is familiar with the problem, but also knows what fate awaits this kind of radical reform. Whoever invents a new word for rose or a new image for a heart is almost begging to be misunderstood. It would be just as romantic and far-reaching to see whether you can innovate and preserve at the same time, in other words, whether you can find a form in which a heart is still a heart and retains its essence without becoming a cliché.

8

At first glance one of Betz's new paintings brings to mind an abstract flower still-life, but the combination of consistently trembling lines and vivid colors also evokes associations with comics and animated cartoons. Those zigzagging lines and harsh colors immediately remind us of drawings of cartoon characters who suddenly lose control and go crazy out of anger or grief or simply because they are going out of their mind. Since Ludwig Wittgenstein drew his famous rabbit-duck illusion, we know that the same lines can represent two completely different figures at the same time. This kind of duality can also be seen in Betz's work, but with an additional twist. A flower bed is a typical bourgeois symbol, while the other impression is in fact one of chaos, of a total loss of control: two incongruities that are not only combined in the same image, but represented by exactly the same lines, colors and shapes.

9

'The artist should not want to be right.' Philip Guston's remark keeps echoing in my mind when I think about Morgan Betz's work. For Guston it was a liberating experience to be able to paint recognizable banalities again: a man smoking, a man who stays in bed too long. The advocates of abstract art did not exactly welcome this, to put it mildly. Why? I think the unsightly everyday reality that Guston introduced into his work was in fact an implicit critique of the glorified aura of abstract painting, a justified critique because precisely the ordinary and the banal are missing from those odes to representations that have been elevated above the commonplace by the inspired hand of the artist.

Here again Betz is trying to achieve a synthesis. His sculptures, drawings and paintings tend to have a striking presence, they are here and cannot easily be overlooked. They ask important questions, give intelligent answers and at the same time refer to everyday things. This does not only have to do with what Betz depicts. It has to do with the humor of the work, an incisive, streetwise humor that provides the necessary contrast to the philosophical aspect of Betz's representations. Those two poles cannot exist without each other—if one gains the upper hand the work becomes too weighty, if the other prevails, it becomes too banal.

We did not only talk about art that day in Berlin. We also discussed stand-up comedy and R & B. And films. Betz recalled muppeteer Jim Henson's *The Dark Crystal*, a film about two endangered tribes: on the one hand the inherently violent Skeksis, on the other the peaceful Mystics. They are threatened with extinction because they exist independently, and it is only at the end, when they literally merge with each other, that they succeed in securing their survival.

10

One of the questions raised by Betz's work has to do with the sharp line that is often drawn between abstraction and figuration, even though artists like Barnett Newman and Warhol both essentially work in the same way. There is a directly perceivable composition whose colors immediately try to grab your attention. Whether you look at it briefly or for a long time, there is nothing else to see, you can't evolve beyond that first glance, only, at best, supplement it with a context, which is an activity of the brain, whereas the physical sensation caused by both abstraction and figuration that is reduced to its essence, is broadly the same.

Abstract images obviously often are also derived from an aspect of reality: a triangle of light on a kitchen floor, a line in a landscape, a shadow, a damp stain. I am quite sure that an abstract painter like Clifford Still took his forms straight from nature.

Betz makes no secret of his sources, he does not erase their traces. The viewer is free to associate them with a neat flower bed or with some character who is losing his mind. With a puzzle piece or a framed patch of sky. With a sun, a balloon, a bomb. With a middle finger or a boat. Take a step back and you see the figuration, take a step forward and the work becomes abstract. It's all a question of the right proportions, of the right distance. Betz's eye for the exact point where the balance can just about be maintained reveals that he is a sculptor—a sculptor who paints, and vice versa. He has learned how to suggest movement with a static form. It's a finely tuned process. A new canvas, depicting a sun or a balloon or a bomb doesn't display that balance yet. 'It is still too boring,' Betz says, opening a can of fluorescent paint. 'I'm going to try this color, but if it doesn't work I'll have to start the canvas all over again.'

11

Researchers in a laboratory have laid two electrically charged atoms on a table. They have the task of finding out when radiation is created. The lead researcher carefully taps the particles towards each other with a screwdriver. Nothing happens, tap, nothing, tap, still nothing, tap, there it is: the electricity.

I—Avoidance

Johan Gustavsson: So I thought the first question should be about your earliest ideas of becoming an artist.

Morgan Betz: I guess it's a long story. It goes way back to my childhood. My father was an illustrator. He studied graphic design and illustration at the School of Visual Arts in New York back in 1956–57 and he became an illustrator and moved to Germany when he was thirty-something years old to design stained glass windows for churches. Eventually, he wound up in Holland, and well, had me. When I was growing up he considered himself an artist. I never agreed on this, because I was probably a terrible son, but I always thought he was too much, how do you say, kind of an illustration of what he did. Even his abstraction was an illustration of abstraction. It wasn't very consciously the way I was thinking...

And how old were you when you understood what the difference was between an artistic practice and an illustrative practice...?

Well, I guess intellectually I didn't understand it, and still do not know exactly, in a sense, but intuitively I did understand it from when I was old enough to talk back. My dad and I would go around together. When we went to New York, for instance, always on the agenda would be to visit a museum. When I was much younger we went to New York and there was a famous painter called Andrew Wyeth. My dad called him up to come and visit his studio. That's one of the first memories I have of art. We were going to visit Wyeth, but then he had a back problem or something and the trip was cancelled. Later we visited another artist, a Dutchman who had made it big as an illustrator, called Braldt Bralds. We visited his studio upstate New York... So those kinds of memories of really technical painters are some of my earliest childhood memories of art. There was also a guy in New York, where my dad's family is from, called Don Eckelberry, who was sort of following in the footsteps of the famous bird painter Audubon. In the 1960's he was a famous bird painter. When I went to New York with my father on holiday we would always wind up at his house, and they would discuss politics and art, and I was a witness to this. He was very intellectual. I was maybe 8 or 9, and I would be involved in these conversations. They didn't really treat me as a kid. Those were my first intellectual or whatever you might want to call it feelings with art from my father's side. When I was even younger, 4 or 5 I think, my mother worked at this wonderful gift shop at the Stedelijk Museum in Amsterdam, and when she was working her shift, sometimes she would bring me along with her, and I could run around the museum. So I remember a lot of art stuff, like an exhibition of the Bauhaus artist Oskar Schlemmer, crazy costumes that were later kind of recycled in videos in the 1980s, and then sculptures like *The Beanery* by Edward Kienholz, and George Segal ...

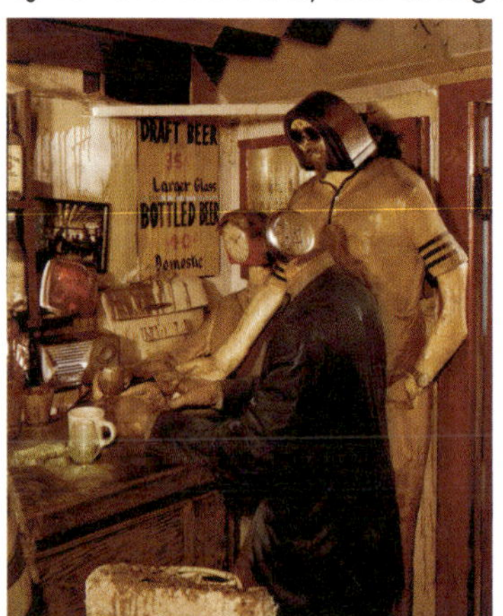

Edward Kienholz, *The Beanery*, 1965 Collection Stedelijk Museum Amsterdam

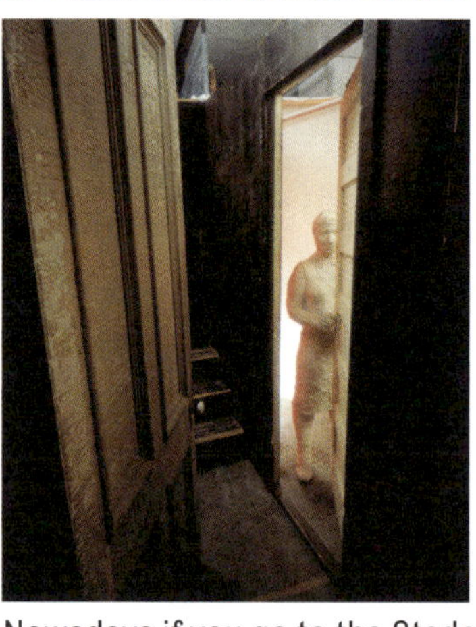

George Segal, *Woman in a Doorway (II)*, 1965 Collection Stedelijk Museum Amsterdam

So those are works that you would...

Nowadays if you go to the Stedelijk there's a guard in front of *The Beanery* and you have twenty seconds or half a minute to go in. I don't know if this is correct, perhaps it's the fog of memory, but I remember that when I was a kid you could just go into this dark space on your own. I really thought this world was interesting, you could just go into this other world. That's my earliest memory, even before the kind of technical painters that my father was interested in. I never thought I would be an artist, but I was making drawings... My father had a steady job making architectural drawings for the national aerospace laboratory in the Netherlands. They would give him a blueprint of a building and he would make a 3D painting. I would go to his studio almost every week and hang out while he was doing his work. He was a very bad employee because—and I guess that later I got a job myself and I copied him—he would hide in the closet or under the table or something like that and when I got a job myself, I was 21 and would do the same. So I guess you get fucked up by your parents.

But it brought you to make art yourself.

Well, I mean I don't blame anyone, it's not like Ivanka Trump is going to be a painter, right? People always think they choose their own path in life, but you're very much informed by your parents, politically, religiously. My father had a steady income and was a sort of artist. But I didn't want to become an artist. We would go to museums and he would be standing with his nose against an Edward Hopper painting, and I would be bored. But now I would really like that.

So when was the moment when you said, okay, I go to art school, the Rietveld Academie, in your case.

Well, I wanted to be a writer. I didn't finish high school, I dropped out and then was basically like Oblomov. Oblomov is this character from a Russian novel who is always detached from the world and sleeping, just hiding in his bedroom, like a clam. I did that for a couple of years, and then, because I wanted to be a writer, I entered a competition where you could win a job as a copywriter at an advertising agency. I was one of the five who won a job. There were five big advertising agencies in Holland. I was placed at a big advertising agency called McCann Erickson. It's actually one of the biggest, oldest advertising agencies in the world. I had no idea what I was doing, because suddenly I went from being unemployed, smoking all day long and writing bad poetry to having a job as a copywriter pretending to know what I was doing. It was kind of crazy, because I was very shy and didn't want to talk to anyone. Of course, in an office situation you have to talk to people. They gave me an office and then said: 'Here's a car, and maybe you'll write some copy, make up some stuff.' I had no idea how to formulate something. I remember one of the first thing that I did was just insane: there was this station wagon and you just had to say how spacious it was. The space of the station wagon was compared to other cars and you could do stuff in the car that you wouldn't normally be able to do, so I said it's big enough to have an affair in or something like that. At the end of the day you would have these different teams and you would have to pitch your idea in front of the creative director. I remember pitching that idea and people were just looking at me thinking, 'What is that? The car is big enough to have an affair in with one of your colleagues in the parking lot?'

And what year was this?

This was in 1995 or 1996. Luckily for me they found an art director who was willing to work with me. He had gone to advertising school so whatever outlandish ideas I came up with, he pulled them back in and made them sort of fit into the normal language of advertising, which is pretty standard fare in the end. So I did that for a year and then realized I didn't want an office job. At the agency, my ideas were mainly visual, but I was supposed to be their copywriter, and although the other guy was a graphic designer, he turned out to be much more verbal in a lot of ways. He would actually be able to write stuff, and I would come up with visuals. So it was a mixture: I did both, he did both, and then I realized, maybe I should not be doing just text stuff, and then I applied to art school. I lived with my father at the time and I made a darkroom in the attic. I had a big old Nikkormat camera and during the weekends I would bike around Amsterdam and go to cemeteries, taking architectural photos which I would then print in the darkroom. I did that while I was working at the advertising agency, so I thought maybe it would be better if I went in that direction. I wanted to be a photographer. I then applied to art school and quit the job.

So you entered the Rietveld with the idea of becoming a photographer, not to paint?

Oh, no way! Not to become a painter. I thought I was going to make drawings or basically some kind of sculptures or something like that. Semi-installation things.

Those were wild years at the Rietveld?

Well, they were very naïve years. I think at least for me. Everyone was rather innocent in their expectations of what it meant to be an artist. Also, there was a business course that you could take in school to prepare you for life after the academy, learning to do bookkeeping and being self-employed. Hardly anyone took that class. And then there were two autonomous directions. One was called simply *free media* and the other was called *audiovisual*. I enrolled in both and wound up going to *free media*. Basically you had a studio and that's it. You just did what you wanted to do and nobody was giving you any kind of input. I didn't feel at the time that there was any kind of ideology in that school. Looking back on it there was probably some kind of ideology, Deleuze and the like, but at the time I didn't have any grand ideas about being an artist.

You were just doing it…

Just doing it. Stupidly doing it.

And when was the moment that you thought, aha, I'm grasping something here?

I think after I had finished. After art school I went to a residency program…

The Ateliers.

Yes, I think I'm somehow a slow person. I have some things that I'm very quick at, but generally I'm very slow at letting things sink in. The Ateliers was kind of a natural continuation of the Rietveld for me, with no interruption. I didn't go out into the real world, I didn't test my work, I went straight from the Rietveld to the Ateliers. I guess I didn't realize what an opportunity it was. Only after I'd finished I realized that if you are programmatic about your approach you can carve out a space or territory as an artist, and even during my time at the Ateliers I didn't consider that. So there were a lot of opportunities, but I think a lot of it was wasted on me. I just didn't want to enter daily life because I had found out that that this office job was not for me. Going to art school and being an artist is kind of luxuriously avoiding normal life.

II—Dependence

Were there people at the Ateliers that influenced your thinking?

When I was at the Rietveld there was certain work that was en vogue. I guess that goes for every generation. In my time it was very much Kippenberger, and through Kippenberger people who associated with him, like Albert Oehlen and Georg Herold. When I saw that Herold was teaching at the Ateliers I thought it would be great to study with him. That's one of the reasons I applied. Kippenberger was very interesting for me. Well, for one thing, I didn't really connect to Dutch art. I couldn't understand this stuff that was happening. There were some people I liked, like Atelier van Lieshout, David Bade. And there was a teacher at the Ateliers whom I liked as well. His name is Toon Verhoef. I liked his paintings at the end of my time at the Rietveld, but other than that I never really felt informed by Dutch art. There was this video scene going on at the time. I dabbled in that a little bit.

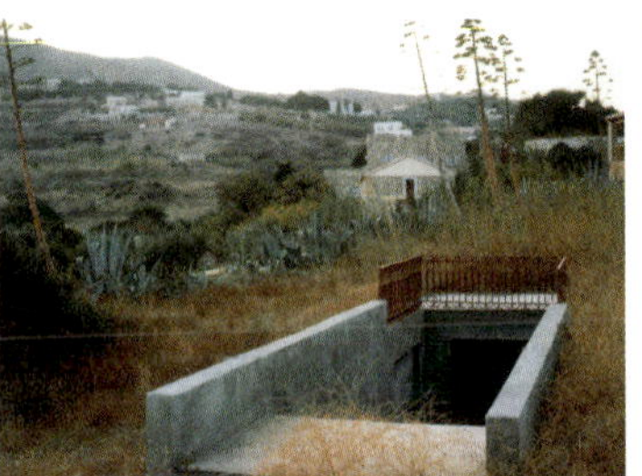

Martin Kippenberger, *Metro Net Subway Entrance*, Kthma Canné, Hrousa, Syros, Greece, 1993
Estate of Martin Kippenberger

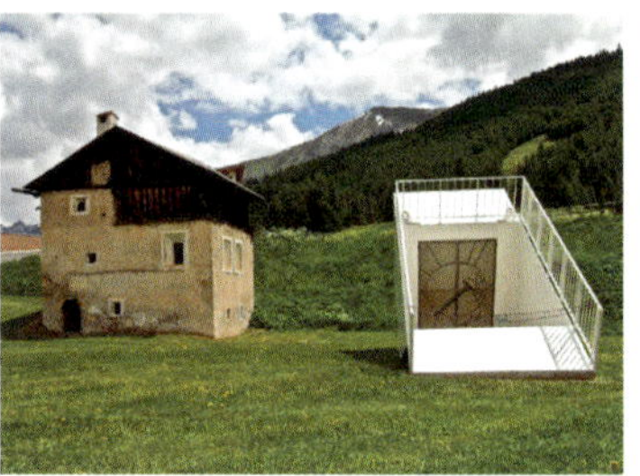

Martin Kippenberger, *Metro Net Subway Entrance*, 1997–2014, Zuoz, Switzerland
Estate of Martin Kippenberger

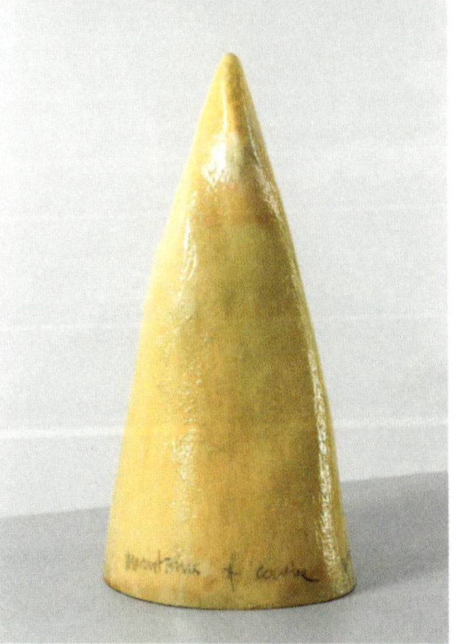

Georg Herold, *Mountains of Cocaine*, 1990
Courtesy Petzel Gallery, New York

So Kippenberger was more exciting...

Kippenberger was much more exciting because he was very distrustful of art, and that appealed to me, and it was very broad as well. He made some fake metro stations across the world. I didn't overtly think of myself as a person who made paintings or drawings, while in fact...

So does it have maybe more to do with the lifestyle rather than the ambition of becoming an artist?

So far I haven't figured out the ideal amalgam. Maybe that is the central issue in me making my work. I stumble over it while making, it is not an issue I project onto it. That is quite contrary to Kippenberger, who in the end was not separable from the work and his lifestyle in an extravert way. In my case there is a reversal: I feel more separable, like a stork delivering a baby. I thinks that's it. Historically, that relates to the advertising job as well, because although that was a job, nobody told you where you were supposed to get your ideas from. There's a history there. We read advertising history and we read about campaigns from the past that were successful. Much like artists look at artists from the past, in advertising they look at creative thinking from the past. You try to model yourself on that but end up with your own version. I guess that carried over into the feeling of being independent as an artist as well. You look at history, but you formulate your own position in relation to what came before you. In the advertising world you do have a job, someone pays your bills, but on the other hand they're still kind of free and *don't* have a master. I guess that somehow appealed to me—like you say, a lifestyle in which you can make your own time independent of history.

In referring to history and the past, in the text for Willem Baars Projects it says: 'What Morgan Betz's art makes clear is that a great deal of present-day art is irrelevant because it does not demonstrate its legitimacy'...

First of all, I didn't write that text...

I know, but it is quite a strong statement: 'Every work of art must be able to answer the question whether it is truly of any added value.'

Well, who am I to say about myself, that's what I'm doing. But I do think that I try to formulate a position that at least sort of tackles that situation. Maybe that's why I got away from making these oil paintings. I felt that within that idiom I was not adding anything to the canon of oil painting, either because I was incapable of doing so or because I felt restricted or choked by the pressure. Although I think some of the paintings I did make were quite sensual—some of them are very bad, but some of them are pretty good painterlywise—, I somehow felt that maybe this river had run its course and was running dry in this direction. I can be the tenth third generation Philip Guston wannabee kind of painter. So I was wrestling with this feeling, and I don't know if I'm answering these questions at the moment in my work. I think at least what I'm doing... maybe it's dated pop art, but at least I feel like I'm building my own vocabulary at the moment.

How do you relate yourself to painters like Philip Guston, because I think in some way there is a lot of these types of traditions that are very present in the works. Some sort of glorification of that period or those aesthetics...

I wouldn't say 'glorification', because I can't imagine people anticipating their own avant-garde position. You simply do what you are made of. How could you find your own voice when you're only trying to be modern. Guston painting figuratively, there's no difference: maybe to people it looked different, but he was just making a painting to the best of his ability. And I like that attitude. I think that if I had to do something else, I would bring the same kind of attitude to it as in making these paintings. Maybe if I became an organic farmer or a ceramist, I would still be whatever it is that drives me to make this, but it would be something else. I don't care, as long as I can stake my own claim, much like people who followed the gold rush and said: 'This is my plot of land, I stake my claim.' In a sense, with these paintings, I stake my own clams.

Has this to do with sincerity, truthfulness...

Anything I do is indebted to what I know of art or of movies or whatever. But I'm trying to create my own sphere, and I try to inhabit it as truly as I can. I don't know what it means to be true or authentic, because being authentic can also mean wearing different masks at the same time—you take one mask off and another mask appears, etc.—and they're all representations of your 'true self'. Maybe behind the masks there is no true self. In a way, these paintings are like masks, but I never want to put out something that I can't really support. Maybe it's very arrogant to say that, but I'm trying to be as objective as possible to myself, and trying to be very harsh about myself as well—maybe I've bungled it. But it's not me, in a way, it's only coming through me, so I try to take that position.

So is there a difference, compared with 10, 15 years ago, with a billion images that are uploaded yearly and the number of artists, both professionals and hobby artists, an incredible amount of image-makers, does that in any way influence the way you work?

This may sound a little bit esoteric, but I don't think I'm an image-maker. I am probably going to say something stupid, but I very much believe—and I'm not this per se spiritual person—there is this naturalness to art. You can tell, because we are very finely attuned to very small variations—even crude people, even people of whom other people say they don't understand art—, everybody is very attuned to the world. You pick up small signals and variations, and I think art is somehow very connected to that kind of stuff. That's where art is beyond words, it's not verbal, because in a way life is not verbal or intellectual. When you see an artwork, you know when someone is pulling the wool over your eyes, when you're basically putting on airs like this is not me, but I'm going to trick you into thinking that I'm this kind of artist or that I'm smart or that I'm technically gifted. This is horrible, but we're part of some energy or equilibrium, and I think art functions like that as well, it's part of this being part of things. In a sense, that is a natural thing, so I think art is a very artificial natural thing. Like *bonsai*. Sometimes to experience something for real, you have to actually stage it. It's this human need to connect with whatever it means to be alive.

How do you come about new images, is there something like a trope for making new work?

You know what? I had this idea of making a series of collages—maybe not all at the same time, but incidentally, and on each of them I write 'early space-age art'. This Don Eckelberry I was talking about, was collecting outsider art. He had a self-published art book called *Early Space-Age Art*, which to me sounded very futuristic. I thought it was a promise of what was to come, but actually it referred back to the 1960s and the moon landing. The book was beautiful, a purple hardcover book, and 'early space-age art' in gold letters in a very basic font. I have it here somewhere. It's one of the most beautiful books. Basically, he made his own art style called neo-cubic graphic art. He drew maps of the US, a kind of map-like paintings, and he painted moon-landers and stuff like that. If he were still alive, I bet he would have voted for Donald Trump. It's very patriotic, but there was something so intriguing about this title to me when I was something like ten years old. We were in New York and he made me call this guy who was in California. So I called the guy and told him I was visiting from Europe and he said; 'Who are you?' I said, 'I work for the library in Amsterdam and could we have a copy of your book?' He said, 'Okay, you can buy it,' and so I bought this book. It's a quaint curiosity, but this idea of a trope led me to make a full conceptual idea of something, which in itself could be a concept, in a sincere way. I like this idea of pleasuring myself with these sort of collages, you know, it's sensual, but I felt maybe this is a bit too gratuitous, a bit too pleasuring. So I thought maybe I can trick myself into making them and labelling them as early

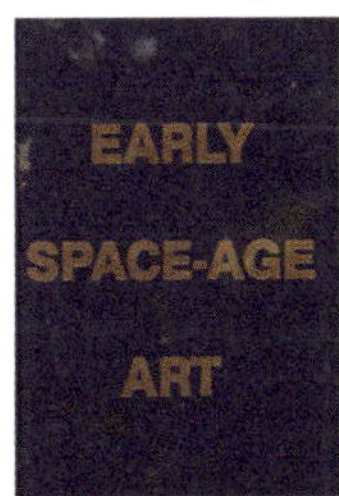

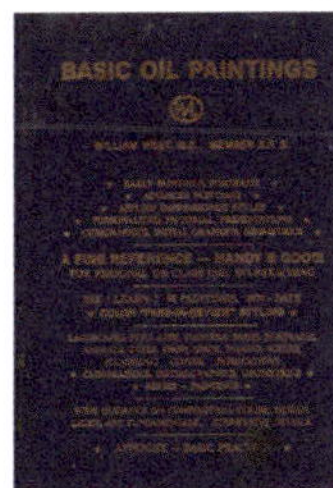

William T. West, *Early Space-Age Art*, Stockton Trade Press, California, 1984

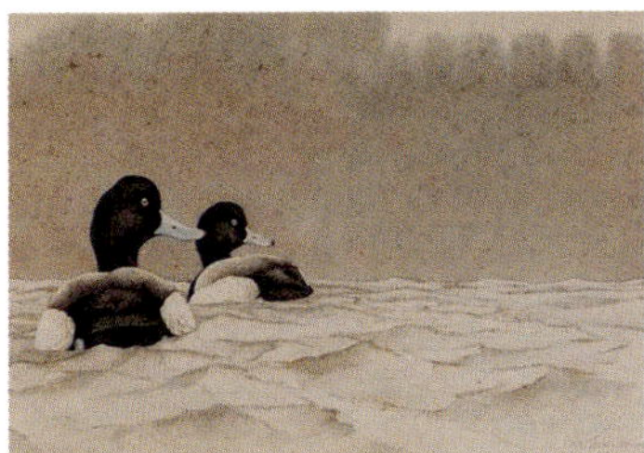

Don Eckelberry, *A pair of Greater Scaup Ducks*, watercolor, private collection. Courtesy Brunk Auctions, Asheville, North Carolina

space-age art, because the idea of space-age art for me was the art that I used to see in science-fiction movies that was always retro at the same time. In *Star Trek 2300* they have Brancusi-like sculptures, modernist stuff. This is a big problem for science-fiction. It's already hard enough to imagine the future of technology, let alone the future of art. I mean, what are they going to have on board of the starship Enterprise? So there is this whole idea of early space-age art, of sort of confusingly playing with this idea. I also find this idea of making art and writing 'art' on it quite funny.

In a nice way, that demonstrates the basic need that exists to produce work, and in the end that will always stay relevant.

There's Buckminster Fuller, from the 1960s, who was a visionary architect. He made these domes called Bucky Balls and wrote a book called *Operating Manual For Spaceship Earth*. He basically says that we're on earth and that earth is a spaceship full of astronauts. There's a lot of very progressive thinking in there. He lays out some sort of broad plan for how we as humans have only finite resources, but our minds are not finite, and we have to find a way to eventually leave earth, but while we're here we have to deal with this situation. It's very utopian, but it's not dreamer-like, you know, it's practical, an operating manual. Science-fiction and science-fiction movies are my favorite topic. It's a sort of promise, there's nothing there but we already know it all, and at some moment we are going to fulfill it, because that's how we are as humans—jet packs, internet in your brain, artificial intelligence—it's all going to happen because we fantasized about it.

Nowadays, when you have a camera with you all the time, and you have this possibility that you didn't have in the past to place something on Instagram, you literally have the same possibilities to create images that tell stories.

But you know what happens with Instagram, right? People are like, 'Oh, that's a cute dog. That would look nice on Instagram.' So they take the photo already thinking that they are going to put it on Instagram, and they put it on Instagram thinking of how many likes they will get for the photo. They're not going to take a photo that nobody likes. So basically, they are just looking for affirmation of their own insecurity or whatever... It's so completely fabricated. It looks spontaneous, but we're becoming more and more unspontaneous: thousands and millions of spontaneous unspontaneous messages. I'm not one to condemn it, I mean everybody does it. I had an Instagram account, and I logged out because I was going to quit it, and now I can't get back into it, it's gone and that's fine. Everybody is the author of his own life, and okay, Andy Warhol: everybody's going to be famous for 15 minutes, everybody's going to be their own brand.

So beauty in itself does not suffice, in the classical sense of the word?

I think artists are very much looking for beauty. That's what artists do. But it's not beauty like Pre-Raphaelite painting, Millais or whatever, but it is beauty because you're looking for a sensual experience. And I believe art is sensual, that's what artists do. With their art they want to connect with the physical world. It's a representation of their connection with the physical world, and the physical world is transcendentally beautiful, nature is transcendentally beautiful. Everything has been thought of by a person, everything else has been conceptualized. Everything else you see is the product of someone else's mind, and so is art.

But at the same time, art is trying to connect with a bigger, mysterious feeling. Even Kippenberger was looking for satisfaction. Even this American punk-performer GG Allin (1956–1993) whose dead body was displayed after he died. He did these performances where he was rolling in his own piss and poo. Even he was probably looking for beauty. I don't believe artists who say they're not looking for beauty or pleasure or some sort of visual, sensual satisfaction, even when conceptually it goes against what's popular or power structures. We relate to the world through our senses and sensuality and experience and art. That is what art does. I think it is very much a sensual relationship: color, shape, volume. Ideas can also have color, shape and volume. Good conceptual art does that, like Lawrence Weiner's work, which is very sensual. It's not graphic at all. It's more like a sensual, ambiguous experience, through the mediation of visuals, texts or whatever. I don't want to make anything that people would be revolted by. Maybe we can make small moves to something else, incrementally: two steps forward, one step back.' I think it's very limiting if you want to piss off or please people consciously.

Art forces the viewer to notice it as a unique object.

To be a good artist, you're probably not an idiot, you're not completely stupid, but you're not a scientist or a philosopher. An artist, in a way, is a jack of all trades, a hustler, to put it negatively. He's not as disciplined as a scientist, he's not as deep a thinker as a philosopher, but he does combine some of both these aspects. There's an interest in philosophy, and there's experimentation that goes into axiomatic science discovery, but I think an artist is maybe somewhere in between, between a scientist and a philosopher, something of a lazy version—definitely someone with time on his hands. I don't think you can rush art, it takes its own time. That's why I think it's good to have a studio practice and not just be a laptop artist The studio also functions as a sort of external brain, stuff flies around, and it hits something else. One day you walk in and you think: these two things that were separate actually belong together, and I could not have thought of that, it had to happen much like penicillin was discovered, by accident. But it needs a lab.

No, I agree with that. It's sitting down and thinking, creating possibilities for mistakes, for things to happen.

Apparently over time you get better at that. In a way you become an editor of mistakes. You have this kind of compost and you know that is going to be rotten, just rotten, but the other stuff is going to ferment and be fertile. So you're like a kind of gardener. Maybe that's why I make some of these images, because they relate to some cycle of life kind of feeling, some kind of meta-microcosm, like in the movies of Matthew Barney—I haven't actually watched all of them, but I like the idea that there is this meta-structure that relates to this inner space. You have the whole country that functions as something within the body, or something out there has a sort of parallel or analog to something which is a physical process. There's this scene where there is a football stadium and there's a zeppelin, and it's basically the sperm entering the uterus or the vagina... I think he's a very good artist. It connects all these layers, politically and personally. It's clever—clever and stupid, because it's not just an intellectual experience, but also an immersive sensual experience. It's thought out, but it's an accident as well, I'm sure, a coincidence.

What does a day in the studio look like for you?

I think an artist needs a project. I don't agree with this idea of just wanton creativity, that you're this creative person and you just poop it out. I think you need a structure. You need the confines of a brief to be creative.

When you don't have a project or a show going, you don't feel the natural need to spend time in your studio?

I might be musing about stuff, but I'm not necessarily the most disciplined person. It's very difficult for me to say, okay, I have nothing to do, I'm just going to go to the studio from nine to five and hash it out. Looking at a white canvas. If that were the case, I would trick myself into a structure, but I need to have something on the horizon. I think you need a limitation to be creative. You can't just say, I'm all over the place just being creative, alleluia. You need some confines. If they aren't external, you can create them yourself. Apparently I'm not the best at doing that, but you definitely need it. There is no formula for inspiration other than hard work.

In the case of having this show coming up now at the Gemeentemuseum, how do you go about something like that? What are your initial thoughts?

It's been growing a little bit, over the past years. I've been making these printed paintings. I somehow see this show as a conclusion to that. When I started to think about the show I was all over the place because I had not tackled the idea of the space yet and I came up with all these different scenarios of how to fill that space. Then it struck me that I didn't have to look for all these ideas. It's already there, in a way. I didn't have to come up with spectacular inventions and wild installations—I was already on a sort of path, making the stuff, so why didn't I just follow it to its ultimate conclusion. I thought, why don't I take all these guilty pleasures that I have and just unify them in a show and try not to feel guilty about it. I'm formulating myself, but at the same time it's a fictional thing, because it's a mask. But if you have enough masks, maybe what you're left with in the end is yourself. So I thought if I could make a series of paintings that deal with all these things that I'm interested in...

What are those things?

Well, visually they are kind of iconic things. Maybe reductive things as well. I used to make paintings that were really full of stuff, and it worked, but it's endless. I like this idea of some more hermetic thing, a few visual symbols, but when you add them up they represent a full-scale life. So I guess in a way, these paintings together are a cycle of life. Funnily enough they relate very much to icons, to emojis. Emoticons are similar. We are going forward, but the way we do that is very primitive. They're the most advanced visual language, and at the same time they're completely archaic: for mail you use an envelope, to express joy you use a smiley face. But emoticons are visceral, and what I do is hopefully more sensual. These paintings function in the same way: a kind of iconic, recognizable, reductive things, masks that you see in the rear view mirror, and that have a visual impact.

The thumbsup that comes back several times...

In ancient Rome the thumbsup meant that the gladiator lived... I also use this kind of rainbow. The rainbow is the most minimal representation of painterliness, with an open prescribed meaning, because it is also a spiritual event, and at the same time it is the opposite of blending, the normal procedure of painting. It's also just color, basically, but everybody associates it with a meaning, let's say hope or nature. For me, it represents the idea of painting. The most reductive representation of a painting, for me, is a rainbow. But it doesn't only come from that, it also comes from this object. You were talking about how things feel—nowadays, stuff feels like shit, it's cheap. I have an heirloom from my grandfather. This object is the sun and a rainbow, to me. My grandfather was a contractor in New York, I never met him, but he used to build houses. My father gave this to me, it is one of the few heirlooms that I have. This is how they used to make stuff. It's like the Chrysler Building, isn't it? For me this is a sort of measure for making something. You could say it is nostalgic, but it is also about efficiency, mind you. It is about ornament but at the same time the form it has, represents meaning. I think good art has no fluff. That's what I appreciate about an object like this. Maybe that's why I was starting using rainbows as well. It's a kind of personal thing.

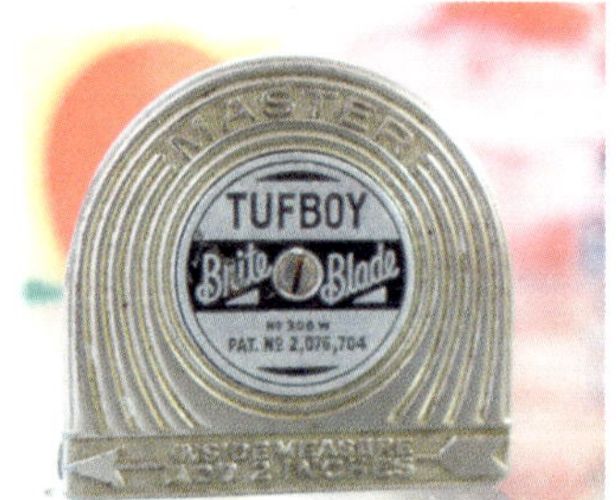

Brite Blade Tufboy Master, measuring tape, metal, no date
Collection of the artist

Back to the kind of symbolism in your work. One of these things is cigarettes, we are looking at an ashtray here. You already mentioned life and death. Cigarettes of course are a really beautiful, clear symbol of pleasure and also of death.

Yeah, this is quite personal. My father died from lung cancer, and I went through the whole process. Even before he got sick, he had this book called *Island* by Aldous Huxley. It's a kind of utopian science fiction story, and I thought about this quote, 'no man is an island'. I always thought that every man is an island in a way, but in a way you're not. When my father got sick, he sort of became this island, and I started relating that to the creative process in the studio and sort of looked back. And then when he was hooked up to machines in the hospital it really started feeling like this kind of hermetic...

within the world there was this even smaller world. Life and death is there, but then suddenly it shrunk, and that is why I was fascinated by cigarettes that symbolized the transience process—Kreislauf, as the Germans say. It was very closely related to my father dying.

In some of the works there are cigarettes going through an apple or going through a tree...

I find this idea of piercing fascinating. I don't know exactly what it is, but... contamination, or trauma. It's like trauma. When my dad was in the hospital, they plugged a tube into the back of his body, into his lung, to suck out the fluid. This collision of the physical world and the mental world. It's injury, a festering wound. That's trauma, I guess. Somehow that's why I do that. I have several examples of it. This is a ketchup bottle, but it gets pierced. I'm working on a sculpture: it will be one tube piercing another tube. I hope it will be realized. I have versions of this always going on, like the cigarette piercing the peach. The peach is very much sensual life, woman—this is horribly sexist, I guess. But I like this kind of contamination or trauma...

It's stuff you are trying to understand. If you don't understand fully what it means to lose a parent in a process like this...

Yeah, but they are not necessarily confessional. I don't want them to appear like that. I hope that they are connected with some larger picture...

Of course they do. We can only understand the world through our own experience and we try to figure out things that touch us. But I'm curious, is there any relation with when something like 9/11 happens or bigger social things?

Graphically, that's a very poignant thing to say. There's a plane that pierced a building, and New York is an apple... You could more easily say that it's a finger going through an apple. Nothing more. You could say that it is a social-political situation, but it is more like a physical representation of a very private process. Trauma is always on a personal scale. Do I react to 9/11 directly like that? No, I don't think so. I don't think I have that kind of agenda, because I feel that would not be sincere. How could I pretend to be that person? Of course, I'm affected by it. I think I can only relate to things on a very private basis.

Artists do struggle to be relevant with regard to what is happening in society.

As much as the next person, I'm tossed by the winds and the seas. But in the end, isn't it relevant enough to make good art? It is a digestive process, right? And what is good art? Like I said, there's something economical about it—the maximum use of minimal means. You don't want to use stuff that's not necessary anywhere els in life either, so why should art be any different? Nobody likes a restaurant with two thousand things on the menu. It's just not necessary.

Was this more traditional or romantic idea of an artist a part of your decision to move to Berlin? In what year did you move here?

In December 2008. I chose Berlin for practical reasons, but it could have been somewhere else. Berlin was just the obvious place to go. Later I went to Japan for four years in a row, from 2012 to 2015. Each time staying several months, and that was very confrontational. I didn't know anyone there, I didn't speak the language. But then I made friends there, I had exhibitions, I did a residency and learned the language. And I think it helped my work as well. Before I went to Japan, I was making these traditional oil paintings. During my residency there, I wanted to make woodcuts and I found out that Hokusai didn't make the woodcuts himself. He just made a drawing and other people carved it in wood, and other people printed it. I didn't know that. It's just something you don't think about. One of the first days of my residency we went to a place to learn how to make woodcuts and I realized it was a lot of work. If I was going to make an exhibition there I would only make one print at the rate that I was going. So I improvised: I went to the DIY shop in the town where I was staying. I thought, what if I replace this woodcut by stenciling? That's how I got into this technique that I'm using now. It came out of practical necessity. It was faster, cheaper and more practical, and it suddenly fit because I had these instant volumes that I found interesting. They filled a space and it wasn't contrived. If I hadn't gone to Japan maybe I would have never arrived at this technique, but now that I did, it felt that is what I was supposed to do. And I wouldn't have done it, if I hadn't tested myself in a foreign and strange environment.

What if someone walked up to you in a bar and you had to describe in a few words what your work is about.

Then I would probably take out my phone and show pictures.

In general, people prefer words, and explanations, because it makes them feel comfortable. A title helps people to understand or to feel that they understand the work. How do you choose these titles?

I think that things land in your lap. I hate this word, but it's like serendipity, you happen upon this stuff at the right moment. Maybe I'm not really thinking about a title, but I think that's how our brain works. Maybe you're reading a book, but you basically latch on to stuff you were already looking for. And it feels like a coincidence afterwards, but basically, you're selecting it yourself—involuntary. I think that's how it works with titles for me. I feel like it's a coincidence landing in my lap. I don't want to be too conscious about constructing it, because I think the way the images come about is similar, in a way, to how the titles come about. At the same time I'm aware that I'm selectively finding these things—they're selectively landing in my lap because I'm looking for a certain thing. My mind probably blocks out other information and just gives me that. And the funny thing about that is that in one way it's generous, it enriches you because you suddenly start seeing a pattern, a sort of matrix, a fabric of life, and at the same time it's limiting because you're blocking out other stuff. Generally speaking, for me, titles work like that. I had this idea of malapropism, where you pronounce or read something differently than how it's meant. A very simple example is therapist, which you can also read as 'the rapist'. It's just a misreading of a word. What your mind makes of it—it morphs or mutilates the word. You get this new reality. And some of the images I use come about in the same way, through miss-seeing or misunderstanding. When I watch movies there's something similar happening in the background. In the foreground there is what you're supposed to be looking at, but in the background there might be a painting or what you think is a painting. Your mind automatically latches on to it and makes an image out of it. Later it might turn out that you didn't see it correctly. But your mind has already taken the most interesting information out of it and changed it into something else. I think that sometimes some of the images I want to use or that I end up fantasizing or mutilating or modifying come from this background—like a flash of recognition of something which wasn't there. In a way that relates to how you build up or construct your own reality.

That's a nice way to describe what you are doing.

Maybe this print is a good example. It's a combination of a lot of these things. It's a bunny with eyes, and the eyes are also breasts. I like this kind of visual contamination, which is much more reliable than something which is clear. Things that are ambiguous are more trustworthy in a way than things that are supposed to be clear. That's how I like the images to have a life of their own. There's this idea that things have a life of their own. There's an old cartoon that I used to read by this guy called Gary Larson, *The Far Side*, and there's one where there are cows standing in the meadow and they're smoking and drinking. Then one cow who is on the lookout says he sees a car coming and all the cows go back to eating grass. I guess it the same idea, like, whether a tree falling in the woods makes a sound if there's nobody there to hear it. We always see these things as they are because we're there. There's this old Jim Henson movie called *The Dark Crystal*, about two dominant life forms on this planet which can't live without each other. They're both a representation of each other's other side, like yin and yang. I had this fantasy about my work that it exists as it is now, but that it would be great to have a night version of it—let's say a version of the same work that I could look at as if I wasn't there. I made this sculpture of a chair, I put objects on it and I placed a tinted perspex hood over it. It's in the gallery space in bright light, but you're looking at it as if it were standing there at night and you're not able to see it. I don't have a factory like Andy Warhol, but I like this sort of minimal serial production through stenciling, with which I can make two versions of a work. Now I have a hand doing a thumbs up in the daytime, but I could have a version of it in a different color. I thought maybe I could exploit this idea a little bit and make two versions of it, and still be conceptually clean about this idea. The reason for doing it is that they're like yin and yang or in the same sphere. You can see them both at the same time. In reality you could not do that, but as a fiction I can produce that situation. That's why for this show I thought about producing two or three of these works within these series but in a different color variation, as if they were in a different time, but they would be there at the same time. This ties in to this sort of ambiguous feeling about your own identity.

Maybe you could still try to explain how you would describe your own work.

I've been asked this question in bars. It really does happen. It's a very difficult question. To begin with, when people ask me what I do, I try to make it a little more bite-size by saying, 'Oh, I make paintings'. Then they ask, 'What kind of paintings do you make? Oil paintings?' Then I say, 'No, I don't make oil paintings, I make work that is somewhere between...' The thing is, it's like poker in a way. They always say when you play poker, you have to imagine your opponent's hand. So when people ask me what kind of painting I make, I try to imagine what kind of painting they think a painting is. Either they are thinking about portraits or landscapes or they think that you're splashing something wildly on a canvas. First I say, 'I'm not splashing something wildly on a canvas and I'm not painting a landscape or a portrait. Luckily, sometimes you can show them your phone, and people go, 'Oh, great'. They are quite easily satisfied.

You refer more to the paintings, but you also make three-dimensional works. Is there a big difference in approach between the two-dimensional and the three-dimensional works?

A painting is like a window, it transports you elsewhere, whereas a sculpture doesn't really do that—you attach it to your locale, to where you are. It's in the same reality as you, whereas a painting somehow always alludes to another place. That's the funny thing about painting, because in a way abstract painting shouldn't do that, but it does actually.

Unplugged
Hans Janssen

Let me begin by confessing that I found the 1990s confusing. This confusion arose from an accumulation of apparent realities. Don't get me wrong. The years running up to the turn of the millennium were exhilarating and fun. Excitement was everywhere: it was eternally spring, with an economy that just couldn't go bust; a clear world order; a marriage between capitalism and socialism that had a liberating effect; a party that seemed to last forever. But something was off—and I wasn't the only one to notice. I looked in the fridge to see what it might be. I couldn't find it. Was it the art of the period that was past its sell-by date? So little of that decade seems to have lasted.

Was it a consequence of the fall of the Berlin Wall? Of the collapse of communism? The idea that the triumph of Wall Street meant the end of history? I don't know. What I do know is that I felt the art debate was getting out of hand. Artists were coming up with *theories*, at first to underpin their work, but soon they were using them to replace the image in all its manifestations or to cover up what was left of it. The gravitas of scientific theory and social commitment became the norm. Relationships and domains were shifting. Culture and art became interchangeable. The difference did not seem to matter anymore. Artists increasingly broke with the practice of making things. A form of art emerged which began to act out accordingly. Swimming on dry land. Art criticism happily joined in, producing a lot of chatter about the world surrounding the artwork, but none about the work itself. There was little or nothing in between. No analysis of the visual, of the image. It was as if there was nothing left to say. Writing or speaking about the artwork itself increasingly became a salvage operation. It was hopeless for someone like me who likes to look at things and to report on what he sees.

Morgan Betz grew up in the 1990s. He was a late bloomer, although it's also possible that he adopted a wait-and-see attitude—and maybe still does. But in spite of his hesitations he is also part of the first *unplugged* generation—hence the introduction. Somewhere around 1997 the internet and mobile phones began to conquer the world. Everyone who came of age after that was part of the first generation that could act freely, free from the burden of history. Or at least, we played the part, the Zeitgeist demanded it. There was no longer any possibility, desire or need to have a grasp of reality or history. Fiction reigned supreme. Everything was made for speed and convenience, everything was pre-prepared. There was a microwave oven in almost every home.

What strategies did a young artist have at his disposal in 1997–98 to prevail in the face of this steadily advancing—but previously unnoticed—reality, giving him the possibility to act and make a visual statement? Should he just go to work? Ignore the developments mentioned above? When you are at a loss, sincere, mild humor is always a good recourse. Not the type of comic effect that results from breaking the rules or transgressing accepted social norms. That kind of cynicism is alien to Morgan Betz. He does enjoy humor that can be expressed at a more technical level: when fiction and reality become intertwined and it is no longer clear who or what is involved, or where. When something opens up or is set free. When something is underpinned and at the same time is divested of its weight. That is what happens in a successful artwork: making something lighter by adding weight, or vice versa. Something like that.

Drawing plays that role in the early work of Morgan Betz. It is as if he has sent himself merrily on an errand into the impenetrable jungle of everyday superficiality. Sometimes it is visible on the surface of individual paintings and drawings, as a vibrating tangle of ideas and suggestions, beautiful lines and visual inventions that tumble over each other and form possible—and sometimes impossible—paintings. Sometimes—especially in a later phase—drawing seems to fade into the background and become part of the act of painting, merely performing its role on the surface of a well-organized canvas. Drawing in this instance mainly has to do with organization. Whether you see it as a breeding ground or as a choreography, both approaches are based on an uncontrolled, implicit organizational talent. Morgan Betz uses drawing in a contemporary manner, as a nimble instrument to transcend or tackle the language of things. For me, the drawing is an object that is meant to be looked at with more than average interest by the viewer. It gives direction to a particularly *visual* way of thinking.

Visual thinking. It is a problematic concept in an age when everyday images mostly come at us like a tsunami, a constant, overwhelming stream that drowns out the power of the individual image and drags everything into the domain of low culture to be exploited as trash. It is an inescapable phenomenon in a world that is driven by internet, globalization and capitalism. Snoopy isn't surprised to meet Tsubaki in a small village in Brittany that still holds out against the Romans, and Sponge Bob engages in a duet with canine piano player Rowlf from Sesame Street in a landscape that looks like Krazy Kat. It is not just cartoon characters that are put through the mill, but also logos, advertisements, graffiti and whatnot. Internet, with all its social media, reigns supreme. There is an incessant exchange of images through digital channels. This has led to an image overload. The art world can use this superabundance and overwhelming chaos as a strategy. It then becomes a method: copy-paste.

This is a tempting option for artists. It may seem like a fun thing to copy this overwhelming world and turn it into art. It is hip and almost always aims to amuse, tongue in cheek. But as images they are all over the place, they serve as pawns and conversation pieces in the bustle of exhibition openings. Far from transcending the moment, they are time-specific and quickly exceed their sell-by date. The resulting artworks are interchangeable and deeply embedded in a commercial art world. Morgan Betz calls them 'Kippenberger light': images as a pastime, as a subject for idle talk.

But are they *visual*? In the worst case, the closer they get to Kippenberger, the more they are. I can't say exactly what this visual aspect implies. It is recognizable for those who are open to it and are not afraid to draw conclusions on the basis of their perception and nothing but their perception. It gives something weight by making it lighter. Something like that. It's not a straightforward matter, because it shirks the whole social and conversational aspect of things and requires a certain susceptibility, leading to untimely conclusions which initially may seem strange, particularly to the makers.

A method that cultivates 'strangeness'. The entire industry of postmodern cultural theory is based on it.[1] A different strategy would be to put the idea of production on hold, and to go in search of powerful images that can survive in the marginal world of the studio. A return to the art of drawing, perhaps? I'm afraid this could only be successful as long as we have no illusions—as long as we do not put on a stern face, and the goal is not the butterfly, but the pupa, or rather, the larva. Only then there is some hope that images could develop that have or may have a right to exist, images that can survive *visually*, that can, as such, attract the gaze of a loving eye. As a maker you can never be sure. 'Whatever happens later,

1
At a recent seminar in Amsterdam on the state of art criticism I heard that it might be preferable to designate that activity in Dutch with the term Theory, with a capital T—it would be a better indication of/what it really means. In my view it is mainly an empty shell, producing only generalizations, which has sacrificed the visual to spreading generally held social views outside the public arena (as it is confined to the domain of art), and therefore is utterly harmless.

2
Letter of Piet Mondrian to Albert van den Briel, March 1927. Published in Piet Mondriaan, *'t Is alles een groote eenheid, Bert. Piet Mondriaan, Albert Driel en hun vriendschap, aan de hand van brieven, documenten en fragmenten*, Haarlem: Joh. Enschedé en zonen, 1988, pp. 12–15.

3
Personal communication with the artist, 5 September 2017.

4
Idem.

you will be outside of it', Piet Mondrian said in 1927, well before things really got underway.[2]

Let's take a closer look at the way Morgan Betz organizes his search for the visual. First let it be said that he often asks himself more or less explicitly how he—or anybody else—should understand artistic practice. What is artistic practice? Is it always wrong, laughable, defenseless? This question is consistent with Mondrian's statement. If anything, according to Morgan Betz, the artist is a 'reluctant participant in reality'.[3] When it comes to the significance of his work in a broader social context, Morgan Betz sees himself primarily as a spectator. Unplugged. He looks at things sideways. The funny thing with that position—especially in the current climate—is that he unintentionally takes on the guise of white male privilege. And to a certain extent this is true, because as an artist, what are you supposed to fight against? The suffering in the world of today? The realities of appearance? Edward Kienholz's *The Beanery* is a good example. It is both an indictment and a prank. For the young Morgan Betz, however, it was also an escape from reality during his expeditions in the Stedelijk Museum of the '80s and '90s.[4] As an image. As a visual manifestation.

Like many others, it steered Morgan Betz towards drawing and painting. Most of his earliest drawings are preparatory sketches for extremely intricate, wrought paintings like *The Island of Dr. Moreau* (2008), in which space is divided by white and light ochre facets, and dark ochre and green combine with blue to suggest a world without a sky. The atmosphere evokes the weary chaos of the science-fiction/horror film that gave the painting its title. Or take *Say Yes to No NO* (2009) and *One House Ago* (2009): these two paintings are based on drawings in which the shallow perspective of space is represented as an accumulation and succession of half overlapping forms, as if the builder of these spaces had to constantly start over again and search within himself because his failing memory prevented that space from taking on a logical aspect.

Examples of this are *Untitled (Study for LM)* (2009), *Untitled* (2009), and *Untitled* (2009), in which the colors stand in the way of the development of space—or control it. Drawing here is like driving into oncoming traffic. The artist bumps into something, and it could easily happen that in turn something bumps into him. The oncoming traffic does not just *look* back at him. It all becomes one big happy mess as the collisions become more intrusive and physical, which in turn influences his driving behavior. Driving becomes the mainly intuitive ability to cautiously steer clear of the rationality of

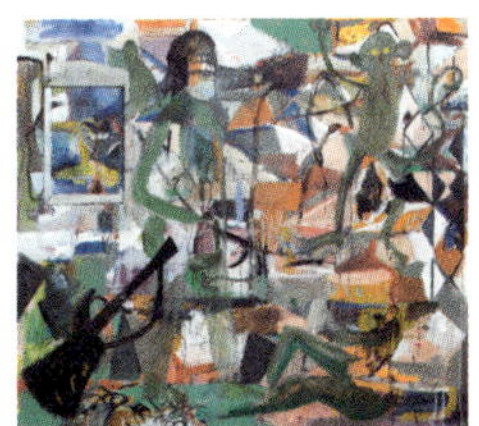

The Island of Dr. Moreau, 2008
Oil on canvas, 180 × 200 cm
Private collection

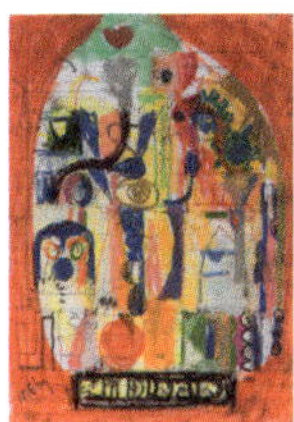

Untitled (Study for LM), 2009
Pencil, fineliner and crayon on paper, 42 × 28.5 cm
Private collection

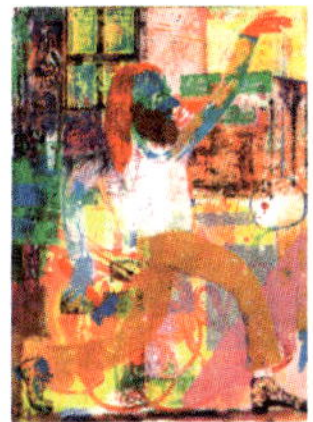

Say Yes to No NO, 2009
Linocut, oil and Flashe vinyl paint on canvas, 118 × 88 cm
Private collection

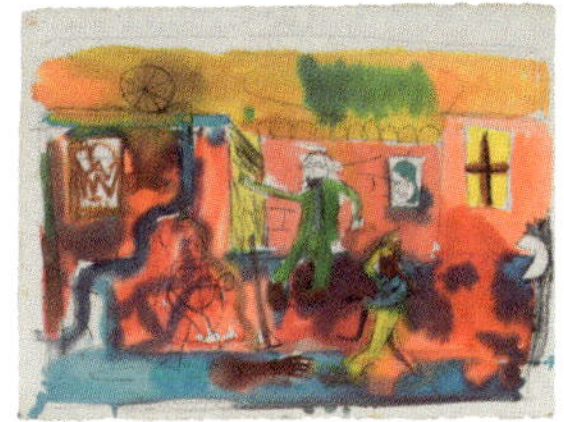

Untitled, 2009
Watercolour and pencil on paper, 58 × 77 cm
Private collection

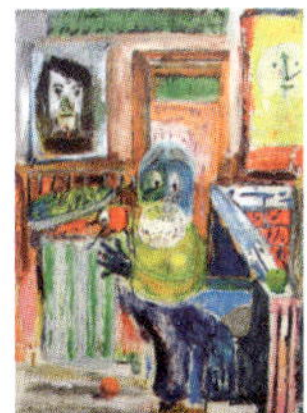

One House Ago, 2009
Oil on canvas, 125 × 90 cm
Collection Auke van der Werff

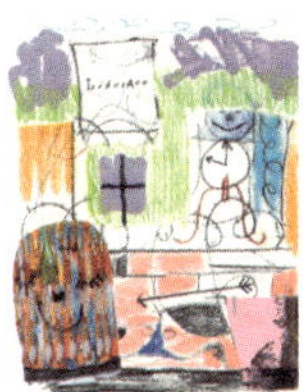

Untitled, 2009
Acrylic, pencil and collage, 40 × 30 cm
Private collection

words and language. Though the resulting paintings may sometimes have a precursor—like *One House Ago* (2009), in which we recognize Kienholz's *The Beanery*—Morgan Betz's early works are not just courageous but also quirky. They stay close to what is essentially possible, to what is strictly necessary—how could it be otherwise—and manage not to trip up over the impossibility of individual elements. Here receptiveness and imperfection are working hand in hand.

This results in a strange dream-like atmosphere. Like in a dream, these images aren't emanations of repressed specters of the past. Rather, they are, in the words of Louis Ferron, guardians at the entrance of the labyrinth where the true horrors may hide.[5] Suggestion is lurking everywhere. Why are foreground and background positioned in such a strange way in relation to each other in *Pinot noir* (2008)? Colors and lines masquerade as fences, webs, tilted tile floors or dark shadows. Is this a symptom of *horror vacui*? Maybe so. But surely in a humorous and relaxed form. As if the true horrors could be teased out and tamed by giving their guardians free rein. A bit like Buster Keaton who already knows the routine he is about to perform will amount to nothing, thereby actually increasing his chances of putting on a brilliant performance that takes on a dream-like quality which can only come about in the moment. It opens up a view on something that is different from the one-dimensional language of the drawing and what it represents, it breaks through to that something, a satire which also gives free rein to fun and fantasy. A tightly orchestrated space.

Why is the light behind that window ochre, green, or yellow? Is it because that is what the external world looks like? Or because the inner world has been provoked to view things that way? Drawing is like dreaming aloud. It allows you to hear yourself, to dig a deep hole in search of something that is protected by the guardians. Something that can't be acquired or even learned. Something that can only be worked out by *doing* it. Morgan Betz approvingly quotes Woody Allen, who pretty much describes the actual process: 'What people who don't write don't understand is that they think you make up the line consciously—but you don't. It proceeds from your unconscious. So it's the same surprise to you when it emerges as it is to the audience when the comic says it. I don't think of the joke and then say it. I say it and then realize what I've said. And I laugh at it, because I'm hearing it for the first time myself.'[6] In most cases there is also an energy at work in the individual line, an energy that is infectious. It stands alone, like an acrobatic trick. It takes its energy from the drawing, energy that has entered the drawing like oncoming traffic. The ability to draw energy from within without effort is what makes someone a good actor or actress.

The earliest drawings already feature numerous windows and doors. And mirrors. These provide Morgan Betz with an opportunity to depict the incidence of light or underlying representations, worlds within worlds. They create space and mitigate the *horror vacui* which he has trouble shaking off during those years. I'm not sure if that is really what happened, but I would like to think that these windows were the starting point for two further developments. In 2010 and 2011, Morgan Betz increasingly considers the sheet of paper as a stage on which something is about to take place.

These stage scenes have earlier counterparts in a number of painted portraits: *Bad Ronald* (2009), *Old Spice* (2009), *Pinkerton* (2009), and *Plaid and Tartan* (2009). I mention them here because they are consistent with the idea of dreaming out loud. They are the subconscious iteration of drawing. They uncover a body and a persona in the process. They place and locate a character who always looks startled and seems to apologize for his sudden and unexpected presence, who has been caught in the act, laughable and helpless. The maker apparently took pleasure in seeing those worlds appear—without really becoming involved. This is reminiscent of the painter in the book by Cervantes who, when asked: 'What do you paint?", answers: 'Whatever it turns out to be.'

Apart from these stage scenes there are drawings that are given by the window itself, through which views of flat other worlds. *Into the night, day of the triffids* (2009) is a case in point. We see the kind of gradually subsiding, unsettled space which Morgan Betz frequently evoked during those years. In the foreground of the picture there is an open window that looks out onto a stage (with yet another window in the background). Even further in the front, like in a Beckman painting, we see a repetition of the viewer, the back of a person who looks on as a triffid extends its voraciously oozing pistils and groping stamen towards the viewer, from the outside—or is it the inside? Triffids are giant, mobile science-fiction creatures that eat people. With hairy bellies and voracious mouths. Once again someone is in danger, hopelessly but not seriously. The visual becomes a catalyst for the gruesome. Behind it lies the maker's anxiety, his sense of dislocation and not-knowing. The idea that you need to express something as an artist, to actually show something of yourself is frightening and has a paralyzing effect,

5
I thank Frank Van den Broeck for pointing me to this quote by Louis Ferron from his novel *Werken van barmhartigheid*, Amsterdam: De Bezige Bij, 2003, p. 65.

6
Carl Fussman, 'Woody Allen: What I've Learned. Interview with Carl Fussman', in: *Esquire*, August 2013, p. 309.

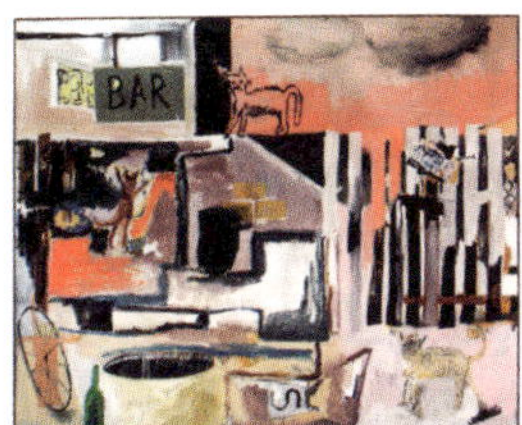

Pinot Noir, 2008
Oil on canvas, 200 × 240 cm
Private collection, Austria

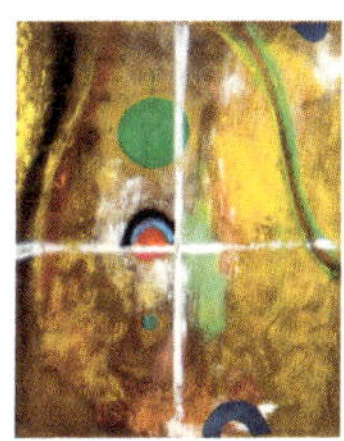

Untitled, 2011
Pigment, paint and collage on canvas, 150 × 120.5 cm
Collection Waldemar Dobrowolski

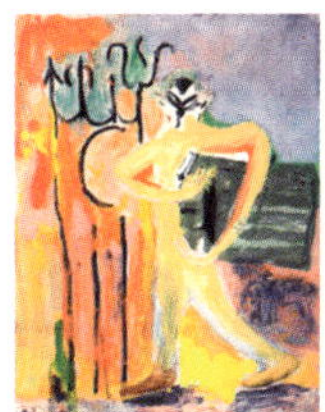

Bad Ronald, 2009
Oil on canvas, 117 × 88 cm
Private collection

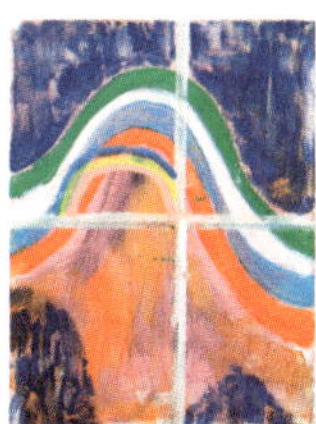

Untitled (Window), 2011
Gouache and water soluble oil paint on canvas, 40 × 30 cm
Private collection, Amsterdam

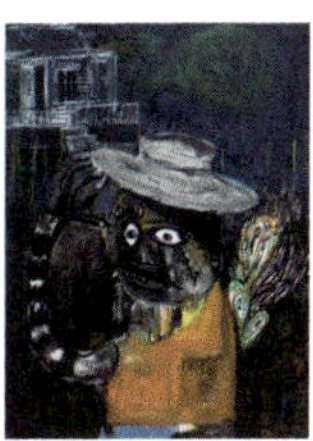

Old Spice, 2009
Oil on canvas, 200 × 150 cm
Private collection

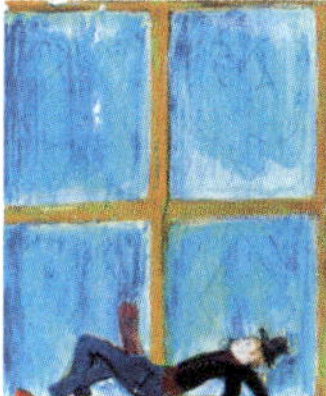

Fairy, 2012
Oil on canvas, 30 × 24 cm
Private collection

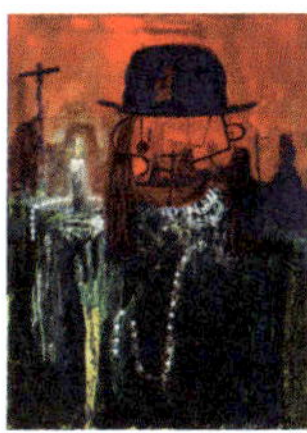

Pinkerton, 2009
Oil on canvas, 80 × 60 cm
Private collection

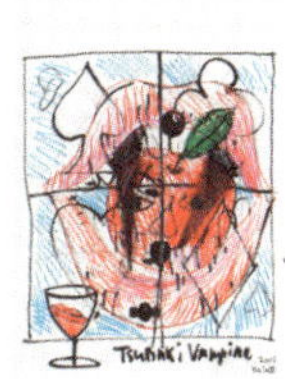

Tsubaki Vampire, 2015
Crayon and ink on inkjet print, 84 × 59.5 cm
Willem Baars Projects, Amsterdam

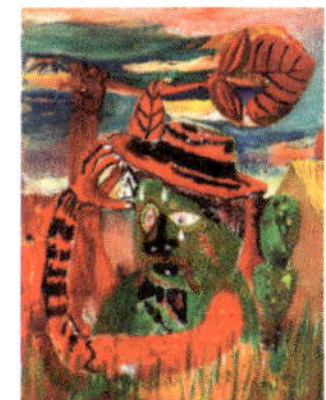

Plaid and Tartan, 2009
Oil on canvas, 118 × 88 cm
Private collection

leading to what could be best described as a displacement activity. Despite the impossibility of it all it can attain a clarity which is disquieting. And which comes about in approximately the same way as Woody Allen describes it.

After 2010 the window becomes a recurring motif. Rooted in a sentimental memory (a window by night in a New York apartment where he was staying with his father as a child, where the curtains weren't closed and the imagination could run wild, or rather, where the mirages of reality took over), it became a way to organize an image. Early examples of this are *Untitled* (2011) and *Untitled (Window)* (2011). A green moon, strange planetoids that stick to the window frame, supernovas and nebulae, a golden spectacle. The planetoids behind the window grow and develop into frightening mountainous rainbows, heat waves, the silhouette of a knee or a breast in the foreground. This is where Betz and Rosenquist converge in real time.

Drawing in his case is a ripple of morphological fields which emerge as works of the mind and of gesture in optima forma like *Fairy* (2012) and *Untitled*, (2011), culminating in *Tsubaki Vampire* (2015). *Tsubaki Vampire* combines the window with a relaxing glass of wine, the world of gambling, crimson camellia lips and a distressed-looking cherry head. It all started with a visual Freudian slip, when Morgan Betz thought he saw a picture of a mouth on a t-shirt in the street with a small mouse where its cute little tongue should be (*Graffiti Walls*, nr. 4).

In *Untitled (Fish Fingers) Day* and *Night*, both from 2015, based on a sketch that was meant as a tattoo design for a friend has been modified via the window motif into a sliding puzzle—*horror vacui* once again—that cannot be solved because there is no empty field. Nevertheless, this quartered world incites us to look for new combinations and repair the visual damage. The artwork itself as oncoming traffic. Composition as disruption and distress. *Untitled (Garden)* (2012) and *Untitled (Couple)* (2014) tell the same distressing story about the body and the way it is perceived in relation to the world. About what has been learned until now. Arms, legs, heads and experiences are lying around and only come alive when they are used thoughtfully. Here we should mention the *decorative* that is currently the subject of much uninformed debate. It is a word that is taken out of storage because 'it needs to be addressed'. It is not enough simply to leave the makers alone, to let the artist do what he does best. To simply leave some room for the humor of a well-placed white dab of paint.

In the years since 2010, Morgan Betz has supplemented drawing as the art of combining

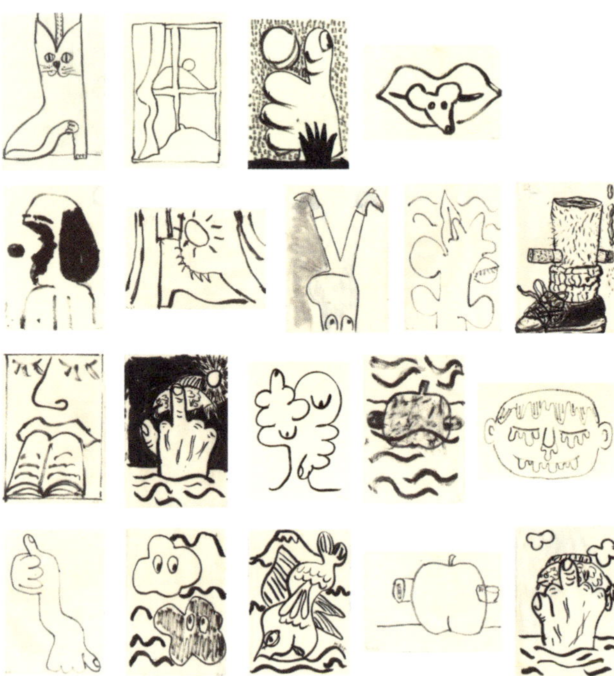

Untitled, 2015–16
Japanese ink, marker pen and charcoal on paper, 14.8 × 21 cm, 19 sheets
Willem Baars Projects, Amsterdam, Private collection

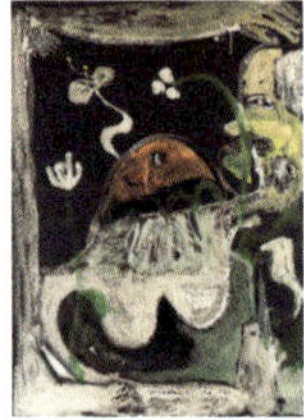

Untitled (Garden), 2012
Gouache on bitumen roofing felt paper, 109 × 79 cm
Private collection, Amsterdam / Berlin

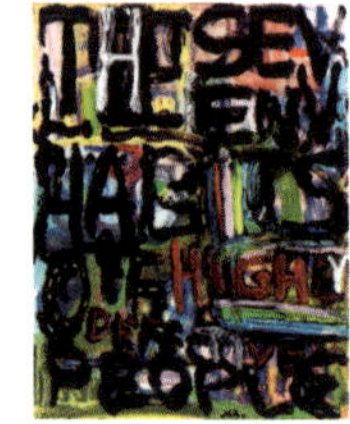

Untitled, 2011
Oil on canvas, 50.5 × 40 cm
Quetzalcoatl Art Collection

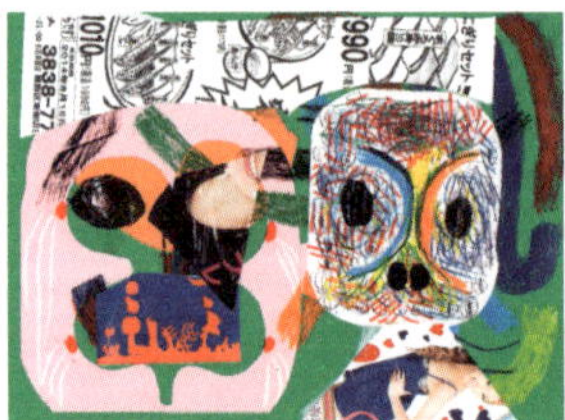

Untitled (Couple), 2014
Collage, business card and oil crayon on paper, 40.5 × 50 cm
Private collection

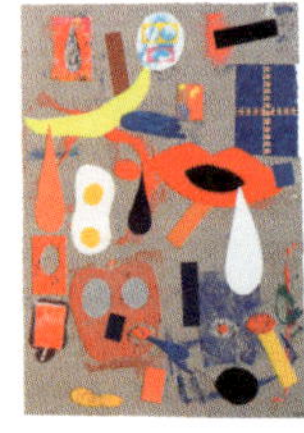

Untitled (Big Collage), 2014
Block printing ink, card, shoe sole, spray paint, plastic adhesive sheet, collage on linen mounted on panel, 210 × 150 cm
Private collection

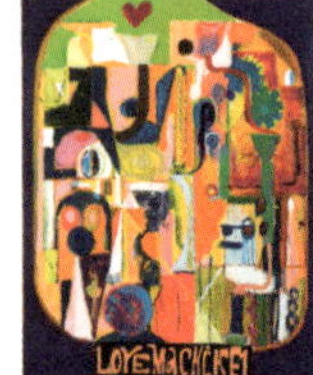

Love Machine, 2009
Oil on canvas, 170 × 130 cm
Quetzalcoatl Art Collection

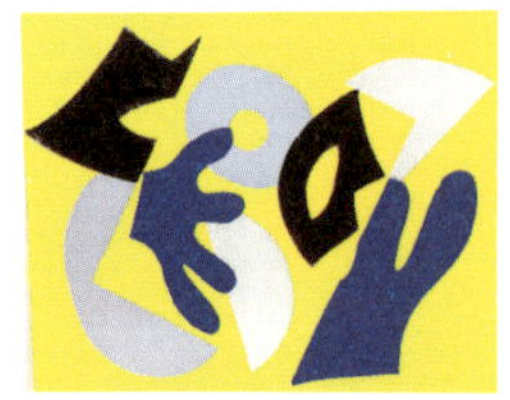

Kabuki, 2014–2015
Acrylic and block printing ink on canvas, 190 × 246 cm
THE EKARD COLLECTION

and as automatism with other mechanisms. The visual entropy that Morgan Betz often mentions—the fact that chaos is more likely to occur than order—decreases as there is more room to fail, the organization of elements takes on more of an improvisational character, and dreaming becomes part of the daily ritual. One might also call this craftsmanship. Overcrowding still plays a role, like in *Untitled (Study for LM)* (2009), which drew on *Love Machine* and anticipated less busy works like *Untitled* (2011) and *Untitled (Big Collage)* (2014). Here forms are becoming increasingly autonomous and simple. The wild fantasies of the mind gradually take shape. Matisse is not far away, but is actually irrelevant as well. Drawing becomes the light-hearted organization of cut-out shapes. Or the freedom to follow the rhythm of your feet, like in *Kabuki* (2014–15). The use of stencils that began in 2012 seems to take us beyond drawing.

Meanwhile there are also drawings that just come out of nothing and that no-one in the organization knows what to do with (nr. 8 and nr. 14 and 15 of *Graffiti Walls*). They become guardians in the studio without any clear assignment, meaning that they can just spend their time loafing around. It is only when they are called to fulfil their duty that they come into action and lose their stylized smugness. As a boy in Amsterdam Morgan Betz learned that you don't always need to run a red light when you're riding a bike. Those drawings, meanwhile, have their counterparts in drawings that were made with a certain intention, like *Graffiti Walls* nr. 10, which Morgan Betz made for a girlfriend or *Graffiti Walls* nr. 1, 6 and 7, which, like a stand-up comedian, want to please, but is also indirectly trying to circumvent trauma and loss.

This applies to an even greater extent to *Graffiti Walls* nr. 9, 13 and 18, which are laconic representations of grim scenes—the piercing or burning of a foot, a peach or an apple with, respectively, a cigarette and a finger. The tongue in cheek approach is no longer an option here, if it ever was (see Woody Allen's narrative). These images tell us parts of a story without revealing its theme. The only thing that they give up as guardians is their form, which sometimes reminds us of Guston, and at others of Warhol, Picasso or Matisse, but which is always fitting for the dark impulses produced by the morphological fields from which they stem. Yet more stage scenes. Worlds without a context. The isolation of a motif.

In an unguarded moment this could also have led to a drawing like *Untitled (genius of love)* (2014). It was made during a sleepless night in a hotel room in Kyoto and shows a cat, a woman and a body that fill the cranium of a despondent self-portrait as a jellyfish. *Untitled* (2011), *Snake on a Bike* (2011) and *Ghost* (2011) have a more remote source, they are more loosely organized and therefore pay more attention to oncoming traffic. It makes them more mellow and upbeat.

This also applies to drawings like *Untitled* (2011), *Untitled* (2011) and *Nostalgia* (2011), in which drawing is no longer a mystery but makes its appearance on the stage of the hilarious. Deformity and floral motifs work together to produce images that transcend the cranium. Here drawing breaks free from words and things, from the anecdotal, the complex, self-depiction and show and tell. Art ceases to be a public event. This creates more room for works like *Untitled* (2013), *Pain du Jour* (2015) or *Early Space-Age Art*, which brilliantly combine breeding ground and choreography and give clear substance to Morgan Betz's unplugged stance. The pure fun of making things? That's the prerogative of the artist. We are allowed to peek at an acoustic world from an appropriate distance. The creative process? Digging a hole is something you would rather do alone. Shovel in hand. Beauty? The pleasure of creating something from a sideways position. And of taking a stroll in the wilderness.

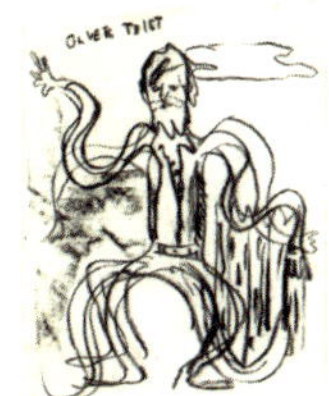

Untitled, 2011
Charcoal on paper, 42 × 31 cm
Private collection

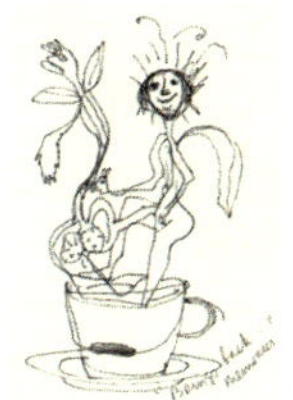

Nostalgia, 2011
Pen on paper, 21 × 14.5 cm
Willem Baars Projects, Amsterdam

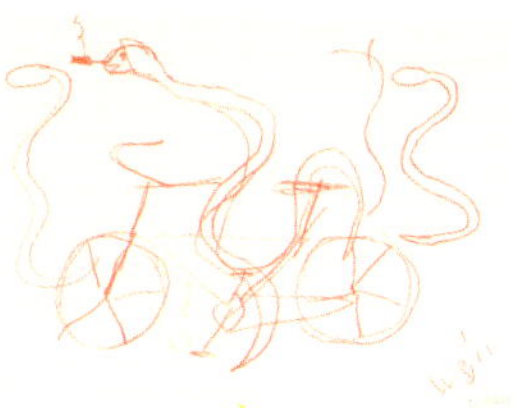

Snake on a Bike, 2011
Color pencil on paper, 25.5 × 34.5 cm
Private collection

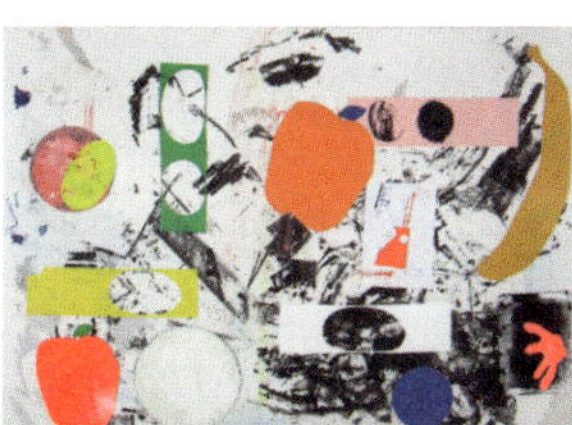

Untitled, 2013
Mixed media on cardboard, 119 × 170 cm
Private collection

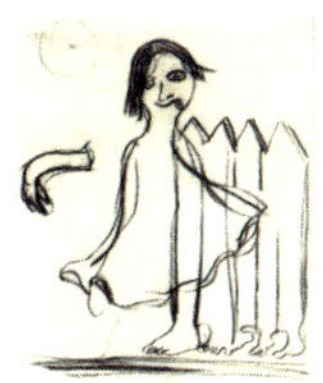

Ghost, 2011
Charcoal on paper, 42 × 31 cm
Private collection

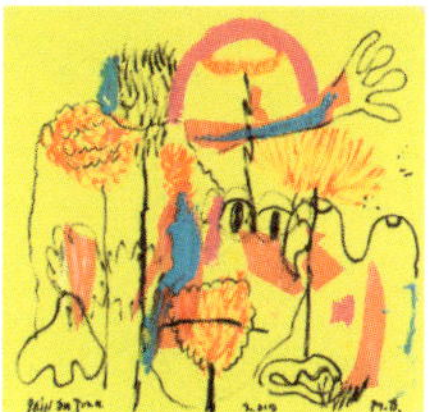

Pain du Jour, 2015
Gouache, self adhesive plastic sheet and ink on paper, 83 × 79.3 cm
Private collection

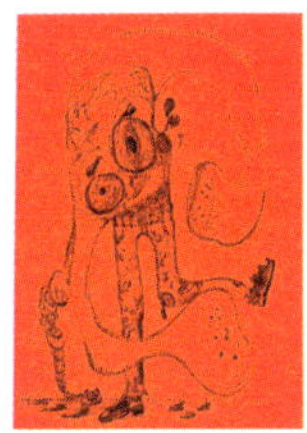

Untitled, 2011
Pencil on paper, 34.5 × 26 cm
Willem Baars Projects, Amsterdam

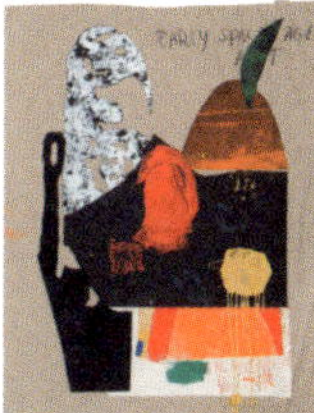

Untitled, 2016
Collage, fabric, charcoal and block printing ink on paper, 107.5 × 84.5 cm
Willem Baars Projects, Amsterdam

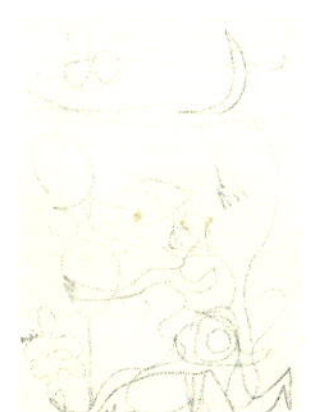

Untitled, 2011
Pencil on paper, 34.5 × 26 cm
Private collection

Morgan Betz

*1974
Lives and works in
Amsterdam/Berlin

Education
Rietveld Academie, Amsterdam
De Ateliers, Amsterdam

Selected
Solo Exhibitions

2018 *Morgan Betz – Flies on Milk, Green Eggs & Ham*, Gemeentemuseum Den Haag, The Hague
2015 *Transformer*, Willem Baars Projects, Amsterdam
2014 *Brussels Cologne Contemporaries*, Galerie Warhus Rittershaus, Cologne
2012 *Ikebanazawa*, KAPO, Kanazawa, Japan
2011 *Morgiana*, Willem Baars Projects, Amsterdam
2009 *Baker Street*, Aschenbach & Hofland Galerie, Amsterdam
2008 *Nova Swing* (with Lutz Driessen), Anna Klinkhammer Galerie, Dusseldorf
Amour Fou, Gallery Hidde van Seggelen, London
2007 *Bermuda Love Triangle* (with Helgi Thorsson), 101 Gallery, Reykjavik
2006 *Die Welt des Essens*, Kunstraum Acapulco, Dusseldorf
2005 *Poep Bruin* (together with Rob Birza), De Overslag, Eindhoven
Cet obscur objet du Plaisir, Ministry of Culture, The Hague

Selected
Group Exhibitions

2017 *Living in Dreams* (curated by Frank Koolen), De Bond, Bruges
2015 *Druck Berlin*, Urban Spree Galerie, Berlin
2014 *Oranžerija* (curated by Zilvinas Landzbergas), Biennale Vilnius, Vilnius
2012 *Murder Ink* (curated by Christof Mascher), Der Grieche, Berlin
Change your desires rather than the order of the world (curated by Zlatko Wurzberg), Willem Baars Projects, Amsterdam
2011 *What's up! De Jongste Schilderkunst in Nederland*, Dordrechts Museum, Dordrecht
Drawing on hands (curated by Serge Onnen), Print Room, Rotterdam
Kjarval Division Nylo, The Living Art Museum, Reykjavik
2010 *Lucy Stein presents LIVING IN ORANGE!!! (easyjetsetters)*, *The Forgotten Bar*, Galerie im Regierungsviertel, Berlin
2009 *Neue Künstler, Richtiger Schnaps*, Galerie Warhus Rittershaus, Cologne
N. t. (with Paul Haworth, Simon Hemmer, Lutz Driessen), Villa Goecke, Krefeld
2008 *KAAP*, Fort Ruigenhoeksedijk, Utrecht
2007 *The Contented Heart*, W139, Amsterdam

Exhibitions
Curated by the Artist

2013 *Il Tenki – Artists from Japan* (curated by Morgan Betz), Willem Baars Projects, Amsterdam

Published by the Gemeentemuseum Den Haag, The Hague and About Books, Zurich/Berlin, with financial support of Willem Baars Projects, Amsterdam on the occasion of the exhibition *Morgan Betz – Flies on Milk, Green Eggs & Ham*, running in the Gemeentemuseum Den Haag, The Hague from February 3 – June 3, 2018

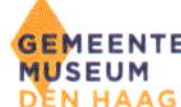

Gemeentemuseum Den Haag
Stadhouderslaan 41
NL-2517 HV Den Haag
gemeentemuseum.nl

Benno Tempel, director
Hans Janssen, Curator at large for modern art

About Books
Flurstrasse 93
CH-8047 Zurich
aboutbooks.ch

Willem Baars Projects
Hoogtekadijk 17hs
NL-1018 BD Amsterdam
baarsprojects.com

Edited by Hans Janssen
Project-management and picture-research by Michiel Simons, Willem Baars Projects
Texts written by Mischa Andriessen, Dominic van den Boogerd, Hans Janssen & Benno Tempel
Interview by Johan Gustavsson, The Hague, conducted in the studio in Berlin of Morgan Betz on September 9, 2017 and edited by Walter van der Star, Hans Janssen & Morgan Betz

Translations by Walter van der Star
Copy-editing by Hans Janssen
Photography by Arend Velsink, Amsterdam & Elsa Quarsell, Berlin

Designed by Bruno Margreth & Martina Brassel, Zurich
Typeset in LL Grey, Lineto
Printing and binding coordination by Ron von Oven
Printed in The Hague by Opmeer *papier pixels projecten*

Gemeentemuseum Den Haag, The Hague & About Books Zurich/Berlin
ISBN 978-3-906946-07-8